Cwmbrân

Volume 1

including

Cwmbrân Village, Upper Cwmbrân, Llanfrechfa, Henllys, Llantarnam, Croesyceiliog, Llanyrafon, Pontnewydd & Pontrhydyrun

Dr Gareth D John
&
Graham H Lawrence

DEDICATION

Old hearts fuse with new minds
to create confidence in a brighter
future for the benefit of all.

Gareth D John
'Hearts and Minds' (2007)

Old Bakehouse Publications

Abertillery

First published in October 2007

ISBN 978-1-905967-03-2

Published in the U.K. by
Old Bakehouse Publications
Church Street,
Abertillery, Gwent NP13 1EA
Telephone: 01495 212600 Fax: 01495 216222
Email: theoldbakeprint@btconnect.com
www: oldbakehouseprint.co.uk

Made and printed in the UK
by J.R. Davies (Printers) Ltd.

British Library Cataloguing in Publication Data: a catalogue record for this book is available from the British Library.

FOREWORD

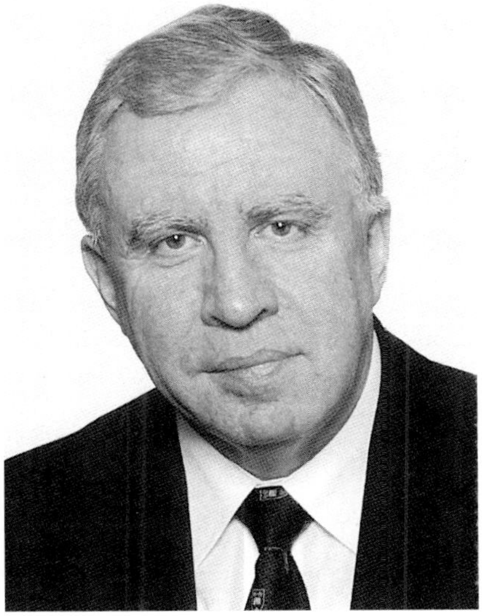

I have enormous pleasure in commending to you this fascinating history of Cwmbrân written by Dr Gareth D John and Graham H Lawrence. They have undertaken a vast amount of research to give us a feast of information about our town. They have especially done us a great service by publishing some fine photographs of people and places.

The authors have decided to devote separate chapters of this book to the individual communities which make up our New Town. This will be particularly useful to Cwmbrân people who have left our valley and who will be interested in their family heritage.

This book has obviously been a 'labour of love' for Gareth and Graham. They are both deeply committed to telling the story of Cwmbrân which will be of great interest to both historians and to the general reader.

Since Cwmbrân is a New Town many people think we have no real history. This excellent book proves otherwise.

Paul Murphy MP
(Formerly Secretary of State for Wales & for Northern Ireland)
July 2007

HOUSE OF COMMONS
LONDON SW1A 0AA

FOREWORD

CONTENTS

INTRODUCTION

1.	CWMBRÂN VILLAGE	6
2.	HENLLYS	23
3.	UPPER CWMBRÂN	47
4.	PONTNEWYDD & PONTRHYDYRUN	55
5.	LLANFRECHFA	70
6.	LLANYRAFON & CROESYCEILIOG	85
7.	LLANTARNAM	106
8.	CWMBRÂN TOWN CENTRE	135

ACKNOWLEDGEMENTS

INTRODUCTION

Cwmbrân is very much an enigma. For from humble beginnings it has grown out of all recognition in the past 100 years or more to become the hub of Torfaen Valley life with an unrivalled shopping experience in the geographical centre of the still existent County of Gwent.

The past half a century has seen many changes and, nowadays, the town of Cwmbrân embraces the former 'satellite' villages of Cwmbrân Village, Upper Cwmbrân, Llanfrechfa, Henllys, Llantarnam, Croesyceiliog, Llanyrafon, Pontnewydd, Pontrhydyrun and the new town centre itself - all awash with housing developments on formerly green pastoral land.

However, this was not always so. Way back in 1909 Cwmbrân was described by G.W. Wade in his guide to South Wales as ***'A Grimy Place'*** abounding in factories, furnaces and rolling mills. This, surely, was fair comment for its growth and success at that time depended on its basic small-scale industries. But during the 1920s both Cwmbrân Colliery and the Vitriol Works were deemed to be no longer viable by ruthless owners intent on exploiting the downtrodden workers to maximise their personal wealth. This resulted in mass unemployment and severe economic hardship. Cwmbrân quickly became a non-entity in the industrial life of the region. The Depression during the 1930s did little to ease matters either. Cwmbrân was seemingly left to languish in relative obscurity. The future looked bleak. Or so everyone thought.

The regeneration of Cwmbrân commenced during 1937-38 when it was recognised by an indifferent central government that something had to be done to improve the lot and appease a hard-pressed people - i.e. the electorate. Enough said. Thus Cwmbrân was designated a ***'special area'*** where with encouragement and suitable financial incentives the industrial base could be expanded and bring much needed employment to so many. With the outbreak of World War II unemployment all but disappeared as local industry geared itself to the war effort. Women also had an important role to play in the workplace.

Finally, dear reader, we hope that you will gain much pleasure from this book. Our purpose is simply to entertain, inform and arouse curiosity about the fascinating heritage of a still burgeoning valley town that rightly belongs to its residents. We have endeavoured to recall glimpses and reflections of the lives of those people responsible for social, political and economic change in years gone by. Our forefathers could never have envisaged the wholesale transformation which would radically change the fortunes of Cwmbrân and its environs for the better.

Remember this: ***'Today's today will become tomorrow's yesterday'***. So appreciate and treasure Cwmbrân's present virtues for we are all responsible for the prosperity of future generations who will judge us and hold us accountable.

G.D.J.
G.H.L.
July 2007

Cwmbrân Village

Until the mid 18th-century Cwmbrân as we know it today was totally unrecognisable - and barely existed at all. The area was dominated by the wealth of Llantarnam Abbey and the Crown. For it was very much a rural and agrarian society with numerous scattered farms and cottages. A society of grasping landowners 'feeding' off the backs of hardworking and downtrodden peasants desperately trying to earn a crust of daily bread to provide for their wives and children. The Industrial Revolution had yet to touch the area. But this was to change. And change dramatically it did with the coming of the canal (1796) and later, during the 1840s and 1850s, the arrival of the railway network when, virtually overnight, Cwmbrân suddenly became a 'boom town'.

Those desperately seeking work swarmed into the area from all over the United Kingdom and Ireland. The consequence, inevitably, was that much of the rolling countryside landscape was buried beneath the development of factories and heavy industry ever belching out their smoke and filth. Neat rows of stone-built terraced cottages sprung up like mushrooms in season. Cwmbrân, it seemed, offered a new-found prosperity and a gateway to a far better way of life. For a few it did. For most little really changed for the better as historical accounts all too readily testify and in many respects the poor became even poorer.

THE OLD POLICE STATION

While the present building in Victoria Street is currently used by Cwmbrân Community Council, this was not always the case. Throughout the 19th-century, criminal cases from the vicinity were heard in Caerleon Magistrates Court. As the old village became increasingly industrialised lawlessness became rife, with the vast majority of cases related to being 'Drunk and Disorderly' and offences of petty theft. Times do not appear to have changed. Cwmbrân urgently needed its very own Police Station and Magistrates Court. The premises were built in Victoria Street in 1898 and comprised police offices, two cells, a recreation yard for miscreants, a magistrates court and a caretaker's accommodation. Most commodious for the time. The first case to be heard was on 13th January, 1899, with the defendant being a local collier. He was found guilty of riotous behaviour on Christmas Eve by the presiding magistrate Frank J. Mitchell (owner of Llanfrechfa Grange) and fined 5 shillings, a sum he no doubt could ill afford.

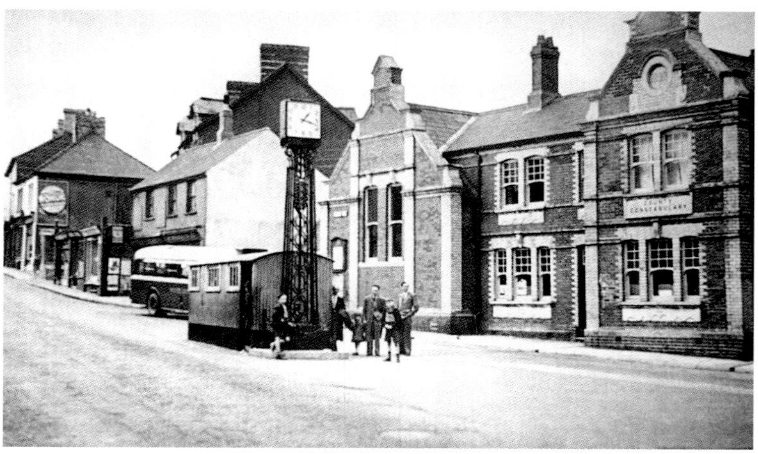

The original police station ca. 1940s with its 'island' village clock.

With population increase and the development of the New Town from 1949 onwards the old facilities in both Cwmbrân and nearby Pontnewydd simply could not cope with the demands placed upon them. So, in 1971 a much larger facility was opened on the old demolished Coronation Street which led to the closure of the two outdated stations. The Old Police Station was then taken over by the Community Council in the 1980s and tastefully refurbished and renamed ***'The Council House'***. The cells are now toilets (how appropriate!) and the Magistrates Room has become a kitchen. The building formerly served the inhabitants of Cwmbrân well for many years in respect of law and order. Will the modern station fulfil its potential? Possibly not, for it is heavily reliant on Newport Central.

THE PASSAGE OF TIME

The memorial Clock Tower in Victoria Street was erected in February 1936 on an island in the middle of the road by Cwmbrân Urban District Council. It was a joint gift from the Cwmbrân branch of the British Women's Temperance Association and the ratepayers of the district ***'In Memory of the Men of Cwmbrân who made the Supreme Sacrifice in the Great War, 1914-1918'***. However, the official unveiling ceremony by Mrs. Annie Kelly, the oldest member of the local Temperance branch, took place later on 18th June of that year. This was attended by hundreds of townspeople and dignitaries who felt it their duty (somewhat belatedly) to pay tribute to those fallen in battle. The dedicatory service was conducted by the much-respected Reverend John Donne, Vicar of Llantarnam. The clock has remained a focal point of the village for some 70 years. The clock is powered by electricity which had only been introduced into the village some 5 years earlier; this innovation readily captured the public's imagination. During the summer of 2007 the clock was taken down for repairs and refurbishment: it was re-dedicated on 7th September. Perhaps it is timely to rededicate the clock to those who fell during World War II.

ELIM CHAPEL & A REMARKABLE TALE!

Elim Independent Chapel was built 1844 in Commercial Street and opened at a time when Cwmbrân had just been catapulted into 'a brave new world' of rapidly growing industrialisation. Straightaway it found favour with workers and their families who held strongly nonconformist beliefs. An adjoining schoolroom was built in 1872 and became a popular centre for religious education, social and sporting activities. Elim offered hope to ordinary folk and a brief respite from the drudgery and grinding deprivation of everyday working life. In recent times, though with diminishing congregations, it continues to play a valuable role within the community.

Within the secluded walled graveyard lies a quite remarkable tale of longevity i.e. that of the oldest British married couple to have been buried together at a combined age of ***211 years***. The headstone, for years obscured by the menacing tentacles of ivy and weathered by the unrelenting march of Time was accidentally stumbled upon by co-author Graham Lawrence while researching his family roots. Still decipherable, the headstone bears the names of Thomas and Elizabeth Morgan. Thomas died on 29th January, 1893, at the ripe old age of 106 years; Elizabeth on 1st January, 1891, aged 105 years. Such longevity was

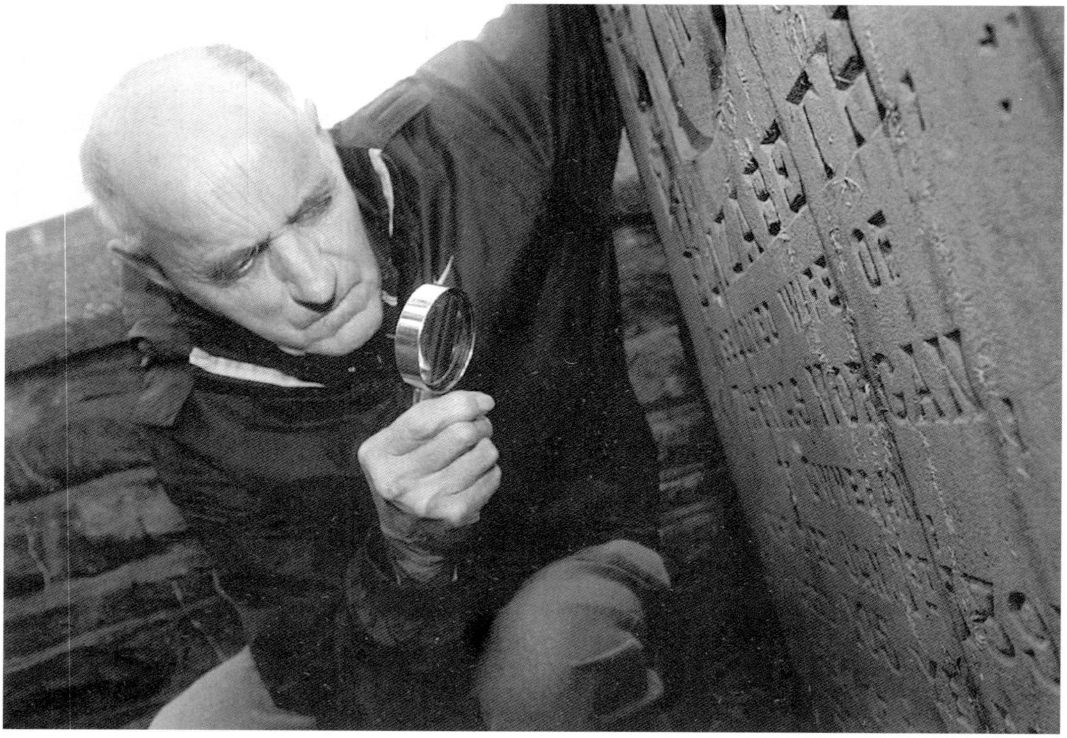

Local historian Graham Lawrence makes a remarkable find!

By courtesy of South Wales Argus

virtually unknown during Victorian times when the average life expectancy was under 40 years. For both partners to exceed 100 years is simply unprecedented - even today. The verse at the bottom of the headstone perfectly sums up their lives together:

IN PEACE WE LIVED
IN PEACE WE DIED
TOGETHER HERE WE REST
DEATH TOOK US FROM YOUR LOVING SIDE
WE DIED ON JESU'S BREAST.

Thomas Morgan was born at Llantrisant on 4th May, 1787, Elizabeth on 17th January, 1786 near Caerleon. Their death certificates held by the registrars in Newport and Abergavenny confirm their ages and the dates on which they died. How the pair met can only be surmised. Thomas most likely came to the area seeking employment. The couple married in Caerleon on 4th May, 1809, and shared their lives together for 82 years. Elizabeth bore him ***15*** children - a veritable tribe! Together, they witnessed the reigns of ***four*** monarchs (from George III to Victoria) and all at a time when the British Empire was a dominant world force. They lived most of their lives in a terraced cottage rented to them by the local Iron Foundry at Forge Row, or Foundry Row (demolished in 1939) just below Clomendy Road. This is recorded in the 1881 National Census.

Thomas became a staunch supporter of industrial and political reform for, like countless others of his time, he believed that the working man had a democratic right for a fair day's pay. He sustained personal injury while protesting in the

Chartist Riots of 1839 (presumably outside the Westgate Hotel in Newport) and ***'to his death's day bore the scar of a wound then received'***. In addition he was an Oddfellow - a fraternity similar to the Freemasons.

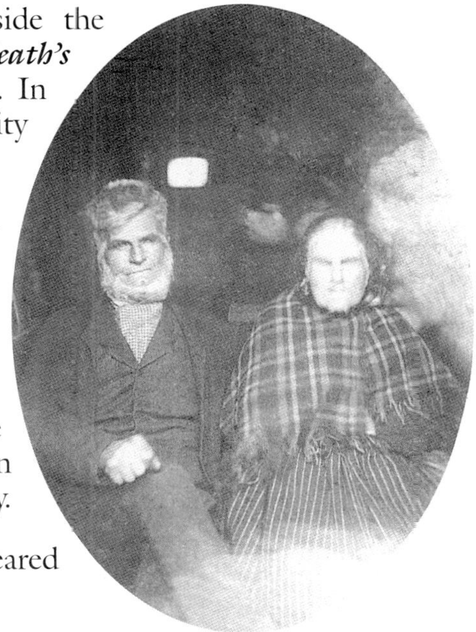

The image of Thomas and Elizabeth Morgan defies the imagination.

Following Elizabeth's death, Thomas lived with his daughter at The Square in Upper Cwmbrân. The funeral arrangements for both Elizabeth and Thomas were undertaken by Messrs. Tovey Brothers of Newport. Unfortunately though, all records of burials before 1911 were lost when a fire ravaged the Funeral Home and it is unknown who attended the services. A great pity, really.

Obituaries for the centenarians' deaths appeared in the ***Monmouthshire Merlin*** (Elizabeth - 23rd January, 1891) and the ***South Wales Weekly Argus*** (Thomas - 4th February, 1893). Oddly, the dates of their births and deaths do not match official sources. Nonetheless, the accounts eulogise the couple's quite remarkable lifespan. It is interesting to note that in later years the Patent Nut & Bolt Company where Thomas had worked ***'allowed Mr. and Mrs. Morgan to live in one of their houses rent free, and have gratuitously supplied them with firing'. 'The neighbours, too, have been remarkably kind to them, the wife of a shopkeeper having daily sent in a hot dinner for the aged couple for many years.'*** The former peasant of Llantrisant and his beloved wife were clearly widely admired and respected.

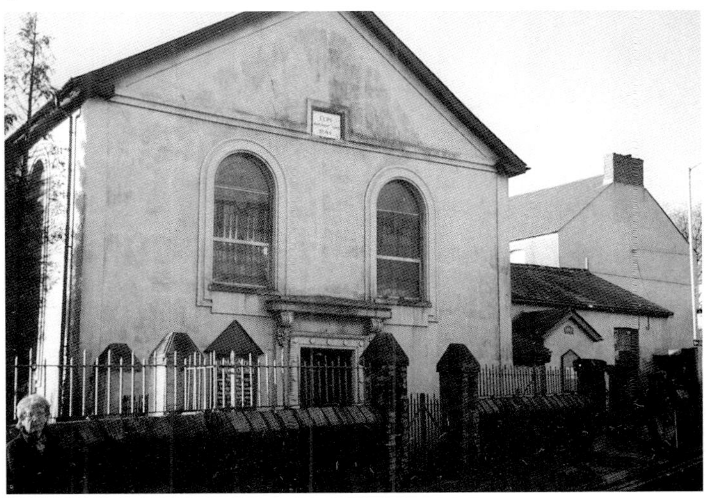

Elim Independent Chapel in Commercial Street.

Some years ago, the overgrown graveyard at Elim was landscaped by the District Council to provide ***'an open space for the quiet enjoyment of the Public'***. Headstones were unceremoniously uprooted and repositioned alongside the west-facing perimeter stone wall. Precisely where the aged couple's remains actually lie is far from certain. On 22nd November, 2004, the couple's ages were authenticated by the ***'Guinness Book of World Records'*** under the category ***'Oldest Married Couple, Aggregate Age'***. A first for the old township of Cwmbrân.

ST. DIALS SCHOOL

The Elementary School was opened in 1874 in Oak Street just off Commercial Street, close to the main thoroughfare of the industrial village. The first Headmaster was Mr. W.J. James who was dedicated to the instruction of unruly and illiterate young children during a period of severe economic depression. He died in 1912 having served the community in that capacity for very many years. To honour his memory a drinking fountain was erected in Cwmbrân Village paid

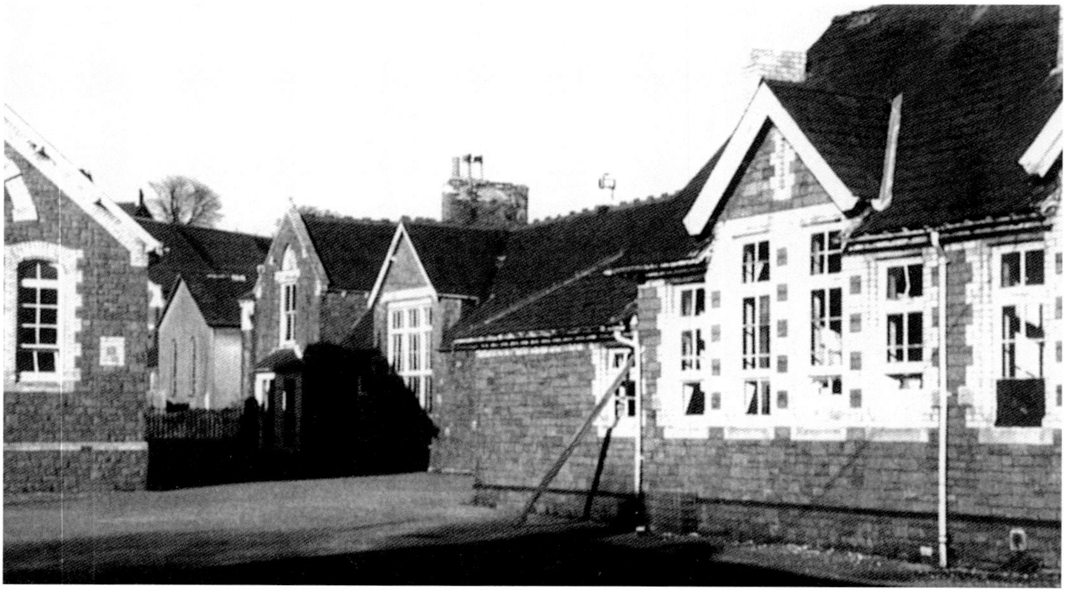

St. Dials Elementary School.

for by public subscription. Following the opening of Cwmbrân Park in 1932 the fountain was transferred there in 1935 and remained a focal point within the park until it was removed in the early 1970s. The greatly respected headmaster is buried in Llantarnam churchyard.

St. Dials School was really two separate schools - a boys and a girls school. The philosophy of the time was that the two sexes should not mix ***'for social interaction would be detrimental to individual educational development'***. Thought provoking. Girls was deemed fit only to be educated in becoming proficient housewives and caring mothers, whereas boys should be taught history, geography, science and woodwork. So girls were instructed mainly in needlework, cookery and good housekeeping. With a lack of proper heating during extremely cold weather the Girls' School log book of 1895 noted that ***'The writing of Standard V is in a very poor condition...the main room has been so cold since Christmas that the girls have been unable to hold their pens...'*** A photograph taken in 1934 (shown opposite) shows the teacher Miss Powell with her young charges. How many of the parents could afford to purchase a copy of their siblings? No doubt very few.

Nonetheless, St. Dials served the elementary educational needs of Old Cwmbrân for almost 100 years before being deemed unfit to serve the best interests of future generations of children. Not surprisingly, the old school records show that the

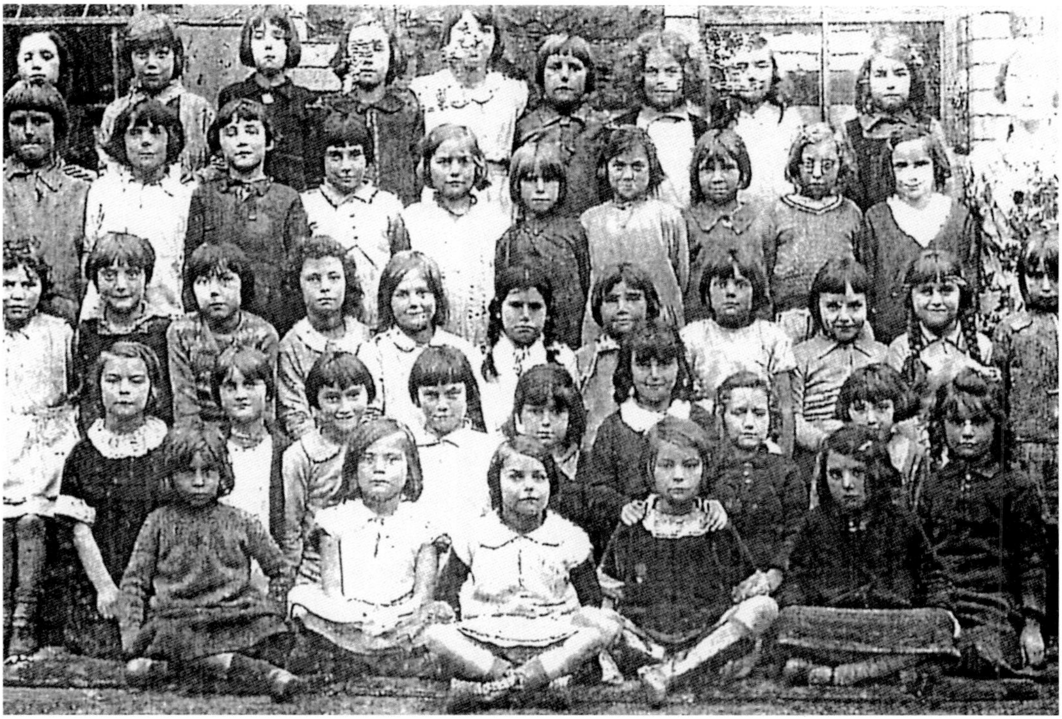

The Likely Girls at St. Dials School 1934.
Back row: Betty Lewis, Gwen Jones, Doreen Thomas, Nina Poulton, Mavis ?, Beryl Jones, Roma Prosser, Olive Sly, Edith Eyre, Miss Powell - Teacher.
Fourth row: Maureen Jones, N. Harris, Irene Jenkins, Nancy Lawrence, Florence Powell, Faith Marasco, Veronica Bird, Pearl Thomas, Gladys Jones, Jessica Phillips.
Third row: Doreen Williams, Doris Wilson, Megan Casley, Irene Jones, Mary Burr, Cissy Gilmore, Doreen Harris, Audrey Simmonds, Betty Flyn, Gwen Jones.
Second row: Ivy Hinwood, Margaret Woods, Frances Mills, Hazel Pritchard, Betty Hurley, Nellie Edwards, Ivy Measures, Rona Beech, Glenys Morgan.
Front row: Edna Akerkley, Jenny Hughes, Rene Davis, Violet Hindwood, Joyce Leighfield.

majority of pupils left school at 14 years ***'For Work'***. Following the opening of Brookfield School in the late 1960s the old school building became redundant, but continued for some years as an educational resource centre and teacher conference venue. The stone-built buildings were demolished in 1983 and a housing complex built on the site for the elderly and disabled - and aptly named School Court. Ironically, its replacement Brookfield School is likely to suffer a similar fate due to supposedly dwindling pupil numbers. But the town centre requires more land to expand its commercial operation. Perhaps the political rationale is of greater importance than the simple educational needs of future generations…

CWMBRÂN PARK

Throughout the difficult years of the 1920s Llantarnam Urban District Council felt that the local populace deserved congenial recreational facilities. After much planning and under considerable financial constraints the park was gradually laid out and officially opened during 1932. A contemporary report waxed lyrical as to the newly-gained amenities:

'The council's enterprise was very much appreciated and Putting was proving very popular. The new public recreation grounds at Penywain are at once a boom to the town which previously had nothing to offer its residents in way of summer entertainment...and the grounds are fast becoming the most successful business undertaking in Cwmbran...the park has been described as the 'Mecca' of Cwmbran's pleasure-seeking public.'

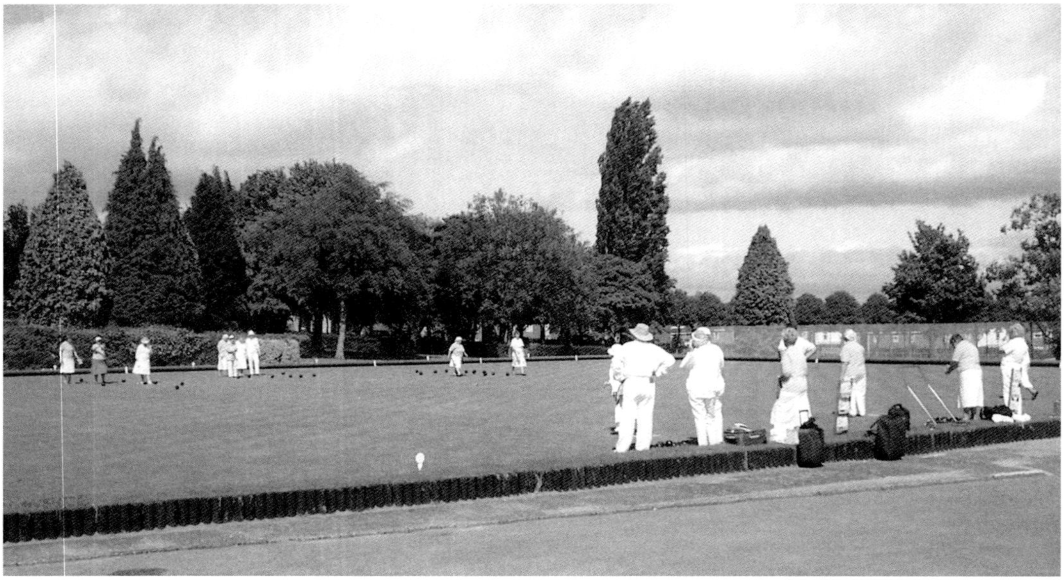

Men and Ladies Bowls Clubs 2007.

For many years a fountain shaded by a large oak tree and dedicated to the memory of Mr. W.J. James, a long-serving former headmaster of St. Dials School, quenched the thirsts of energetic sporting lads and lasses. Both oak and fountain were lost when nearby paths were widened. Why?

Unthinkable by modern standards, the park was closed to all on Sundays during the 1930s, 40s and 50s when religious fervour still held sway. Such traditional beliefs can be traced back to the early 17th-century and the ***'Book of Sports'*** originated by James I which clearly forbade any form of games and revelry on the Sabbath. In 1965 the Urban District Council, after much heated debate, most sensibly relented. Times change, yet the park continues to be much used for football and tennis. Moreover, the men and ladies Bowls Clubs remain highly active and welcome visiting teams from outside the area.

A metal plaque, though long gone, reminded all to respect the facilities available and would be just as relevant today:

Let no one say,
And say to your shame,
That all was beauty here,
Until you came.

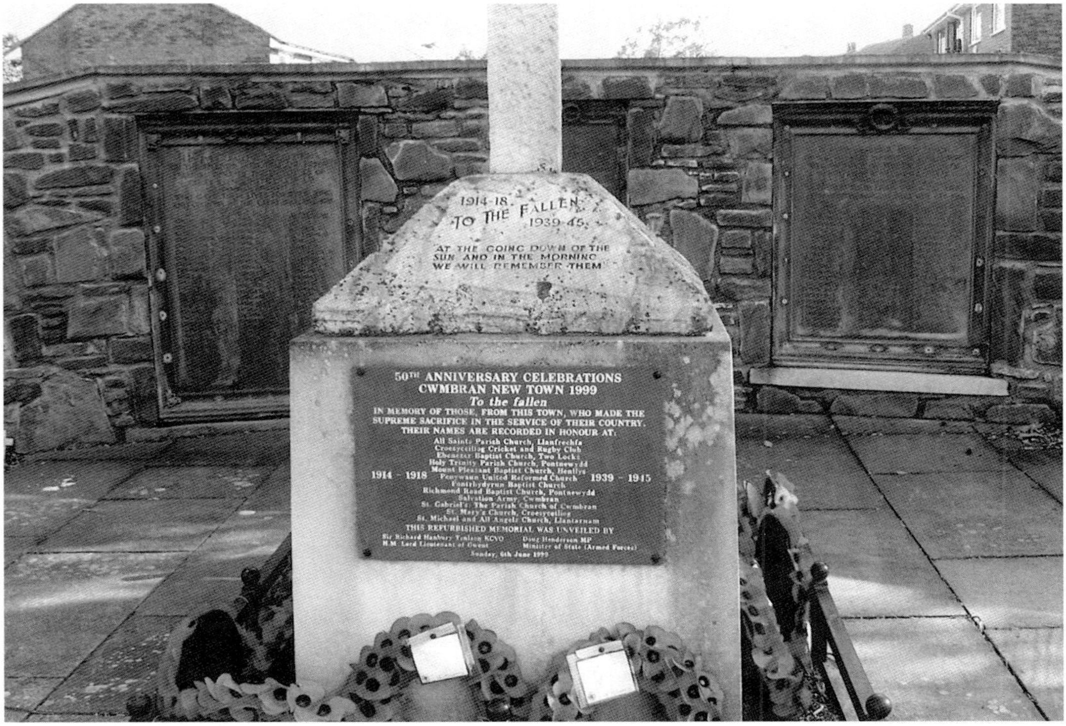

A tribute befitting those who perished in two World Wars.

A small cenotaph in a quiet corner of the park commemorates those who fell during two World Wars. Coinciding with the 50th anniversary celebrations of the New Town the refurbished memorial was unveiled on Sunday, 6th June, 1999, by Sir Richard Hanbury Tenison KCVO, H.M. Lord Lieutenant of Gwent. Three bronze plaques mounted on the stone-walled enclosure were originally displayed at the former Guest, Keen & Nettlefold administrative offices at Forge Hammer and list the names of 84 men from Cwmbrân Colliery and 66 from the Cwmbrân Works who perished in the Great War. When the latter works closed the plaques were eventually transferred to their present site in the park. A stone tablet on the cenotaph's body names the churches and chapels within the Cwmbrân area which honour those lost in the epic conflicts against the forces of aggression and tyranny.

PENYWAUN CONGREGATIONAL CHURCH

The rise and demise of Penywaun Congregational Church and Chapel began when meetings took place during the 17th-century in Henllys House, the home of a very pious woman Margaret Jones. The descendants of those early worshippers were to establish a church in 1741 called Penywaun in the parish of Henllys: during 1818 the first sanctuary was erected when the old farmhouse became a place of prayer. The land was generously given by a Mrs. Margaret Walters and her son William of Ton Farm. The Reverend D. Davies became the first pastor, but with a congregation of only eight they could only offer him food and shelter. To supplement his meagre existence he ran a day school in the same building for the poor children of the area. In 1851 a new larger day school was opened on adjoining land.

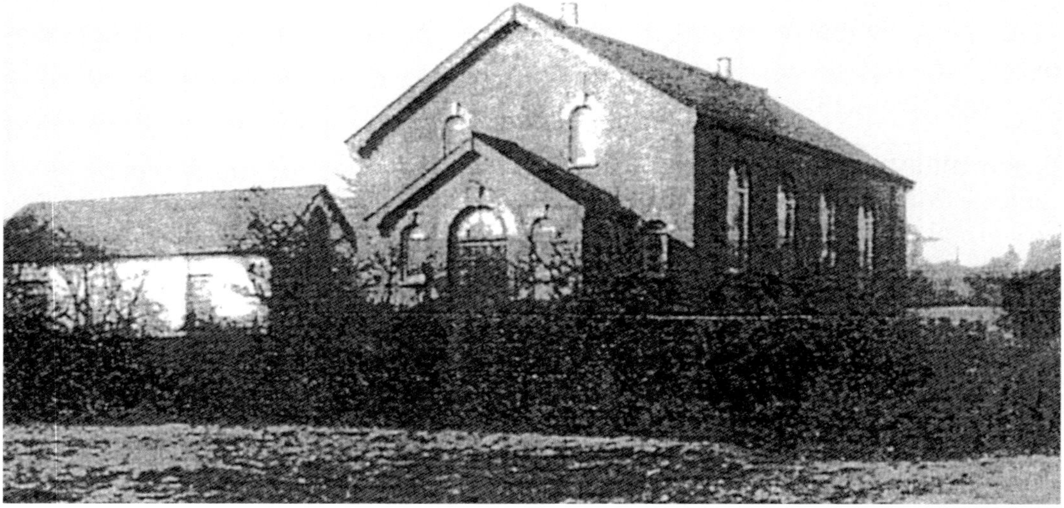

Penywaun Church and Chapel stand shoulder to shoulder.

By 1902 the small chapel could not cope with its fast-growing membership. A new, much larger church was needed. Land adjacent to the chapel was purchased, but no money was readily available to erect the building. So with their own endeavours the faithful rallied round and built most of the structure themselves. The specialist work such as carpentry, seating, heating and lighting was put out to tender. The cost of the new building was £900 - a very hefty sum in those days. The opening ceremony of the new church took place on 17th January, 1907. For decades the larger church building served the spiritual needs of an essentially rural

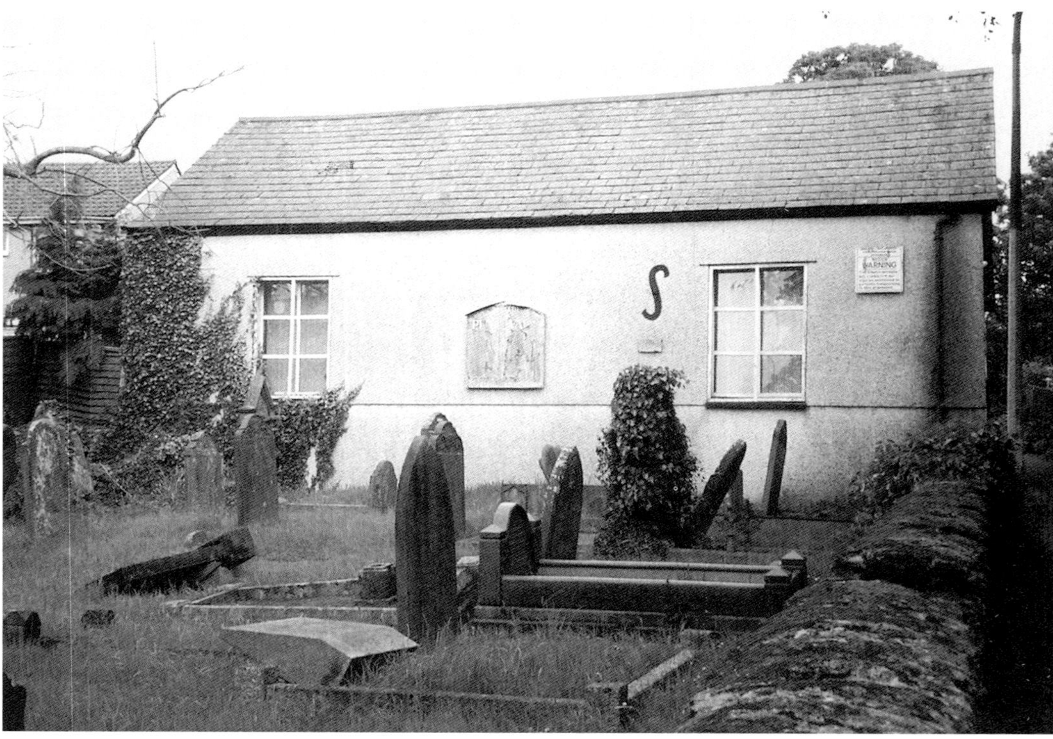

Penywaun Chapel in its present forlorn state.

community. But industrialisation was encroaching fast. And as its numbers swelled rapidly it also became a focus for diverse secular activities. As elsewhere, over time religious belief gave way to materialism and the numbers attending dwindled steadily throughout the 1960s.

A new minister, the Reverend Gordon Lang, a native of Monmouth and a former Labour Member of Parliament from 1931-45 for a Cheshire division, was welcomed to Penywaun in 1956. A year earlier he was appointed to the board of Cwmbrân Development Corporation on which he served tirelessly until 1964.

Unfortunately, the church's foundations gradually became ever more unstable and the entire building was ultimately condemned and demolished in 1986. A housing development has taken its place. During 2004 the ancient Penywaun Chapel itself closed and now stands forlorn, all but ignored and forgotten. The future of this once thriving religious institution and churchyard is uncertain and vulnerable to the hand of Fate - or fall prey to more property developers. What else...

EBENEZER BAPTIST CHAPEL

After long and hard hours working in the iron and coal trade, and with very little leisure time, men would regularly seek solace in the nearest ale-house. The result was that drunkenness was rife. Employers were increasingly concerned about men turning up for work in no fit state to do so. This problem had to some extent been addressed with the establishing of Elim and Penywaun chapels in the heart of the village. A committee met at New House Farm in February 1860 with the respected Ebenezer Williams, pastor of Siloam, Upper Cwmbrân, as its chairman.

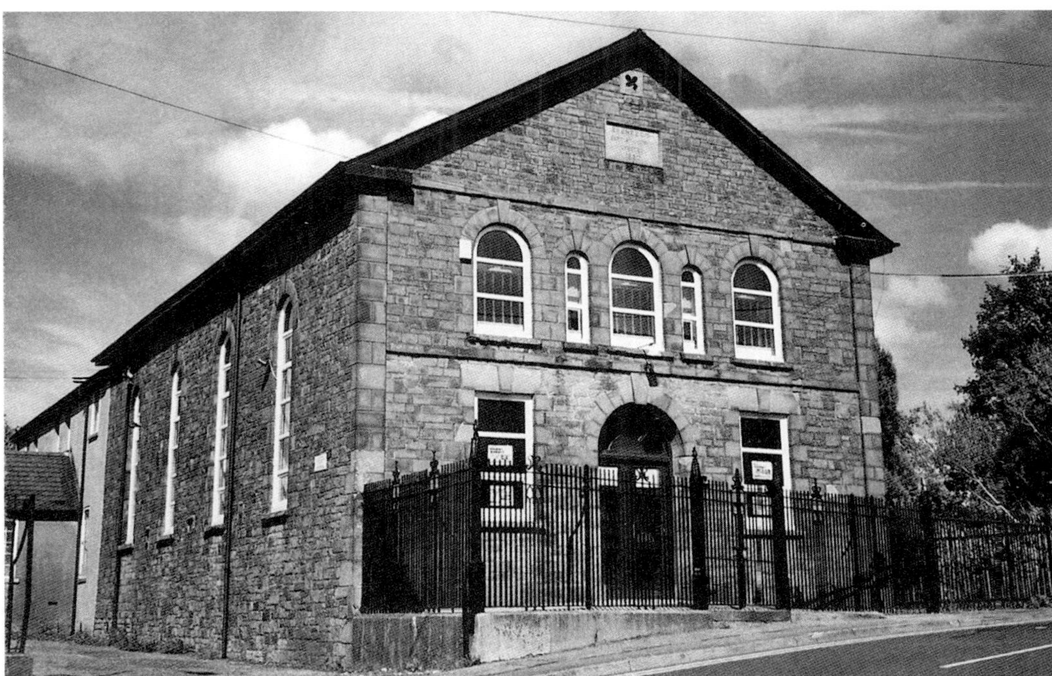

Ebenezer Baptist Chapel.

And it was decided to build a chapel for the Baptist community a short distance from the new village at Two Locks in the Oakfield district. The land was generously donated by Mr. John Samuel of Penyfan, Bassaleg. The owner of Henllys Brickworks, Cyrus Hanson, himself a staunch Baptist, provided some 500 tons of stone free of charge. The foundation stone-laying ceremony took place on 2nd September, 1860, by Miss Samuel of Penyfan. Worthy of note is that during construction work in excess of 20 people were baptised in the nearby Cocker Brook. The chapel was dedicated and opened on Sunday, 3rd November, 1861, and named after Reverend Ebenezer Williams whose religious zeal for the well-being of all was recognised. He must have felt humbled yet a proud man.

The chapel attracted a large congregation and in 1889 it was renovated to include side galleries to accommodate the growing membership of worshippers. Even this was not enough for in 1903 the building was extended to include a lecture hall and **ten** classrooms for the Sunday School. The chapel remains a thriving religious and secular institution and plays an important role in the social fabric of today's society.

CLOMENDY FARM

The village of Cwmbrân was built on Clomendy farmland as was the industrial complex of the Nut & Bolt works which later became Messrs Guest, Keen & Nettlefold and subsequently was one of the GKN holdings. The farm was almost certainly originally a 'Grange Farm' owned and cultivated by the Cistercian monks of nearby Llantarnam Abbey until the Dissolution of the monastery in 1536 when ownership transferred to the Crown. It was later sold to one of the King's loyal servants as gratitude for his dubious patronage. The original farm extended over many acres with fields and orchards before the blight of industry and the houses constructed in and around Commercial Street and Victoria Street. All that remains of what appears to resemble a small and simple early Elizabethan farmhouse is set back in a lane off Commercial Street and is a private dwelling. The modern red-tiled roof replaced the thatch of old and its walls are 'white-washed'. Nevertheless, with its tiny windows in its eaves it retains much of its original character. Possibly Thomas Morgan, centenarian, laboured there during his early lifetime as he was described variously as an outdoor worker. Certainly, he and his wife Elizabeth lived very close by.

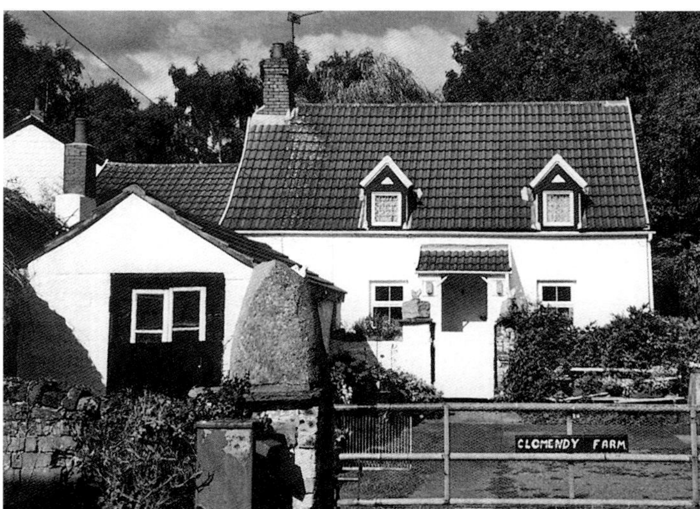

Clomendy Farmhouse.

CWMBRÂN RAILWAY STATION

The Eastern Valley railway through Cwmbrân Village was intended primarily to transport heavy mineral wealth of the upper valley rather than to provide a passenger service. Yet, essentially it was a branch line, not a main route northwards to the Midlands and Shrewsbury, but a direct link to the port of Newport and beyond. The station stood at the rear of Victoria Street and was opened in 1852.

A much published and vaunted photograph is that of the 'future' King Edward VIII during his historic tour of depression-hit South East Wales in November 1936. He wished for little ceremony as possible so that he could ***'...devote the whole of the time available to studying the conditions of the unemployed...'*** He is seen being greeted by local dignitaries outside the station. But little really changed until the war years which brought about the full employment so desperately needed by the population.

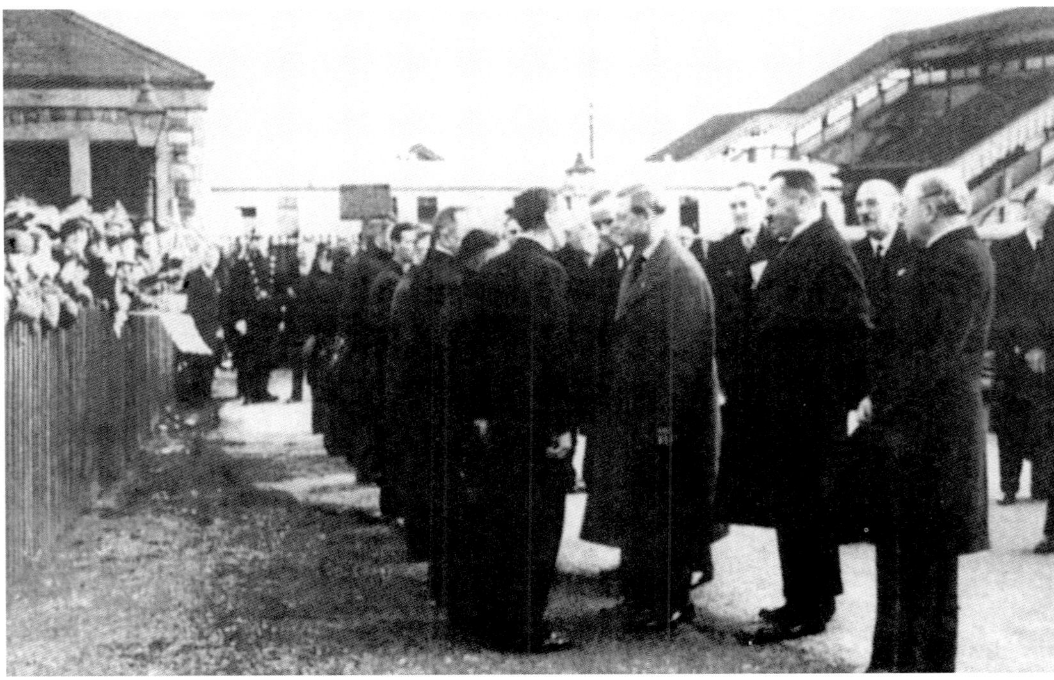

A 'future' King Edward VIII upon arrival at the station in 1936.

Steam traction was replaced in 1957 by diesel multiple units as the photograph overleaf clearly shows a bustling station. Yet only a few years later the line was deemed unprofitable and closure inevitable. What a shame that as Chairman of the British Railways Board Dr. Beeching's infamous 'knife' was not blunted much earlier by a ruthless government. But with competition from buses and an increasing loss of passenger revenue he actually had little choice other than to use the proverbial 'axe' to withdraw services which had provided the locals with transport since 1852. The last passenger train to stop at the valley station ran on 30th April, 1962, from Newport to Blaenafon. Mineral and parcel traffic continued to pass over the 'metals' until 1966 when over 100 years of railway history had reached the 'end of the line'.

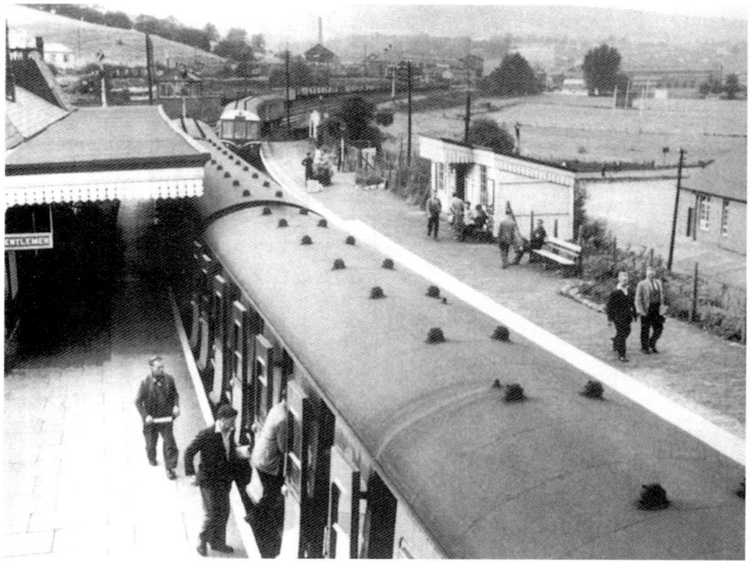

Cwmbrân Station shortly before its closure in 1962.

The whole system was later dismantled; the station buildings and bridges were demolished and the track pulled up and replaced by a public car park and the Village Surgery. Even relics of the earlier railway at Abbey Road and Commercial Street which was abandoned as a third passenger route into Cwmbrân station (Oakfield) in 1879 were obliterated to make way for Cwmbrân Drive - much to the convenience of the rapidly increasing number of motorists. The village with its original railway as seen from the old stone-built bridge will bring fond memories to those old enough to remember. The lack of all transport links by rail isolated a burgeoning new town from the 'outside world'. No-one in authority seemed to care. After all, the future lay in the development of the road infrastructure. Was this really in the name of progress? Clearly not and something to ponder over...

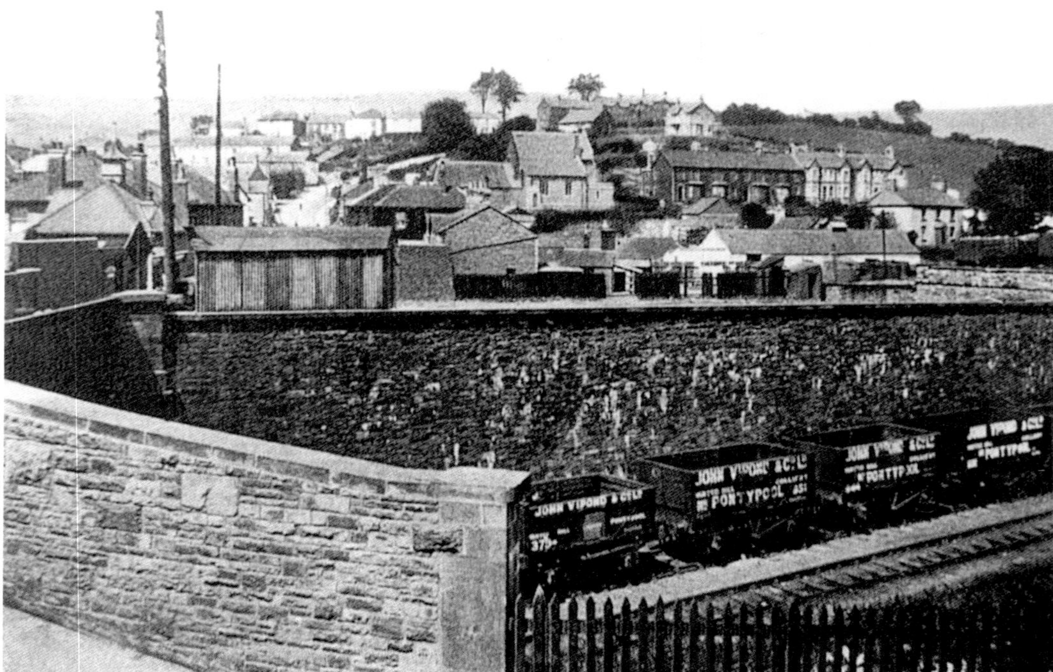

The village and original railway as viewed from the old stone bridge.

A BRIEF LOOK AT THE INDUSTRIAL AND MANUFACTURING SCENE

The emergence of Cwmbrân as a centre of industrial prosperity is all too well documented. Nowadays, the manufacturing scene is a mere shadow of its former self. This subject along with the history of several former industries such as Oakfield Wire Works and Guest, Keen & Nettlefold will be dealt with in a future book. Also, the short-lived but dominant presence of Forge Hammer with its

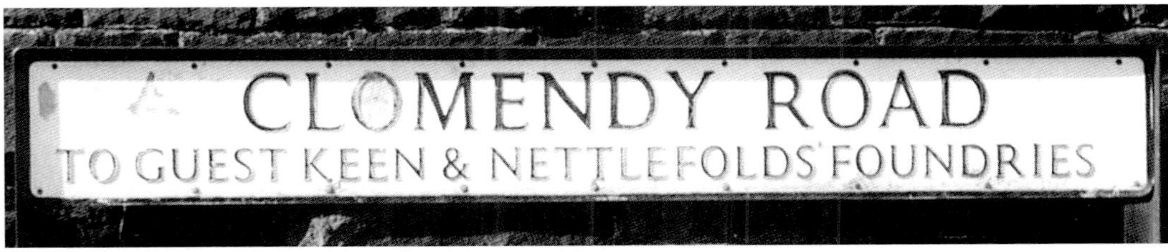

A reminder of an industrial giant.

primarily Irish Catholic community who regularly suffered physical and verbal abuse from their largely English Protestant neighbours. Clearly, history shows us that sectarian prejudice is nothing new. Nonetheless, it is important to recount the history of Cwmbrân Colliery of which little has been presented for public perusal and which helped shape the district and, ultimately, would in years to follow lead to the success of 'light' and economically viable business enterprises.

CWMBRÂN COLLIERY

In 1879 the Patent Nut & Bolt Company opened Cwmbrân Colliery at the head of Springvale Valley. This was an adit mine i.e. a horizontal entrance or passage into the hillside to tap into the underground coal seam. Deep mining was unnecessary hereabouts as the coal was easily accessible. A coke-oven plant, fed

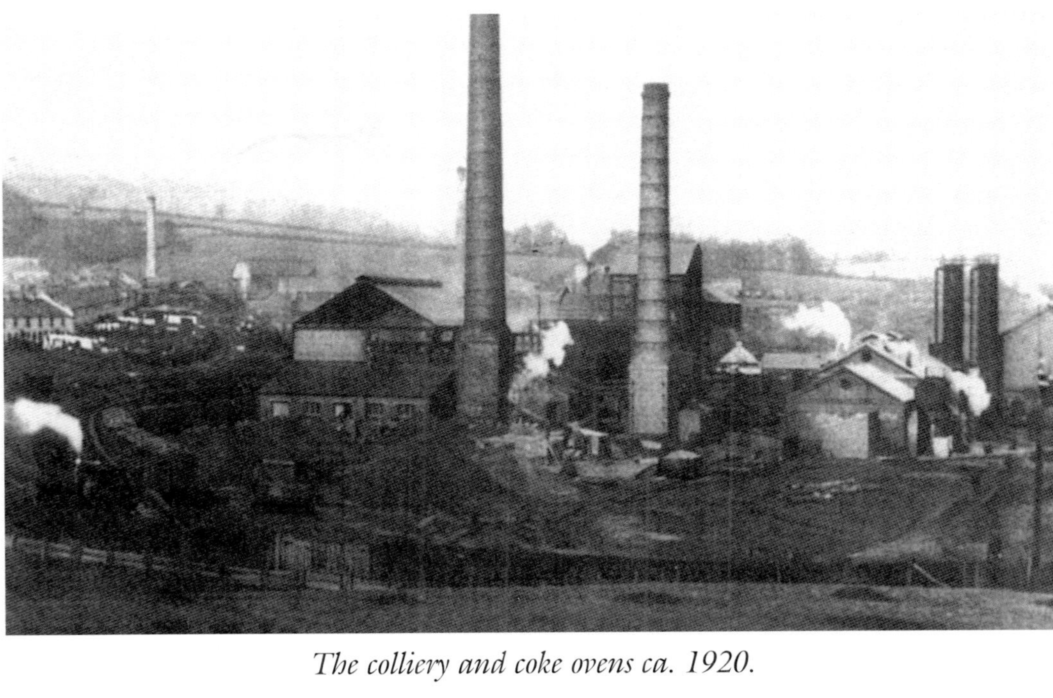

The colliery and coke ovens ca. 1920.

from the mine by conveyor belt, was built nearby soon afterwards to provide the fuel needed for the blast furnaces and foundries which had sprung up alongside the canal. By 1900 the colliery was also servicing the large works of Guest, Keen & Nettlefold.

On the previous page a rare view of the coke ovens and colliery taken around the early 1920s shows a thriving 'works'; on the mid left are the Springvale Company houses which are long since gone. At its peak the colliery employed over 1,000 men. Cwmbrân was certainly 'booming'. However, an ill-fated strike by the miners in 1926 led to the closure of the colliery in the following year causing severe unemployment and economic hardship to the miners and their families.

Water has always presented a problem in the mining industry and the adit mine was no exception. Following its closure there was an abundance of water pouring out of the disused mine shaft. The former Cwmbrân Urban District Council was the water authority until 1961 and as such was responsible for the public water supply. During periods of relative drought, water was pumped from the mine to a filter house in Upper Cwmbrân which then passed directly into the supply system. Domestic water was often discoloured due to seepage of mineral deposits in the long disused shaft. People knew when 'adit water' was 'switched on tap' because it was tainted though they were told that it was still perfectly safe to drink. Hmm...

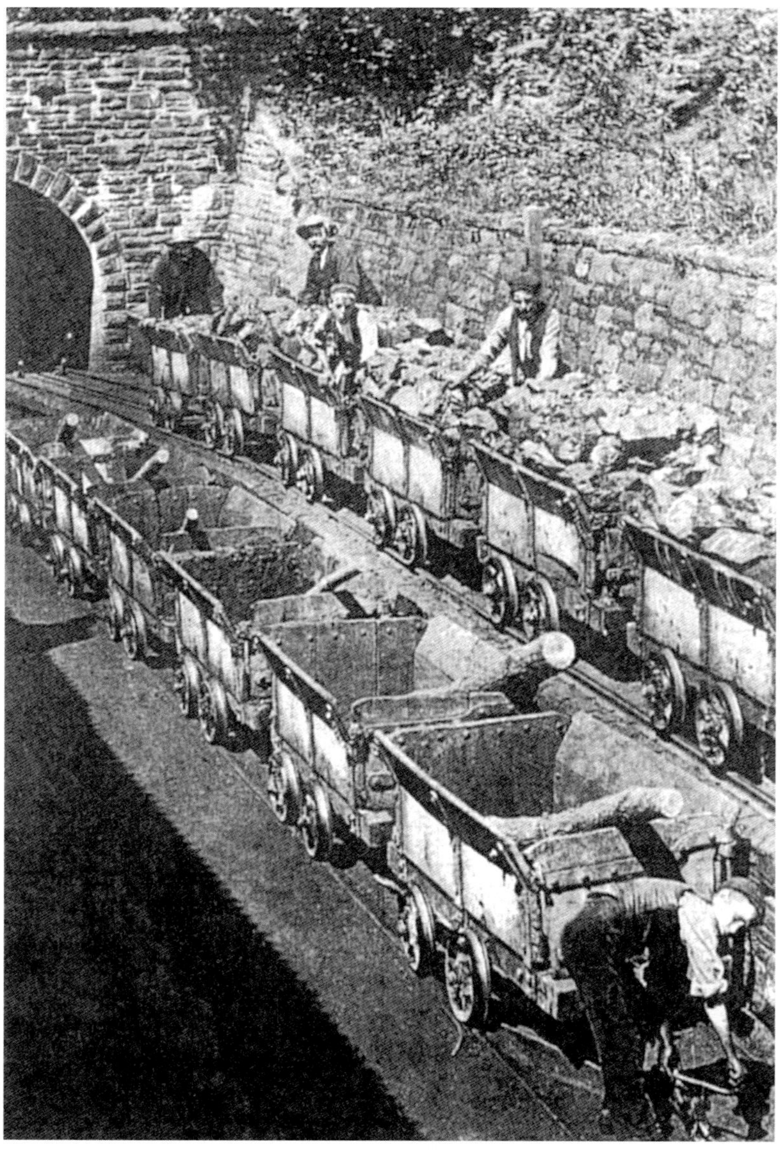

Entrance to the adit mine with young boys hard at work.

The colliery had a relatively short lifespan of barely 50 years, but was an important source of employment and later a provider of water to the population. The photograph showing the entrance to the mine, together with coal and pit-prop trams, offers a fascinating insight into the reality of mining life when young boys were expected to do a man's job. But not for a man's wage. The entrance, though closed off and overgrown by ivy and vegetation, can still be seen and is a reminder of Cwmbrân's industrial heritage.

GIRLING LIMITED

Girling, a member of the Joseph Lucas group, had several factories across the United Kingdom. Its Cwmbrân operation began in 1938 on a 12-acre site alongside Grange Road where it manufactured brakes and equipment for the motor, agricultural and railway industries designed by Captain A.H. Girling. It supplied parts to many of the largest vehicle manufacturers in Europe. Originally a war-time shadow factory, the works went on to produce many thousands of brakes and shock absorbers using automatic machines on the then latest 'flow-line' technology. By the early 1960s it had become a major employer in the area with over 4,000 workers engaged in the production of drum brakes for cars and commercial vehicles. However, world markets are invariably competitive and volatile. Its 'heady' days of extreme success are long over. In recent years the company changed ownership to become Lucas Varity and is now owned wholly by the powerful American company of Arvin Meritor. Nonetheless, to ageing local residents it is still remembered simply as Girlings.

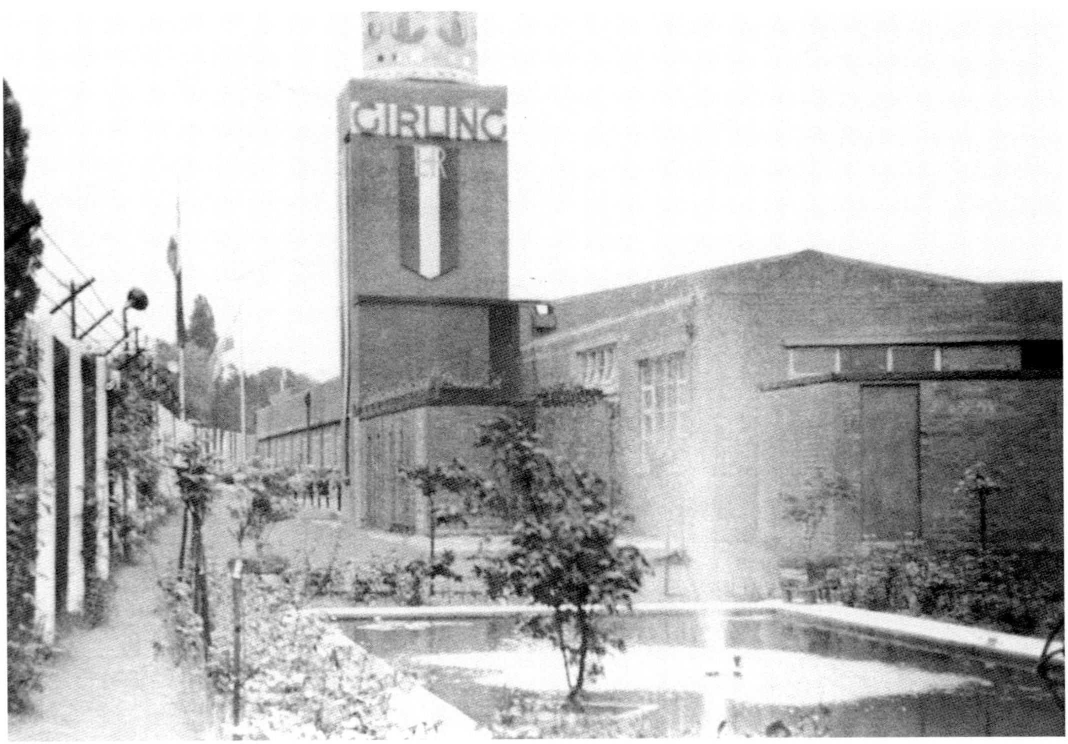

A fountain of hope which ran out of steam.

SAUNDERS VALVE COMPANY

Arriving from the Midlands, the company established its engineering works alongside Grange Road industrial estate during October 1939 and was officially opened by Alderman Arthur Jenkins M.P. for Pontypool. Invented in South Africa by engineer P.K. Saunders in 1929, the original rubber weir-type diaphragm valve was an immediate success as a means of reducing leakage in compressed air pipelines of the Rand gold mines. The innovative valve quickly found further applications in the chemical, petroleum, food and drink, steel and atomic energy industries, in waterworks and sewage plants.

With substantial financial backing from the Government to increase employment in a depressed area the company was destined to flourish: the original workforce of 250 steadily grew to over 1,500. Its outstanding export record was recognised in 1966 by a Queen's Award to Industry. Recent years have seen the company taken over by Alfa Laval and by the Crane Company.

The reliance upon the former heavy industries of coal and iron production are now well and truly in the past and merely a fading memory. Much former 'brown-site' land has been reclaimed for new 'lighter' industrial estates. The development of the town has attracted much growth and inward investment in promoting manufacturing, technological and service industries. The future looks bright - or so we wish to assume. But who can say?

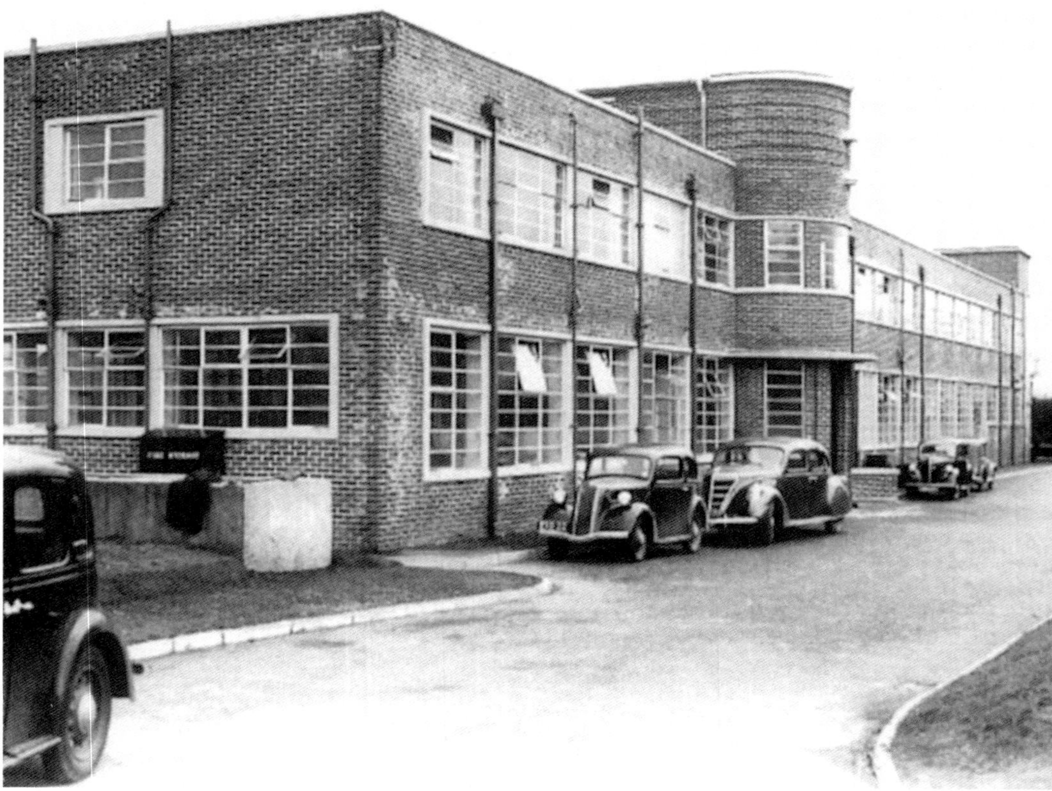

A new arrival - complete with valves.

Henllys

The parish of Henllys stretches from the Nant-y-Milwr brook in the north of the village to Bettws in the south. The older part of Henllys typifies everything that is good and fine about the rural landscape. Though in splendid isolation, it remains a gem where warblers greet the ethereal breeze while shrill skylarks spiral invisibly high overhead; and where wayside brooks endlessly voice the music of timelessness itself. In such quietude and dignity there is a sense of transience, of other worldliness, a spiritual experience which extols the sheer beauty and tranquillity of God's chosen acre.

Henllys in Welsh simply means ***'Old Court'***, which suggests it refers to a place where in pre-Norman times an important chieftain or ruler held ***'court'***. It is easy to speculate this may have stood on the site of an ancient farmhouse high on the slope below Twm Barlwm and a mile beyond the church, and which bears the name ***'Cwrt Henllys'***. The latter translates as ***'Court Old Court'***. Most confusing.

CASTELL-Y-BŴCH

Castell-y-Bŵch is most certainly a name to conjure with, one that rolls off a Welshman's lips with the sheer lyricism of poetry. Situated on the western flank of the ancient trackway between Llantarnam and Henllys it overlooks the enchanting Vale of Henllys. But what does it mean? Bŵch in Welsh simply means ***'buck'*** (as in that of a male deer). The English translation ***'Buck's Castle'*** is prosaic and hardly likely to stir the imagination.

In folklore the name has long been associated with the giant, Bŵch Gawr (Bŵch the Giant) who lived in the neighbourhood. Little is known about him, except that he fathered six sons each of whom grew to their father's stature. The giant's wife must have been a veritable amazon! Poor Bŵch ended his days by having his head cut off. Why, remains unanswered. His sons survived and prospered, and had ***'castles'*** of their own, some locally and others over the border in Glamorgan. Another legend maintains that a former Lord Tredegar was hunting deer in the surrounding countryside when a frightened stag sought refuge beside ***'a petrified tree near the pub'*** - hence the name. Both tales seem equally implausible to modern-day folk, but are a valuable part of country lore.

Castell-y-Bŵch remains an isolated hamlet on a ridge aptly named ***Cefn Vynoche***, that is, the ***'monks' ridge'***. To this very day, the heart of the community revolves around the ancient inn of the same name. The inn was largely rebuilt some 80 years or more ago, but the original building probably dates back to the 17th-century, if not much earlier.

In the distant past, monks regularly journeyed from Llantarnam Abbey en route to the holy and mystical tumulus of Twm Barlwm on the crown of the southern end of Mynydd Maen. They surely paused at the inn to seek sustenance and rest their weary legs. And no doubt took the opportunity to imbibe the odd pint or two of home-brewed beer or cider. Presumably, the monks' libations on the outward trek were eagerly anticipated. And, equally, on the return journey too!

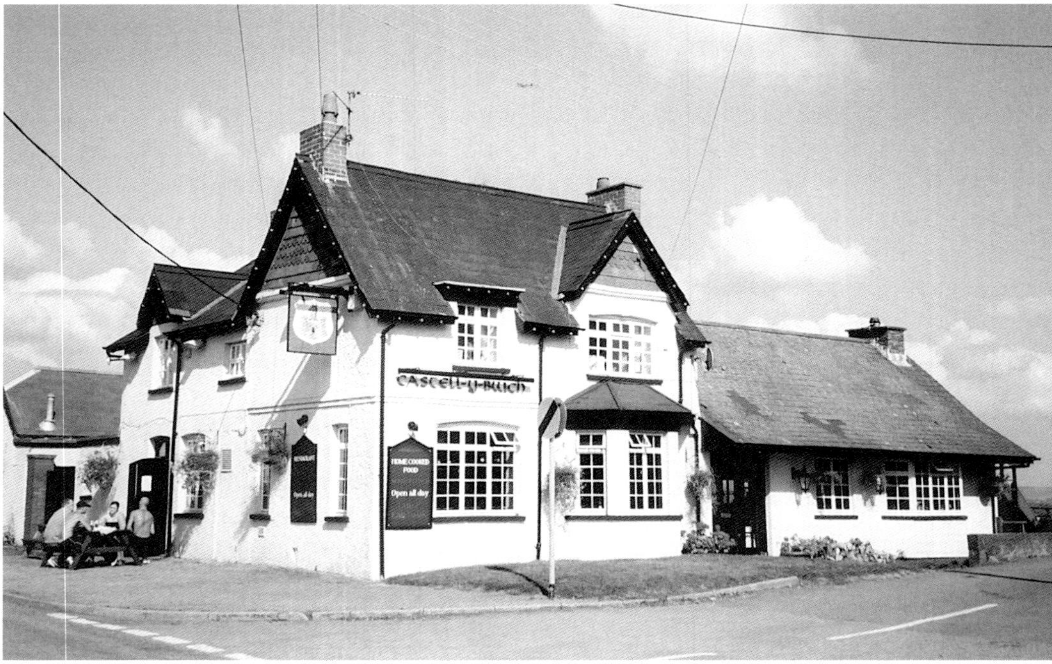

Castell-y-Bŵch inn.

An insight into a former way of life and ***'mountain tastes'*** was vividly described by that famous son of Gwent, Arthur Machen, in ***'Far Off Things'*** (1922): ***'I once saw a woman putting the last touches to a flat apple tart in a little tavern called Castell-y-bŵch...She drew out the tart from the oven, prised open the lid of pastry, and inserted some half-pound of butter and half-pound of moist Demerara sugar; and then put back the lid and replaced the pastry in the oven: so that apple juice, sugar, butter should fuse all together. That is a fair sample of hill cookery: other people of the hills...would buy 'green' Caerphilly cheese, still melting from the press: and they loved to plaster butter heavily on hot new bread and then crown all with an equal depth of golden honey.'*** The mouth waters as the taste buds excite at such a prospect.

No doubt the tramp-poet W.H. Davies also strolled idly through the winding leafy lane from Llantarnam, paused at the old manor-house of Pentre Bach before making the steep ascent to the top of the ridge, there to slake his thirst at the inn with a pint or two of fine mild ale. And to muse and marvel at the wonders of Nature all around, there to watch the sun dip slowly over the softening contours and hues of the purple mountain ranges.

For well over 100 years members of the Samuel family were associated with the inn; during the late 19th-century they were also closely involved with the nearby Dorallt Inn in Henllys village itself.

Though extensively modernised, the Castell-y-Bŵch inn retains much of its original character, such as stout oak beams and flagstone floors and, in winter, the glorious smell of woodsmoke pervades the bar area. It is a thriving public house which offers a fine choice of ales, wines and excellent cuisine.

ZOAR BAPTIST CHAPEL

Within but a few yards from the inn stands Zoar Baptist Chapel which is no longer in use. This simple stone building opened in 1836 when the population of Henllys was a little over 200 to fulfil the spiritual needs of nonconformist parishioners disenchanted by the pomp and idolatry of the Established Church. Its austere interior had no gallery and the minister preached from behind a low railed platform to the congregation seated in box pews along the sides and on open-backed benches in the centre.

Inevitably, times change and the need for religious succour held little relevance to daily life. After generations of support, congregations steadily dwindled. Eventually, unable to sustain itself, it closed its doors for the last time during the 1980s - abandoned after over a century-and-a-half by those it had served so faithfully. Presently, the semi-derelict shell is undergoing renovation as a dwelling. Far better than being consigned to oblivion.

The formerly small overgrown walled burial ground with its stone stile fronting the passing highway has many fascinating tombstones which, though mellowed by age, are now placed around the 'garden'; these mirror the lives of those who toiled daily upon the land hereabouts.

Zoar has many tales to tell: full congregations, an active Sunday School, memorable Harvest Festivals (particularly meaningful in a rural community), and religious and secular events. These are now but a fading memory. Nonetheless, in 1974 the late Mrs. Brenda Samuel, who lived in the village, penned a quite remarkable essay entitled ***'STORIES IN STONE'*** which chronicles Zoar's history and reminisces about those who worshipped there. Though far too lengthy to include in its entirety, certain relevant extracts are worth recounting.

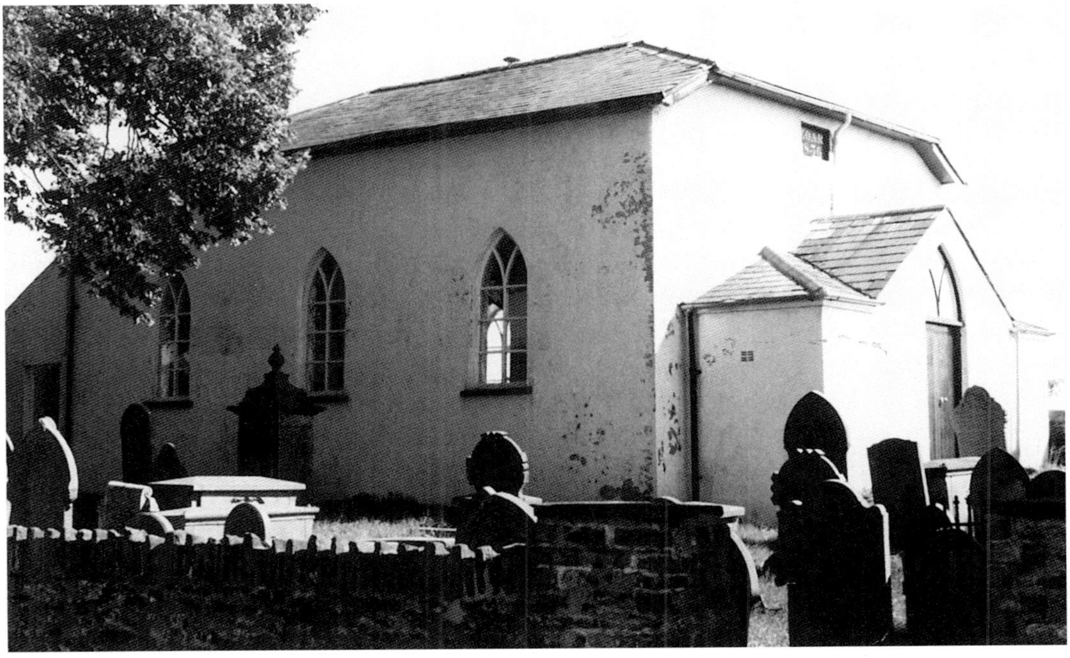

Zoar Baptist Chapel 1986.

'The stone stile...would have overheard the conversation about the man who stole sheep from the pound just up the road...and was hanged for the offence - the last man in Monmouthshire to be hanged for sheep stealing.'

The next is equally worthy of today's moral liberalism: *'...the people were talking about a wedding in Henllys Church which had been stopped at the altar in the nick of time when it was found out that the couple were both males. They probably said to themselves: We're glad it wasn't in our chapel!'*

Drunkenness was prevalent during the latter part of the 19th-century and the Castell-y-Bŵch inn was no exception for ale could be had at all times of the day. The following shows that even clerics are known to enjoy the odd tipple or more. *'In 1897 one David Lewis accepted a call to Zoar...A frail little man, in 1901 he committed a deadly sin...after visiting some parishioners one Saturday evening and partaking of some home-made wine. He enjoyed it and being rather drowsy upon leaving the farmhouse...he lay down by the roadside and fell asleep'.*

'His dear wife became worried when he did not return home by midnight and went to the Castell-y-Bŵch Inn to tell them...a search party was organised and eventually in the early hours of the morning the hapless Mr. Lewis was found and brought home in the horse and trap pleasantly snoring. A chapel meeting was called...and Mr. Lewis was asked to resign...The couple moved to a little cottage at the top of Henllys on the side of the Incline and he became full minister at Mount Pleasant, a chapel founded later in the north of the parish.' Following his wife's death in 1910, the once disgraced cleric lived alone and died in 1913, leaving all his worldly possessions to his new ministry. A wholly charming account showing the folly of men, whatever their station in life.

One particular headstone in the old graveyard is dedicated to the Reverend Harry Samuel. During one of his Christmas sermons in the early 1900s, he commented *'to our sorrow we hear that it is not for the commemoration of Jesus Christ, but chiefly to enjoy ourselves in eating, drinking and making merry'*. A most pertinent statement, for exactly the same can be said of today's Yuletide festivities as celebrated by the vast majority of adults.

An article celebrating the centenary of Zoar (originally and more aptly known as the Farmers' Church) appeared, surprisingly, in the ***Daily Express*** in 1936 and offers a graphic insight into former religious practice. It states: *'For generations people were baptised in a nearby mountain stream, but torrential rains made the ceremony extremely difficult. A brick baptistry was constructed in a field at Gelli Vach nearby...where the black-robed candidates from the chapel were immersed; (this) is one of the few churches carrying out baptism in the open air.'*

The essay concludes: *'The stones go on standing, listening to the swish of cars as they hurry by...and think of quieter days and murmur one to another that this world has changed and they want no part in it!'* Surely a fitting summary to a fine piece of prose. For the stones of Time have seen and know it all...

Both inn and chapel overlook the lush pastoral that is Henllys Vale with its fertile fields and quietly hidden copses, picturesque stone cottages and scattered white-washed farmsteads.

Castell-y-Bŵch is indeed fortunate for it is largely unspoilt by the passage of centuries. Also, the rural way of life has hardly changed and is much the same as in the past. May the threatening tentacles of urban sprawl never encroach upon this idyll in the same way it has already all but destroyed the character of a once proud Henllys village centre.

HENLLYS CHURCH

Henllys Church is a simple medieval church standing alone in open hill country on the western side of the Valley of the Crow and some considerable distance from the heart of the village itself. The earliest mention of it dates from 1230-40. Unlike many churches, it possesses few adornments or elaborate monuments to long-forgotten noble families. Therein lies its charm for its rural simplicity allows worshippers to come close to God without distraction.

The church dedicated to St. Peter is overshadowed by the vast range of Mynydd Maen which acts as a backcloth silhouetted starkly against a wondrous and expansive skyline. The building is largely screened by an ancient yew. Much-needed restoration was carried out during the 1870s and again 100 years later. Yet the structure still retains an old stone roof. Very recently, the exterior walls were 'white washed' using modern sealant agents; it is now resplendent in its original Norman glory.

The slim Perpendicular embattled west tower built in two stages has a stair-turret rising well clear of the parapet. It houses three bells: the smallest is dated ca. 1350 and is probably the oldest in the County of the type known as ***'Bristol Bells'***, because such bells were cast at the great medieval foundry at Bristol. This bell may have been a gift to the church from grateful parishioners who survived a virulent plague which ravaged South-East Wales in 1348. The other two bear the dates 1656 and 1711. All three bells remain in working order.

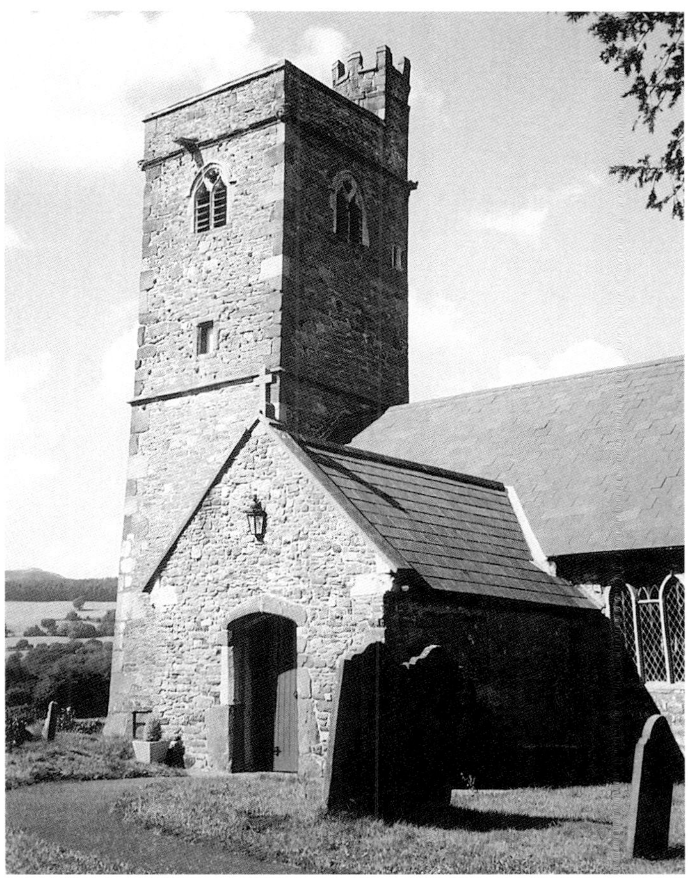

The Church of St. Peter as seen over centuries.

The chancel with its barrel roof divided into compartments with frames of oak and nave

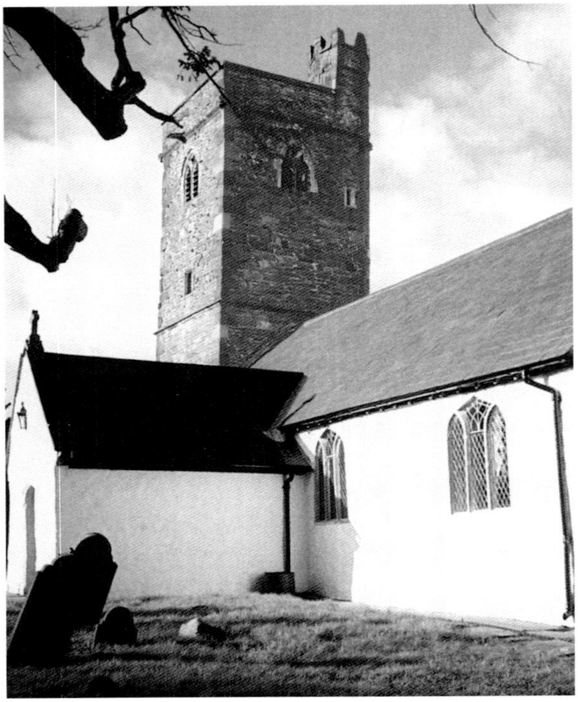

The Church recently 'white-washed' to its original glory.

hold little of architectural merit. Medieval wall paintings, though flaking badly after so long a time, were lost forever when the decaying plaster was removed during the more recent restorative work; only a few traces of the once highly-coloured murals are still visible.

Above the 14th-century windows runs a course decorated at each corner with a quaint stone face and a peculiar animal. Several such figure-heads also look outwards from the upper part of the tower. The common belief was that dragons and demons wished to usurp the will of God. These often grotesque carvings were a means of defiance, a way of protecting the church from such evil forces. More significantly, perhaps, they were a reminder to those who entered the sanctity of the building to leave immoral passions outside.

The octagonal font is ancient and, unusually, of red granite. It stands close to the main entrance and symbolises the entry of the newly christened into the life of God's holy church. The church registers date from around 1754.

Henllys and nearby Bettws were former chapelries under Bassaleg, but the former was constituted a rectory in the late 19th-century. The parish has long been fortunate in securing the services of well-educated incumbents, surely reflecting the status and affluence of this rural part of the County. Two early members of the clergy were Edward Lewis, M.A., appointed 1791, followed by John Leyson, B.A., University College and St. Alban Hall, Oxford, in 1814, the son of Thomas Leyson the vicar of Bassaleg.

The longest serving rector was David Jesse Evans whose devotion to his parishioners from 1900 until his retirement in 1936 at the age of 81 years was much admired. Upon his death in 1941 he was buried in the churchyard. In his will he bequeathed £150 for improvements to his beloved church, a considerable sum even at that time.

The walls of the interior display few memorial inscriptions of interest. However, a wooden plaque on the south wall of the nave remembers the kind disposition of ***'David Williams, Yeoman, of the parish of Henllys left by his will dated 30th December 1809 one hundred pounds, the interest of which to be divided annually amongst the poor of the said parish'***. A flat gravestone in the nave recalls Charles

John who died on 25th April, 1785, aged 89 years. Under the floorboards of the pews lie many ancient if well-worn tombstones. A 'mural tablet' on the north wall to Adam Thomas muses on mortality. The third verse reads:

Consider then and be not proud,
Thy time will come to wear a shroud,
With me and them that's gone before
To lie with worms, which craves for more.

Several of the headstones in the churchyard bear verses in Welsh alone, but the lettering has all but been obliterated by the weathering of centuries. Arthur Machen, while working in ***'the tents of Fleet Street'***, described the church with its ***'graves with flourished inscriptions, deeply cut, and queer Welsh rhymes'***. A fragment of an ancient preaching cross has a base of four steps surmounted by the stump of the original column; its 'head' almost certainly destroyed during the Reformation when any form of religious imagery was deemed anathema.

A flat stone beside the great yew marks the resting place of several members of the Winsloe family who lived at Vale Farm during the 19th-century where ***'Mother Winsloe's Soothing Syrup'*** was brewed. According to the church registers, Mrs. Elizabeth Winsloe had four children, three of whom, two boys and a girl, died in infancy. Her ***'Soothing Syrup'*** may have benefited others but, unfortunately, had little effect in prolonging the life-span of her own siblings. Yet bear in mind that child mortality in those days was very high indeed. Mrs. Winsloe herself died in 1859 aged 54 years. There is no mention of her husband, John Hodges Winsloe, nor of their third son, John. They most likely moved away from the farm which held such painful memories.

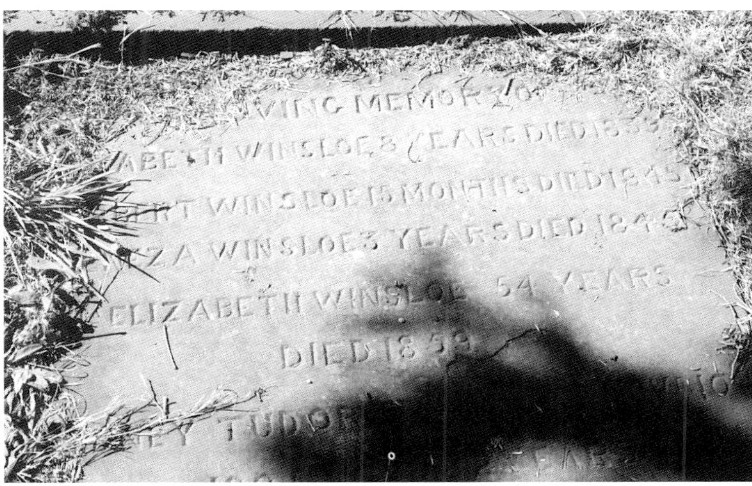

Mother Winsloe's grave.

The great yew is remarkable for its trunk has a girth of some 14 feet; its spreading canopy is around 40 feet in diameter and several of its side branches are supported by wooden props! The following lines penned by the poet Walter De La Mare in his poem ***'Trees'*** are both perceptive and wholly appropriate as they refer to the red fleshy cups that protect the yew seeds, ***'little flames amidst sombre foliage'***:

Of all the trees in England,
Oak, Elder, Elm and Thorn,
The yew alone burns lamps of peace,
For them that lie forlorn.

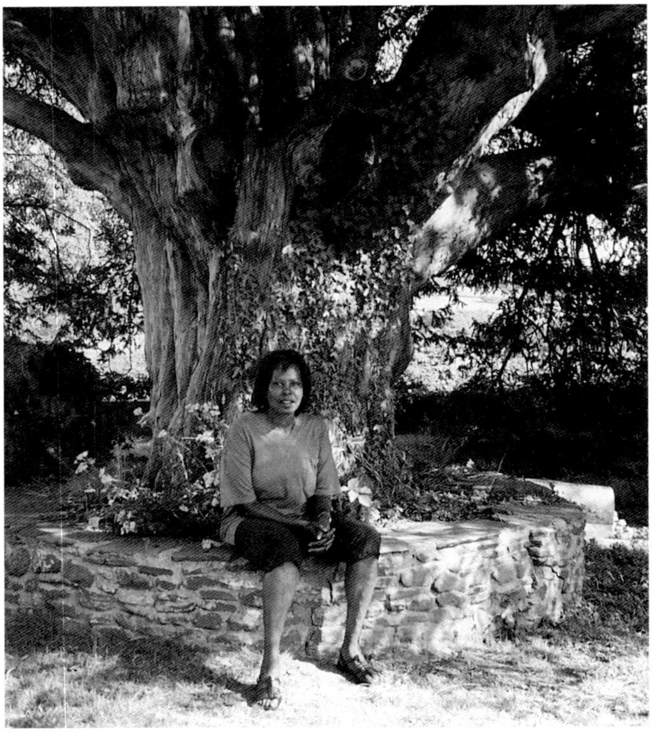

The great yew's girth is staggering.

A stone seat squared around its base provides for rest and contemplation. This venerable tree, reckoned to be at least 300 years old, stands alongside the main pathway and entrance to the church via the south porch. It is impossible to miss!

An upright stone presents an enigma. For John Button, Esq., of Penlangwyn, Llantarnam, who died in May 1891, aged 92 years, together with his wife, Eliza, who joined him later in the same year, aged 75 years, rest here. Why were they not buried in St. Michael's churchyard, Llantarnam?

PANT-YR-EOS

A short distance from St. Peter's Church is Pant-yr-Eos reservoir. The name translates as ***'the hollow or valley of the nightingale'***, a beautiful and meaningful expression both in Welsh and English as this great pool of water nestles into its very own hollow on the lower slopes of the 'pimple' that is Twm Barlwm, yet overlooking the serenity of Cwrt Henllys Farm just below. The reservoir helps supply water to the neighbouring City of Newport, several miles to the south east.

VALE FARM

Sometimes known as Henllys Farm, Vale Farm is found just before the ascent to Castell-y-Bŵch on the magical journey from Llantarnam. Probably built early in the 17th-century, its appearance resembles that of an ecclesiastical building rather than a humble farmhouse. The house is in three distinct parts: the middle section suggests that it may have been used for religious worship by devout Catholics during the religious persecutions of the time. After all, members of the Morgan family at nearby Pentre Bach and Llantarnam Abbey were instrumental in the vain attempt to place Mary, Queen of Scots, on the throne of England rather than the Protestant Elizabeth.

The farm has been in the Richards family for well nigh on 100 years and like many old houses probably harbours tales of haunting to delight the folklorist. Do ghosts frequent modern dwellings? An interesting thought.

The house has several distinguishing features. Two upright stone slabs in the boundary wall that abuts the lane close by, referred to as stiles, once formed the entrance to the house. Within the house are several window-seats with walls nearly 3-feet thick and oak frames. Compare that with today's flimsy housing construction! Long ago, the building had some 46 windows, but with the introduction of the dreaded ***'Window Tax'*** or levy on windows, or ***'openings for light'*** in 1696 during the reign of William III, those above six in number were bricked in to reduce the expense of taxation. To gain extra revenue, in 1825 the windows taxable went up to eight and became ***'House Duty'***. This ceased in 1851. And we complain about excessive taxation in this, the 21st-century!

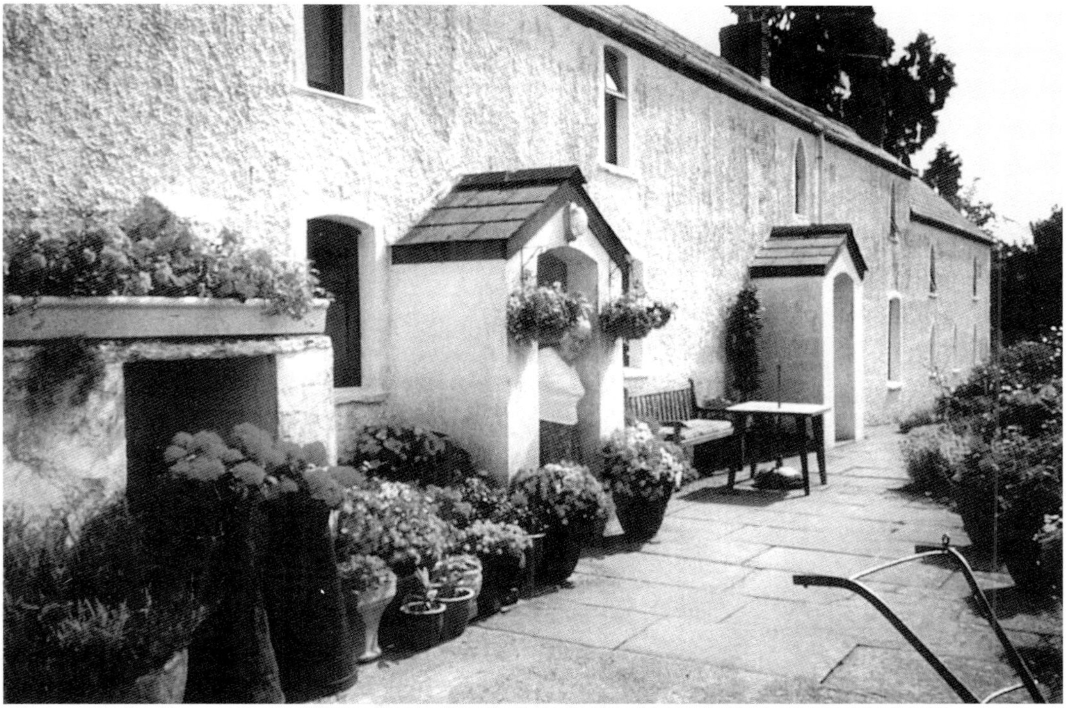

Vale Farm with Mrs. Richards admiring her blooms.

The rear of the house provided a coaching stop complete with stables, a granary (formerly the servants' sleeping quarters) and a cider-house. Moreover, there was an external kitchen with a bake-oven, cheese-press and two boilers. But why two boilers?

Apparently members of the Winsloe family, together with a Mr. Henry Francis of Church Cottage, Henllys Mill, collected herbs from the surrounding countryside and stewed them in the boilers. The resultant brew was bottled and sold locally as ***'Mother Winsloe's Soothing Syrup'***. The recipe was a closely guarded secret. At Primrose Cottage, just opposite the farm, Mrs. Winsloe held surgery and dispensed her potion to grateful folk; it became renowned as a remedy for inducing or 'hushing' infants to sleep. Mrs. Winsloe's ***'FAMILY ALMANAC & DOMESTIC RECEIPT BOOK'*** was published in 1874 and contains many fascinating remedies for a vast variety of ailments. For centuries certain herbs have

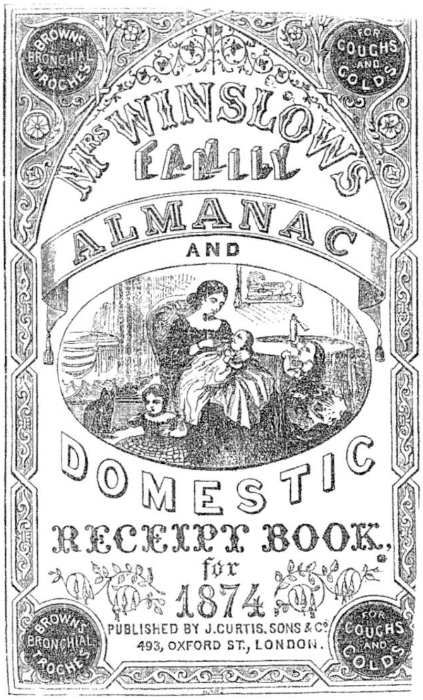

The front cover of Mrs. Winsloe's herbal recipe book.

been deemed to possess soporific properties. Prior to modern medicines, folk naturally pinned their faith in such traditional remedies; Bile Beans for a persistent cough and strong herbal wine. A glass or two of the latter still induces a state of relaxation and contentment.

Vale Farm also played a significant role in the social life of the village. From the early 1920s onwards, Henllys Village A.F.C. held many games there, amongst other venues, in the Newport & District Football League. The challenge of competition was an essential part of everyday life which brought the community together through often dark and troubled times.

And what of the youngsters of today? There can be no dearth of talent.

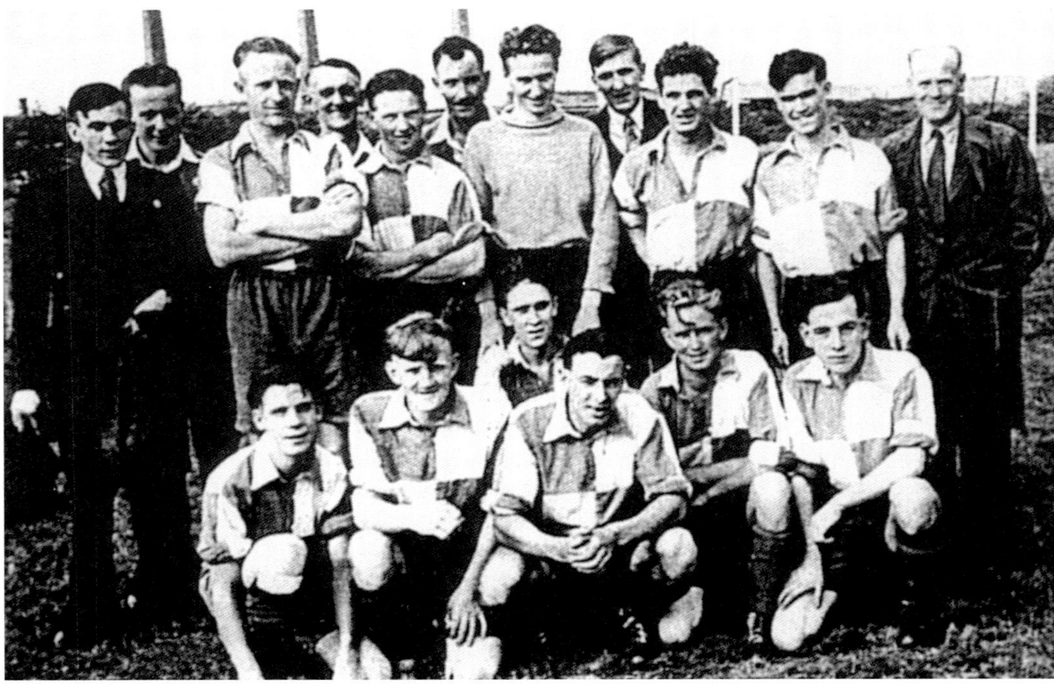

Henllys A.F.C. at Vale Farm during the late 1940s.
Back row: Trevor Roderick, Wally Jones, Bryn Richards, Ralph Prosser, Ron Roberts, Lyn Reeks, Rowland Barton, David Roderick, Derek Prosser, Alan Higgs, Aubrey Smith.
Front row: Maurice Reeks, Ray Tamplin, Byron Reeks, Mervyn Doody (Captain), Jim Roberts, Albert Phillips.

GOLD IN THEM THERE HILLS!

Gold in Henllys? What could seem more unlikely? Yet in the past people of sturdy stock really believed so. An old and very rare picture post card possibly dating from around the 1870s shows Pandy Bach Farm (long gone). Two women standing in the front garden are dressed in traditional Welsh costume and provide an emphatic reminder that during the 19th-century Welsh was the spoken language of the area. Yet of greater significance is the clear wording ***'THE NEW GOLDMINE'***. Most intriguing.

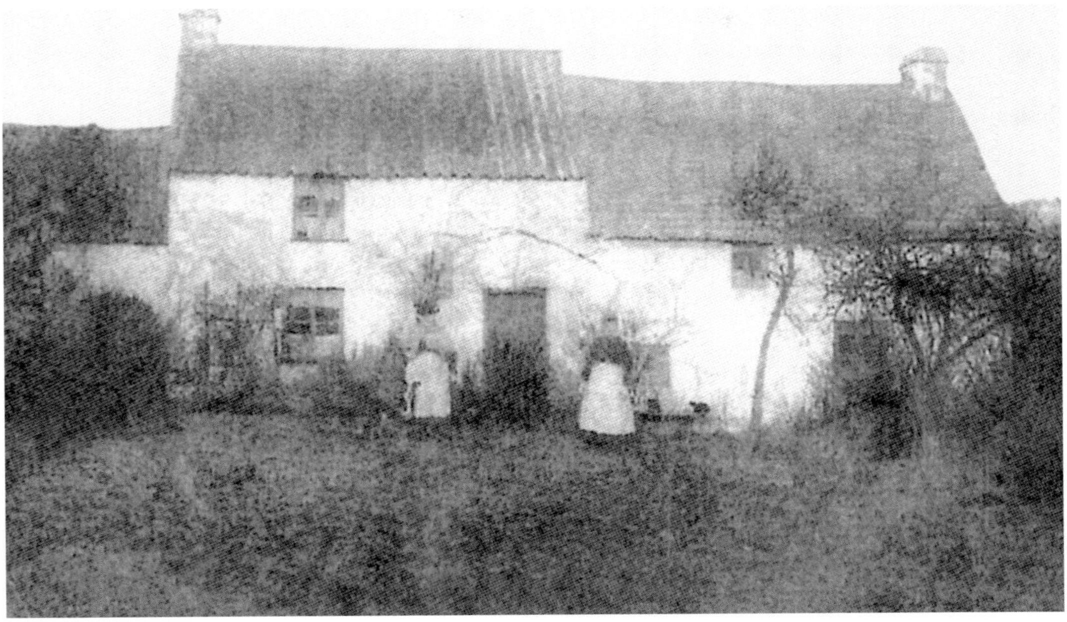

Pandy Bach Farm ca. 1870s, scene of 'Gold Fever'.

Legend tells of gold being discovered in the Nant-y-Pandy whose crystal clear waters emanate from a spring high on the steep slopes of Mynydd Henllys and which sally and bicker until meeting the Nant Henllys before joining the Pant-yr-Eos brook; then meandering silently through the ***'valley of the nightingales'*** towards Bettws Brook, Malpas Brook and finally to merge with the murky waters of the tidal River Usk. Quite a delightful journey.

An elderly couple were panning in the brook close to their garden when, suddenly, the cry went out that ***'gold had been found'***, but ***'not enough to work a mine'***. Word spread quickly throughout the scattered community (the 1881 census lists just over 330 inhabitants). **'Gold Fever'** was in the air. The old folk guarded the 'strike' day and night with a gun and a dog to protect their claim. Children were warned not to venture to the Pandy as it was far too dangerous!

It seems likely that the couple had stumbled across 'fool's gold', a lookalike but worthless sample of iron pyrites commonly found throughout South-East Wales and a remnant from previous coal workings on the mountainside high above. Moreover, with no further finds, rumours quickly circulated that the couple just wanted to sell the cottage and that the supposed 'gold strike' was a shrewd means of enhancing the value of the property. Which may well have been true.

Certainly, Wales is renowned for the precious metal. (England has none.) And panning is still practised in many streams throughout the Principality. The likelihood of a rich strike remains the dream of many even today. Incidentally, and not generally common knowledge, the Queen's wedding ring is made of rare Welsh gold: antique and modern jewellery containing Welsh gold commands a high price.

It is interesting to speculate whether the ladies pictured on the card actually made the clothes they were wearing and were part of the cloth trade. After all, the name ***'Pandy'*** means ***'Fulling Mill'***, which suggests that during the 18th and 19th-centuries a small cottage industry flourished there. 'Fulling' is the process of cleaning, shrinking and thickening cloth by moisture, heat and pressure. The Nant-y-Pandy could certainly have provided sufficient water power to operate a nearby mill. However, there is little evidence to support this assumption, but such industry was fairly common throughout the rural areas of the County.

The card itself has journeyed the world for it was taken to Australia by men seeking fortune in the famous gold rush of the time. An original copy survives and returned to its Welsh roots only a few years ago.

The foregoing makes fascinating reading. And the postcard is genuine. But is the story true? No matter. For it has become firmly ingrained in the area's folklore. When myth becomes legend, believe the legend! Just a ***'flash in the pan'***. Or was it?

SHEEPDOG TRIALS

The annual sheepdog trials marked an eagerly anticipated event in the countryside calendar. (It still does in the neighbouring parish of Mynydd Islwyn.) The first trials at Henllys began in 1889 and were held thereafter every August, but ended in the early 1960s when the housing development of Cwmbrân New Town began to impinge upon the outskirts of this peaceful village.

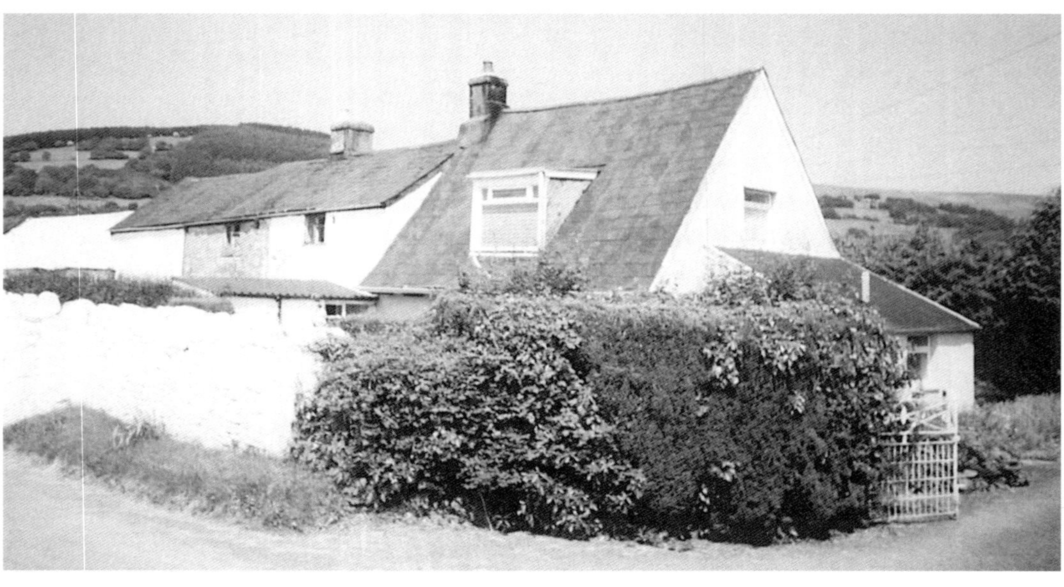

Cock-y-North Farm.

The trials were held at Cock-y-North Farm where those unable to pay the entry fee could sit and enjoy the entertainment from the slope overlooking the fields called *'The Park'*. Competitors came not just from the locality, but from all over the country. Such was the appeal of the occasion.

Competitions ranged from Welsh Mountain Sheep (open to hill farmers only), Welsh Ewes and lambs, and Ram Lamb, all under the control of well-trained sheepdogs. Yet there were other attractions too, with displays of produce, cookery, handicrafts, flower arrangements, sporting events and so on. In the Produce and Home Section prizes were awarded for Best Six White Eggs, Best Six Brown Eggs, Best Dressed Cockerel, Best Cake, Best Sponge, Best Six Welsh Cakes, Best Home Preserves, Best Hand-knitted Jumper, Child's Cardigan, Pullover, Best Hand-embroidered Afternoon Cloth, Cushion Cover, Chair Back or Tray Cloth and Best Collection of Garden Flowers. How many modern housewives are adept in culinary skills or making clothes? Our grandmothers had little option and practised 'household' skills handed down to them by their mothers. Those were the days...

The following two vintage photographs of officials and judges date from 1935. The smaller picture shows Mr. John Edmunds (Henllys) with Mr. Henry Richards (Cwmbrân), both of whom worked dogs in the very first trials many years earlier. The latter was the father of the famous marathon runner, Tom Richards, who won a silver medal in the 1948 Olympics held in London.

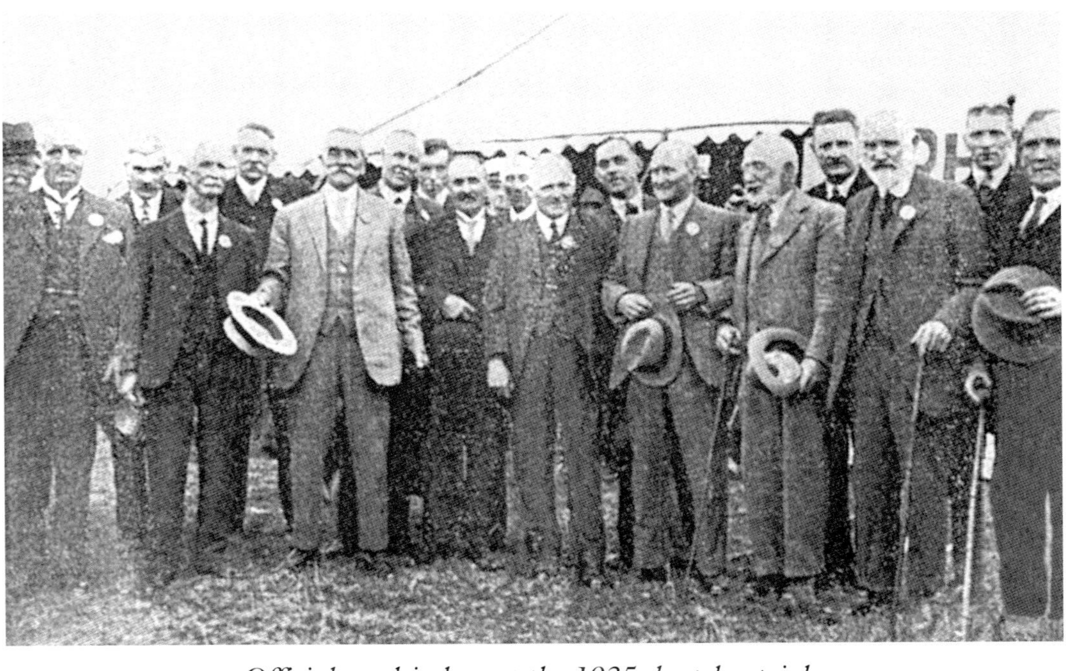

Officials and judges at the 1935 sheepdog trials.
The group includes W.H. Florida, John Herbert, B.V. Thomas, R. Dando, E. John, Fred Lloyd, F.C. Chappell, J. Lawrence, A. Williams, H. Richards, Thomas Lloyd (Chairman), W. Chappell (Treasurer), R.F. Roberts (Secretary).

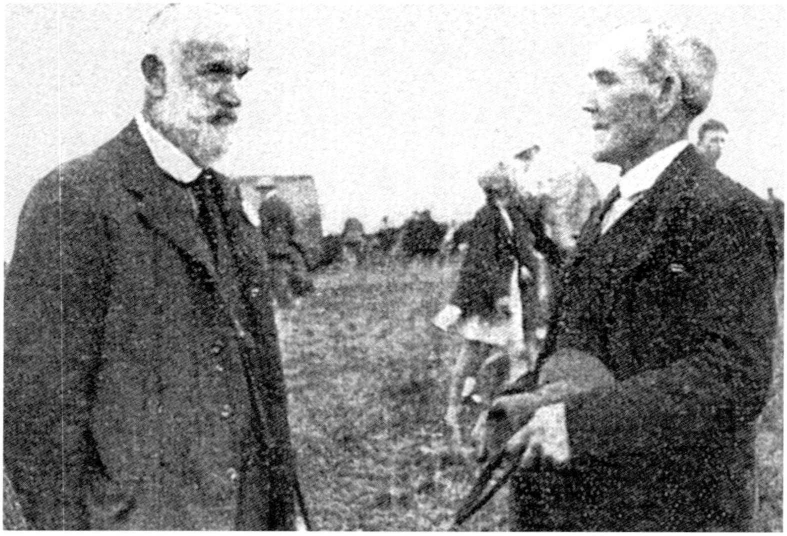

Veteran sheepdog experts John Edmunds and Henry Richards discuss the 1935 trials.

The day's celebrations concluded with a social evening and dance lasting from 9 till 1 a.m. at ***'The Ranch'***, the nickname for the community hall. As was the custom of the day, no alcoholic beverages were available at the hall. No doubt many men repaired to the local hostelries, the Castell-y-Bŵch or The Dorallt Inn, there to enjoy a tankard or two of fine ale. Just another instance of country life which, sadly, has been lost forever. For such rural existence was truly uplifting in the hearts and minds of our forefathers. Have we really moved with the times? Hmm…

THE VILLAGE HALL

During the early 1930s, the community felt they needed somewhere to socialise on a regular basis and for activities and entertainments. A village hall was the obvious answer. It was hoped to raise sufficient funds through public subscription, but this fell well short of the target. Fortunately, the Henllys Conservative & Unionist Association came to the rescue with financial aid and ***'The Ranch'*** was built, so-called because of its appearance and location surrounded by fields away from the actual village centre.The hall was much used for all sorts of functions. There were frequent sixpenny (old money) Hop Dances, usually on Saturdays, ever popular with the younger generations and those not so young at heart.

During the war years, there was an army camp at Graigllwarch Farm and the soldiers looked forward to the Saturday 'hop' at the village hall. This proved a blessing as one night in 1943 German bombers dropped two bombs on the area, one fell at Duffryn Wood and the other near the army base. Mercifully, there was no loss of human life, but several cows were killed. The bomb sites became an attraction, especially among children who collected shrapnel as souvenirs. Exciting for the youngsters maybe, but harrowing times for the adults. At the end of the war, a ***'Welcome Home'*** party was held in the hall to celebrate the safe return of twenty-nine local men and one woman from war service. Following a collection totalling £530, each 'war hero' was given the princely sum of £17 as a mark of respect by a grateful community.

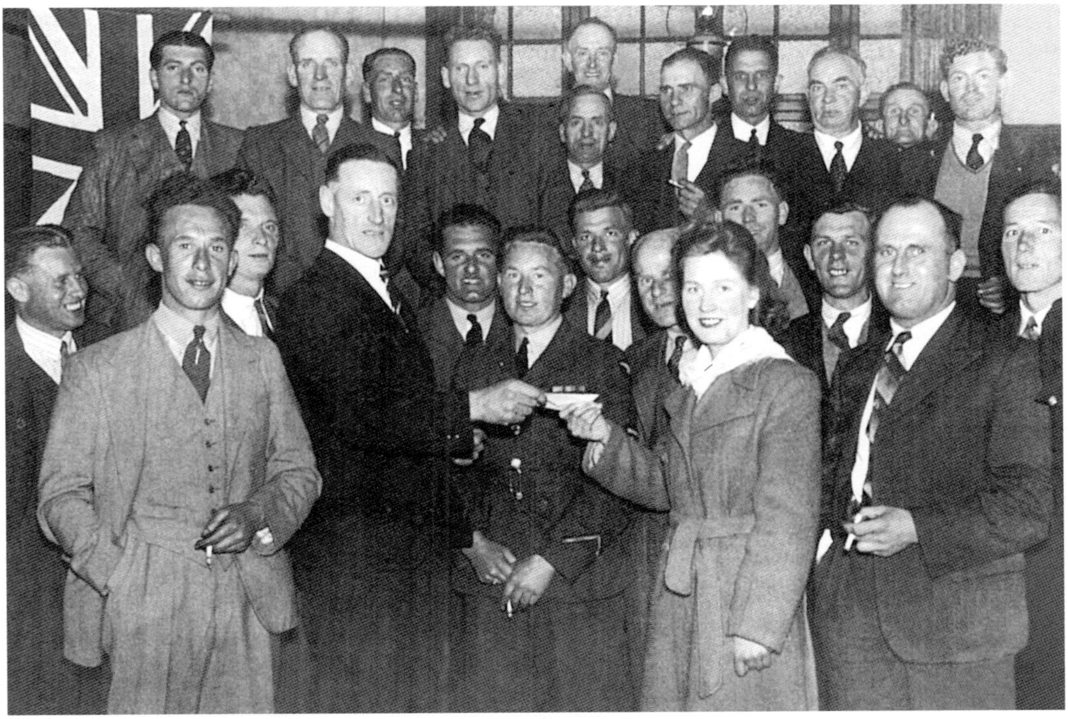

'Welcome Home' Celebration 1945.
Amongst those present: William Hill, William Jones, Gordon Lloyd, Fred Higgs, Wilf Higgs, Fred Richards, Philip Blackledge, Arthur Blackledge, Fred Roberts, Laurence Lloyd, Idris Higgs, Ron Carpenter, Percy Roderick, Vic Russell, Roger Chapman, Doug Welling, Frank Lewis, Aubrey Smith, Leah Samuel, Ivor Higgs, Eddy Reeks, Doug Davis, Pryce Williams.

During 1974 the old hall was demolished and an unattractive modern facility erected on the same site. In 1999 the Community Council pledged to build a new community centre in the heart of Henllys...to revitalise village life. It has yet to come to fruition. The 1970s hall continued in use for children's parties, club meetings, etc. The founders of some 75 years ago would hardly recognise the village landscape nowadays; the population in 1930 was a mere 400 or so; currently, it exceeds 2,000 and will escalate in the coming years.

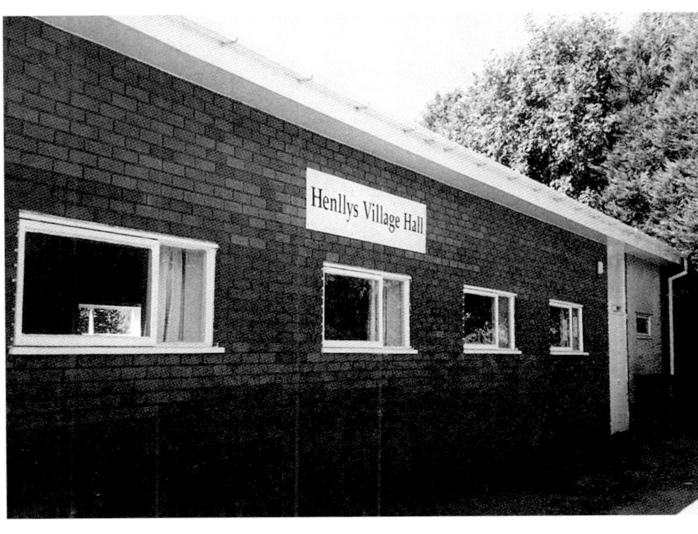

The 'modern' Village Hall in splendid isolation!

HENLLYS BOARD SCHOOL

The Elementary School was established by the Rogerstone & Henllys School Board and opened on 31st October, 1878, with a certain amount of ceremony. Tea was given free to all children in the parish during the afternoon; the evening saw the adults turn with several addresses by dignitaries and entertainment at the not so lowly cost of one shilling (old money). A new chapter in the life and times of the village was about to unfold. Previous attempts during the 18th-century to provide organised education for small communities through a ***'circulating school'*** had attracted little interest.

In 1883 the school gained a degree of notoriety when the Clerk to the School Board was declared bankrupt: several discrepancies in his accounting were found and he was summarily dismissed.

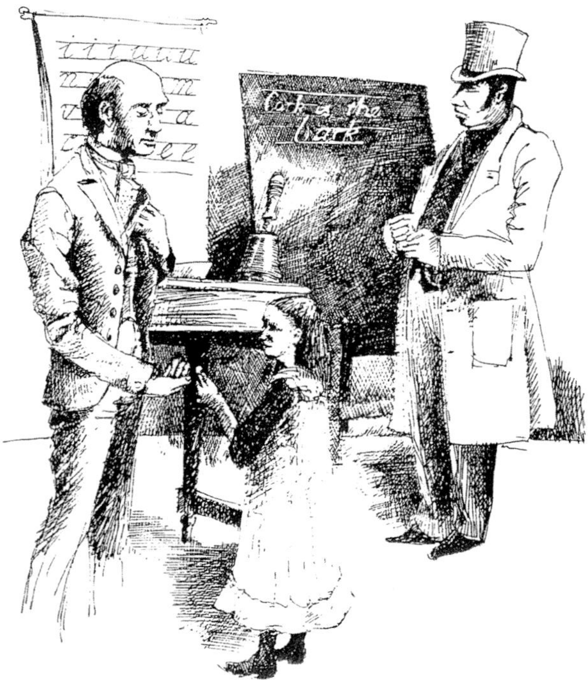

'School Pence' - M. Mather

The school was subject to regular inspection: in the year ending 31st May, 1889, pupils were assessed on their competence in the 3 Rs, i.e. reading, writing and arithmetic. Not surprisingly, the results were less than heartening. At the time 50 children attended, but this gradually increased over the following years.

Being a Board School, parents had to pay for their children to receive an education. On average the charge was two 'old' pennies per week per child. The levy was based upon the number of children attending from each household. But there were discounts. Three from the same family were only charged for two and so forth. ***'School Pence'*** was finally abolished in 1891.

In the late 1890s Sir Joseph Bradney wrote in his ***'History of Monmouthshire'... 'All the parishioners speak Welsh'***, which is questionable as pupils suffered the indignity and humiliation of the notorious ***'Welsh Not'***, a form of cultural genocide, whereby it was forbidden to speak their mother tongue in the classroom. English was the order of the day. This was ruthlessly enforced by English schoolteachers who regarded Welsh as an inferior and gutter language. Youngsters who transgressed were shamed by being forced to wear a rope or knot around their necks. Why was this? Workers from English counties came to the area seeking work in Henllys Colliery and the quarries, and their language prevailed to the detriment of Welsh which slowly began to die out. Curiously, with the passage of time things have turned 'full circle' and the teaching of the Welsh language and its culture now features on every curriculum. Rather late in the day…

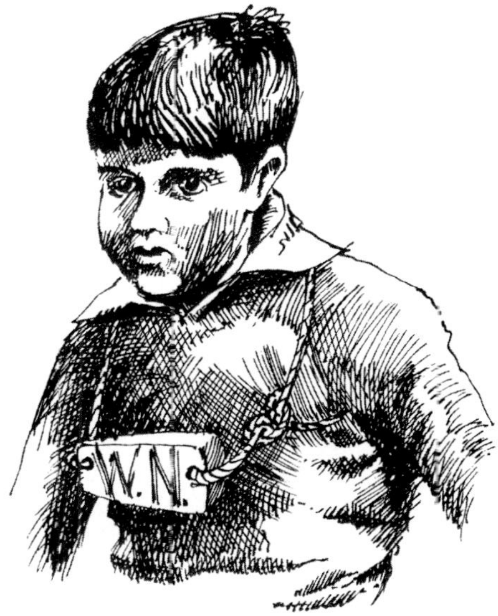
'The Welsh Not' - M. Mather

The school log books and inspectors' reports show that insanitary conditions prevailed at the school and ***'inclement weather contributed to illness and absences'***. The roads, little more than mud tracks, were often impassable for young children after heavy rain. An inspector's report (1914) read ***'...the isolated position of the school militates against the efficiency of the school'***. The records further illustrate the hardships of the time. In 1879 youngsters suffered deprivation. ***'Girl absent owing to her being without shoes...'*** By 1925 little had changed due to a shortage of boots! Over many years mention is made of families leaving the district owing to the lack of employment. In 1900 ***'The attendance still keeps very low...indeed the rows are quite deserted...'***

All too often, children arrived at school in a filthy state and were promptly sent home to clean themselves before returning. Boys and girls brought up under such adverse circumstances had little chance of bettering themselves through education. By contrast, the siblings from middle-class parentage had far greater opportunities to become learned in the professions. A single example will suffice. Both the headmaster, Mr. Evan Griffith Edwards, his wife and three children were all trained in the profession of teaching. The log of 1905 states: ***'Master out of school from 3 p.m. today...son in charge...'*** Moreover, in 1917 ***'Leslie Edwards starts as a temporary teacher...'*** and ***'...Miss Mary Edwards resumes charge of infant class...'*** Well, that's certainly keeping things within the family!

Discipline was strict and misdemeanours punished harshly by use of the cane; for persistent disobedience pupils were either made to go without a proper dinner or detained after school (the modern equivalent of ***'detention'***). Truancy (during Victorian times it was called ***'mitching'*** - just as it is today!) was also a significant and ongoing problem, often affected by events such as ploughing matches, hedging and ditching competitions, the annual Sheepdog Trials and, of course, ***'bringing in the harvest'***.

By the 1920s the curriculum had widened and pupils were taught about their immediate environment. They were taken out into the fields to study the wild flowers. One particular flower was found only around the Nant-y-Pandy. Flowers were collected, identified, pressed and dried, and placed in the individual's school book. Today, the subject is presented as Nature or Rural Studies. (As an aside, Henllys Bog and Woodland area are Sites of Special Scientific Interest, the habitat of several rare species of flora and fauna.)

During the Second World War the school catered for groups of evacuees from the bombings of London. The accompanying photograph shows infants and juniors during the 1943-44 school year. Amongst those shown is a Bill Dowler from the east-end of London, the eldest of 21 children! He was later adopted and became known as William Calder; his sons and grandchildren still reside in the Cwmbrân area.

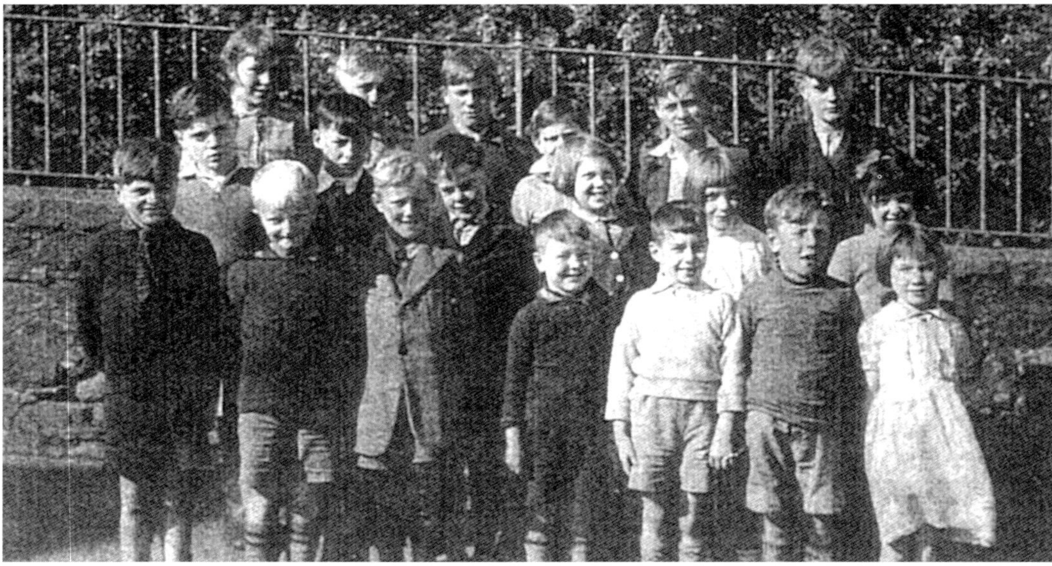

Evacuees from London during World War Two. Bill Dowler as a lad is among the cheerful faces. But which is he?

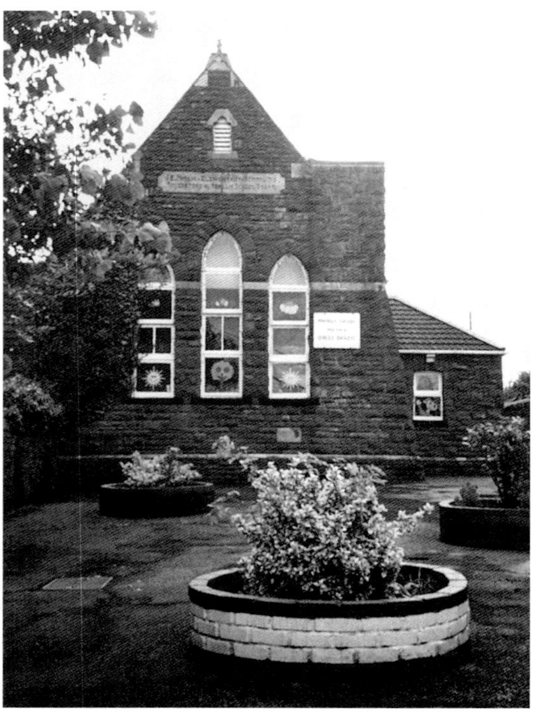

Henllys 'old' school has become a children's nursery.

For over 100 years, generations of children received a rudimentary education at the school. Yet like so many rural schools elsewhere it became unviable and on 24th July, 1991, it closed and all 18 pupils transferred to a brand new Church in Wales school on the outskirts of the old village.

Shortly before its closure a young pupil by the name of Sarah Baulch penned the following lines: ***'Henllys is a lovely old village. There are old farmhouses and no air pollution...I live in an old Welsh longhouse. It is called Dorallt Fach, which is Welsh for 'little forest'. The house is about four hundred years old...Wild flowers in the hedges bloom out and the colours dazzle your eyes. Fields of buttercups look like a carpet of gold and the hay and corn sway in the breeze...The cows sit in the***

shade and those in the sun flick their tails lazily at the flies...The evening comes and the cows go in for milking. The work is all done and the farmer whistles to his dog...The darkness falls and the barn owl can only be heard.' A truly wonderful and evocative piece of writing from someone so young.

Oddly though, the original building was not demolished (unlike Llanfrechfa and St. Dials, Old Cwmbrân) and continues to find use as a children's nursery, thereby remaining part of the education system and social fabric of the community.

HENLLYS MALE VOICE CHOIR

Many villages and towns throughout the County had their own Male Voice Choir. They epitomised both nonconformist beliefs during the religious revival of the 19th-century and the hardship and deprivation of industrial life. Their repertoire consisted largely of the great Welsh hymns.

The choir at Henllys was formed during the early 1930s. Some 30 or more strong, they practised at the Board School and performed for the pleasure of others. They competed in several eisteddfodau with some success. However, their existence was short-lived with the onset of World War II. Blackout restrictions forced them to leave the school and move higher up the valley side to Mount Pleasant Church. Predictably, many of the songsters were called up for war service and the choir was disbanded.

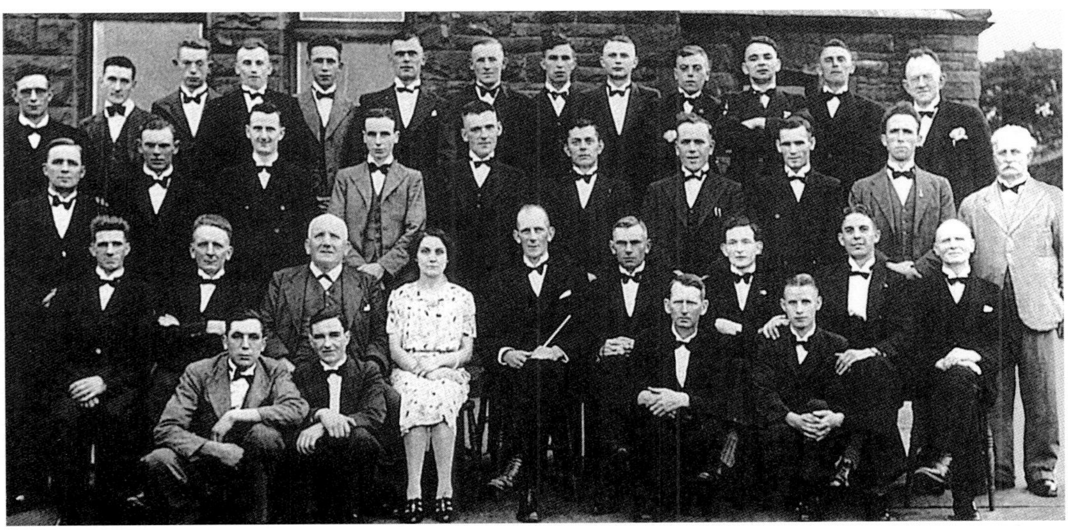

Henllys Male Voice Choir 1939.
Back row: Not known, Percy Jenkins, Bill Roberts, Mel Carpenter, Percy Roderick, Basil Marsh, George Pritchard, Bill Pennells, Ken Marsh, Ron Edwards, Ithel Salter, Reg Marsh, Harold Marsh.
2nd row: Mervyn Jones, Alf Price, Not known, Not known, Roy Cable, Jack Marsh, Cecil Stephens, Ed Smith, Tom Roderick, Harry Calder.
1st row: Bill Jones, Ern Stephens, John Stephens (Deputy Conductor), Emily Petheram (Pianist), Albert Cocker (Conductor), Alwyn Marsh, Not known, Arthur Blackledge, W. Petheram.
Front row: Wyndham Roderick, Not known, Luke Poole, Ron Carpenter.

The photograph, taken in 1939, shows the choir with their conductor, Albert Cocker, and pianist Emily Petheram. Also, six members of the 'Marsh' family, namely, Alwyn, Basil, Harold, Jack, Ken and Reg. Could this be a record in the history of Welsh choirs? Maybe. Following the cessation of hostilities the choir never reformed. A real shame and a loss to the community.

THE DORALLT INN

The Dorallt Inn set high on the slopes of Mynydd Maen affords spectacular views over the valley floor far below with the shining, silver-ribboned Severn Sea beckoning in the distance. For over 100 years the hostelry has been the focal point for much of the adult social life of Henllys village.

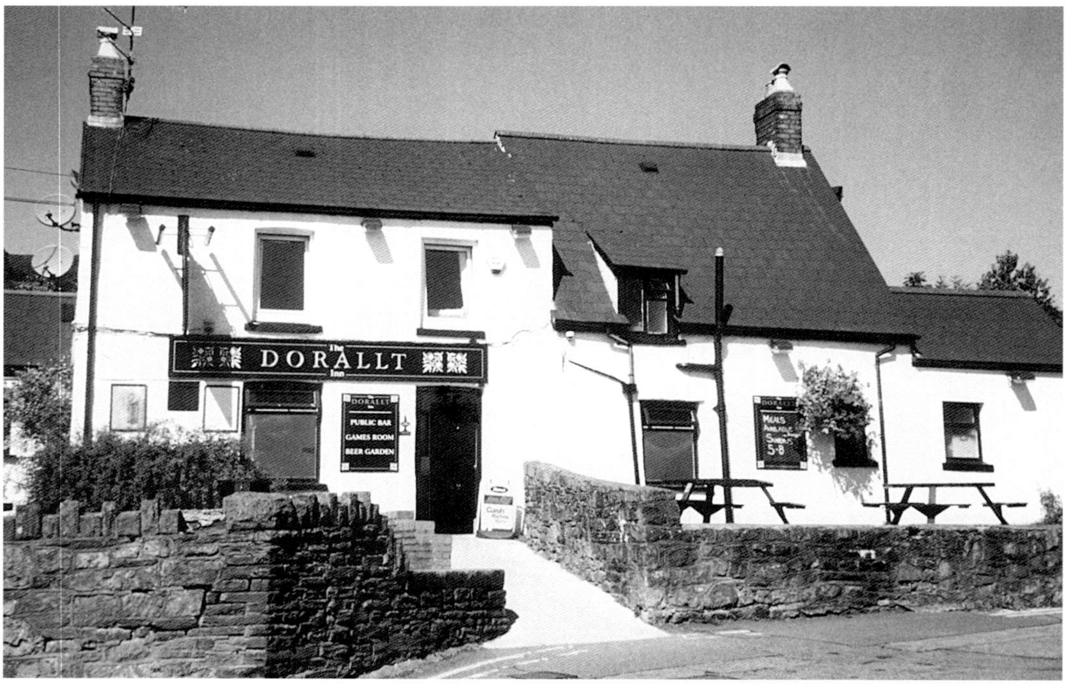

The Dorallt Inn.

Originally, there were two small farms adjacent to one another, the Dorallt Mawr and Dorallt Fach. The latter was demolished quite some time ago and today the Cwrt Henllys hotel stands on the site. An early census classified the Dorallt Mawr as a farm only, yet the 1881 census records it as a farm and public house; Thomas Howells was the innkeeper who also farmed some 17 acres of land. The Howells family were later connected with the Mount Pleasant Inn in Cwmbrân Village for many years. Only in the 1891 census is the Dorallt first mentioned as an inn run by a James Roberts.

There is an earlier mention of a Miners Arms, also known as a shop and off-licence at the top of Belle Vue Terrace, a little higher up the mountainside. No record seems to describe how and when it ceased trading.

Though extended and modernised, the bar area retains its flagstone floor and much of its original character. In winter, what could be more welcoming than the sight of a crackling log fire: the pub's exterior, too, looks much as it would have done a century or so ago. The Dorallt continues to be a popular venue for locals to enjoy convivial conversation, imbibe fine cask ales and sample wholesome fayre.

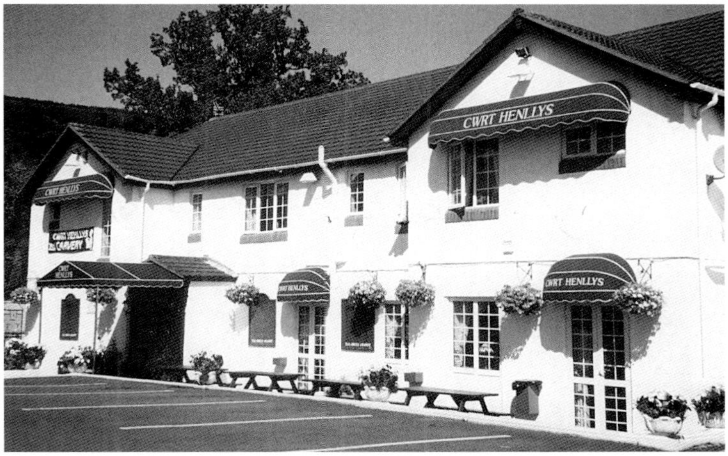

Cwrt Henllys hotel.

By contrast, the Cwrt Henllys hotel opposite is a modern luxurious establishment offering 'all the trimmings' at affordable prices.

INDUSTRIAL HERITAGE

What industrial heritage does Henllys possess? It seems so improbable to people today. Yet high on the steep-sided mountainside was one of the earliest scenes of coal production in the 19th-century. Outcrops of coal had been discovered and in 1814 Joshua Flesher Hanson of Backwell, Somerset, with considerable foresight, took out a lease from Sir Charles Morgan on the land and promptly developed a small colliery to exploit the valuable mineral resource. To ensure the coal would reach a lucrative market, he took out a further lease for a tram road or incline to connect with the Monmouthshire Canal at Two Locks, Cwmbrân Village, where he built a Coal Works and Barge Basin.

On a site close to the canal the 'Henllys Coal, Firebrick And Retort Works' was established under Cyrus Hanson who in 1842 had taken over the business from his father. He had also found good quality fireclay in the slopes above the village - a valuable commodity. Together with coal production, fireclay, quarries for stone and limestone, he developed a thriving business which made him an even wealthier man. Typically, the workforce received but a pittance for their labours. The white firebricks made from fireclay were used extensively throughout South Wales and the South West of England as linings for domestic fireplaces and industrial furnaces. Ebenezer Baptist Chapel at Two Locks, Cwmbrân, was built with stone donated by the industrialist.

Small neat rows of houses and cottages sprung up in close proximity to the colliery and canal to house the workers and their families. The names typify the onset of English industrialisation: Kiln Cottages or Tip Terrace, Old Row, New Road, Bellevue Terrace (shown overleaf), Ladies Row or Four Houses, Machine Cottage, Machine House, Incline Terrace and others besides. Though mundane, such names reflected the nature of the employees' work. Many of these dwellings remain for all to see.

By the mid 1920s the upper coal seams were all but worked out and the Henllys side of the business closed down: the tram road became redundant. This had a

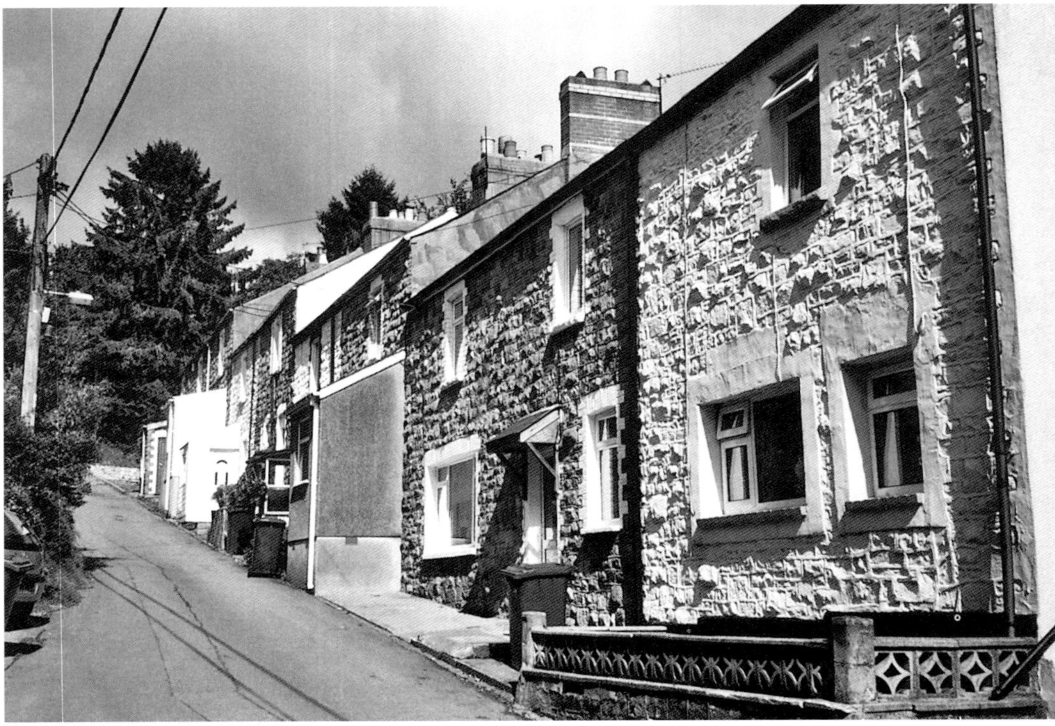

Belle Vue Terrace, built for the miners of Henllys Colliery.

devastating effect on the community. Some men found work at Cwmcarn Colliery some distance away and had to trudge daily over Mynydd Maen and down into the Ebbw Valley. A former resident of Henllys recalls as a young boy in the early 1930s ***'watching the men walk over the mountain in the dark with their lamps showing the way and meeting up with their butties from Upper Cwmbrân'***. These men were desperate for employment and accustomed to hardship. Though hard as nails, they cared deeply about the well-being of their loved ones and showed fortitude in their daily trek to work and back in all winds and weather, particularly after a strenuous shift underground.

In July 1928 the Henllys Estate was put up for sale by auction at the Half Way Hotel, Cwmbrân. Many of the properties remained unsold, but times were difficult. The country was inextricably moving towards The Depression of the 1930s and money was in short supply. The wages of those fortunate to gain work were very low. The 'White Yard' in Two Locks, Cwmbrân, where the firebricks were made was bought by Guest, Keen & Nettlefold. Long closed down, it inevitably became the site of yet another housing complex.

Nowadays, there is little evidence of the early coal-workings at Henllys apart from the spoil heaps long grown over and verdant, and which blend with the natural contour of the mountainside.

MOUNT PLEASANT BAPTIST CHURCH

Apart from Zoar Chapel at Castell-y-Bŵch, Henllys has another Baptist Chapel in the parish which appeared on the religious scene somewhat later, much a consequence of the coal-mining activities in the vicinity. The establishing of the chapel at Penheol-y-Buedd was detailed by an unknown author at around the turn of the 20th-century who stated: ***'After the starting of the coal works here the population considerably increased and the need of a Sunday School, and means of grace was felt...Towards the end of the year 1860 a branch Sunday School was opened here in a dwelling house by some few local brethren.'***

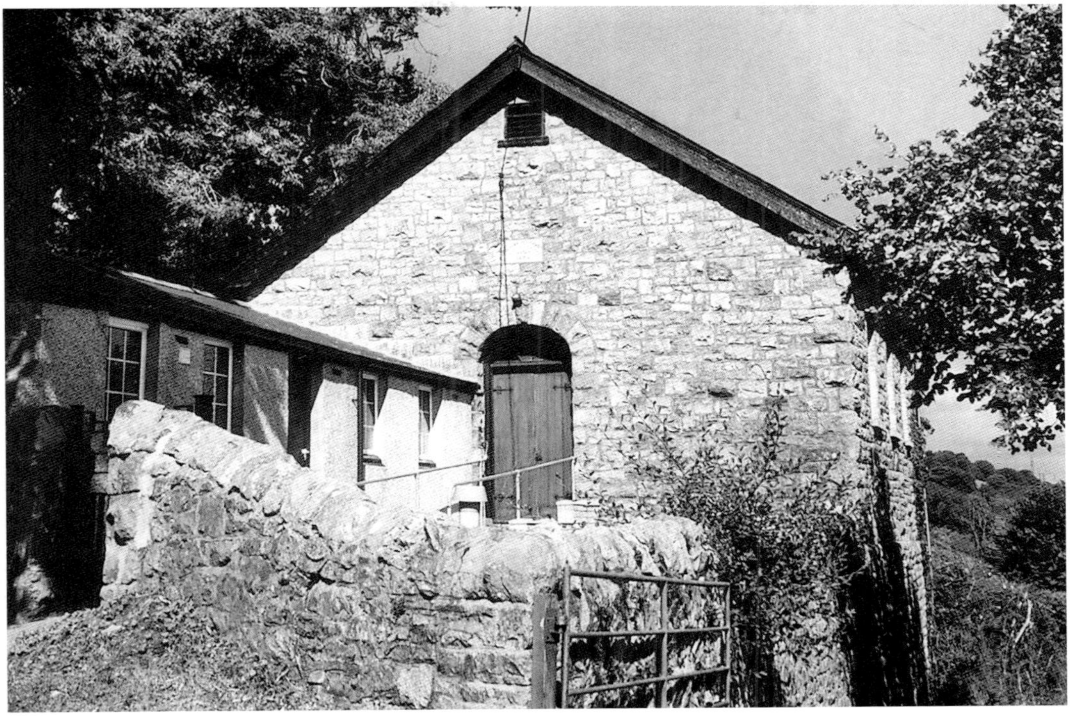

Mount Pleasant Baptist Church clinging to the hillside.

The school flourished for some 10 years, but gradually families left the district as the menfolk sought jobs in the burgeoning coal and iron industry throughout the valley and the number of children attending fell to a handful. ***'At this trying time it was chiefly held up by Mr. Edward Edmunds, a deacon of Siloam Church, Upper Cwmbrân.'***

In 1874 the numbers swelled to sixty and the schoolroom proved far too small and cramped. Many felt the only solution was to build a suitable chapel. The churches at Zoar and Siloam were also interested parties in the venture. However, there was dissension as to the best way forward and the Henllys representatives withdrew their support. The matter was left in the capable hands of Siloam's pastor, Mr. Thomas Cocker. At the annual meeting of the Monmouthshire Association of Baptist Chapels held at Lower Beaufort early in 1876, a resolution was passed ***'that we heartily encourage our brethren at Upper Cwmbrân to establish a preaching school at Penheol-y-Buedd'***.

Without delay a site was secured under a lease of 99 years for the nominal sum of one penny (old money) per annum. Hardly a charge at all. It was commented that if the site had not been obtained then ***'the Wesleyans would have snatched it and occupied the sphere for their denomination'***. So much for religious harmony!

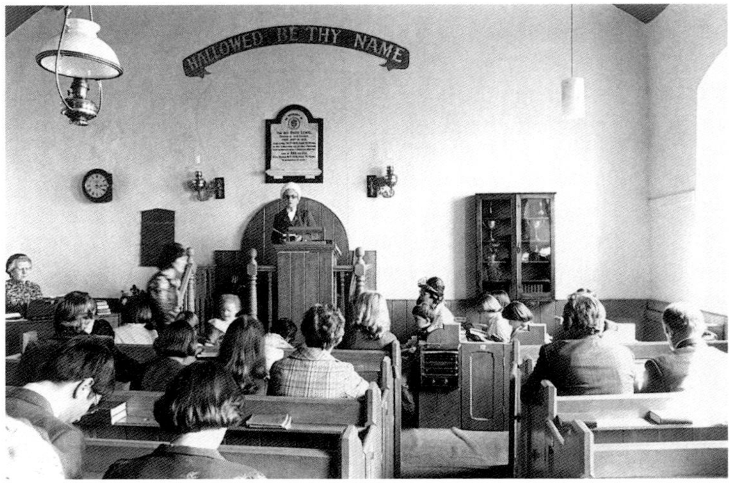

A Sunday prayer meeting.

A plain and simple chapel was built at a cost of £220 and publicly opened on Christmas Day, 1876. In 1885 the chapel formally became a 'church'. Most of its ministers preached here every other Sunday as several held ties with the neighbouring chapels at Zoar and at Pontnewydd.

The church has a large memorial plaque which honours the men from **'THE PARISH OF HENLLYS & NEWTOWN'** who gave their lives in **'The Great War' (1914-19)**. The names of those who also served in the war but returned home safely are listed on either side. So, there actually was an area described as **'Newtown'** long before the present New Town of Cwmbrân was even thought of. Curiously, following the war the plaque was erected at the former village school. Why? Upon the school's closure, it seemed that the plaque was all but lost to the people of Henllys. Yet members of the chapel were eager to display it in their House of God. Mount Pleasant has maintained regular congregations down the years and services are still held for the faithful each Sunday. In 2006 it celebrated its 130th anniversary.

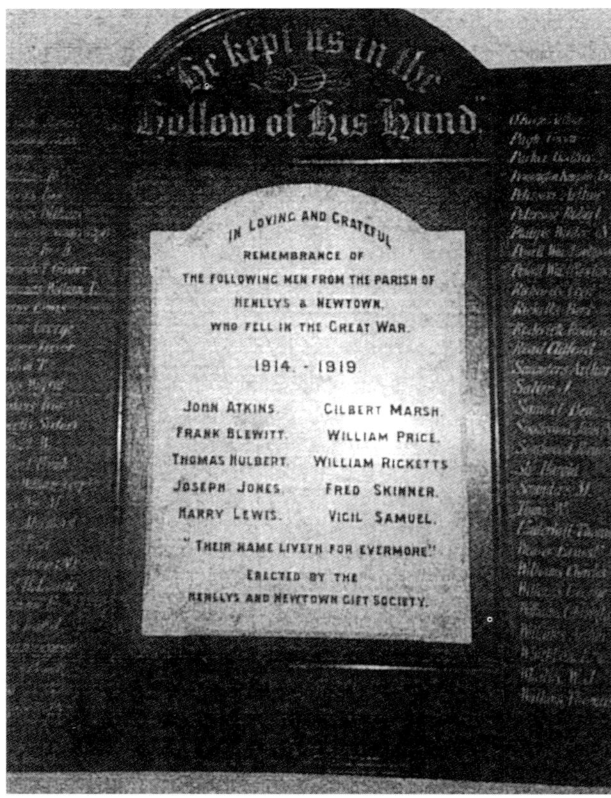

Memorial plaque to honour those fallen in the Great War.

In 1974, Henllys was officially absorbed into Cwmbrân New Town area designate. The result? As elsewhere lush pastureland became awash with houses. Notwithstanding this, the greater part of the Vale of Henllys has retained its rural identity which offers delightful walks along sequestered byways, a wonderful legacy for future generations to enjoy and treasure.

Upper Cwmbrân

The original Cwmbrân, or Cwmbrâen, began as an isolated hamlet high on the steep slopes of Mynydd Maen, in Welsh the ***'Mountain of Stone'***. Little is known about its early history except that it was once part of the ancient Manor of Edlogan. During Norman times it was probably part of the Welshry. This whole upland area with its spectacular views over the valley far below was better suited to pastoral farming than to the cultivation of crops, which remains true to this very day. The need to distinguish 'Upper Cwmbrân' from 'Lower Cwmbrân' lay very much in the future when the latter developed as the result of the iron industry and the 'arrival' of the Monmouthshire Canal and railway network.

Coal outcrops hereabouts were recognised and worked many centuries ago, chiefly by the monks of Llantarnam Abbey. Possibly even earlier by those who in around 550 A.D. founded a small religious cell at Llanderfel and who were converted to Christianity by Derfel Gadarn, or Derfel the Strong, reputedly a great warrior in the days of King Arthur and who in later life gave up his warlike ways and turned to religion. Strange that in later life the most barbarous of humans frequently turn to belief in the afterlife in the hope of redemption from former 'sins'. Precious little remains of this ancient church and monastic ***'seat'*** of ***'the Tribe of the Saint'*** which was of considerable importance until around 1175. What is virtually certain is that this 'hermitage' was the forerunner of Llantarnam Abbey. And yet, unwittingly, the original 'chapel' was built over a coal seam just a few inches below the surface. What irony!

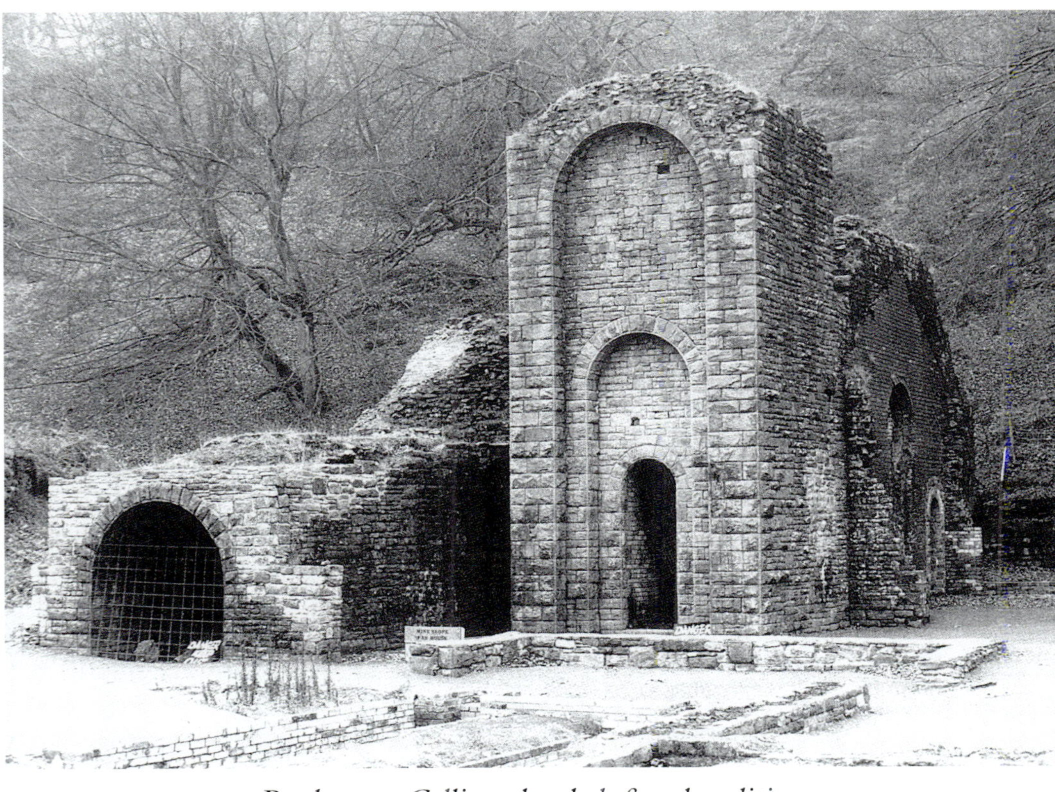

Porthmawr Colliery shortly before demolition.

By the early 17th-century, Upper Cwmbrân had become the centre of a thriving if somewhat scattered community with its own mill (referred to in 1610 as 'Melyn-y-vran') powered by the waters of the Nant Brân. These were simple shallow coal workings, or 'bell pits', and are still visible to the discerning eye. The potential of the coalstock embedded in the mountainside was quickly realised by Major John Hanbury who acquired Thomas Arnold's small-scale 'Colework' in 1698 and expanded operations. By the middle of the 18th-century his 'mine' was supplying coal to the tin works at Caerleon and Ponthir.

Further investment really began in earnest in 1793 when Thomas Stoughton, who had already married into the Hanbury family, saw the potential for exploiting the wealth of 'black gold' in the area and decided to invest heavily in the existing workings. For a ridiculously small price he secured the lease of the land from Mr. Jones of Glyn Brân Farm ***'for the purpose of mining coal and iron ore'***. A shrewd decision which was to make him an even richer man.

But it was Reginald James Blewitt of Llantarnam Abbey who seriously began to mine the coalstock when he established the Porthmawr Colliery or the 'Fire Clay Level' in 1837. During 1843 the miners went on strike following a reduction in their wages. Sadly, they suffered further humiliation for breaking their contracts when the indignity of one month's hard labour was enforced upon them, or told to seek work elsewhere. With no shortage of an influx of men from the deepest corners of England eager for any form of work the striking miners had little choice other than to give in and return to work for an even lesser pittance. But why did the honourable Member of Parliament inflict such a severe reduction in wages? Simply because he had overspent on restoration of a largely derelict Abbey. Being heavily in debt he was forced to sell his mining interests when the Monmouth & Glamorgan Bank from which he had borrowed heavily collapsed in 1851. The mine then became the property of John Lawrence, noted sportsman and industrialist, who not only bought the land and mineral rights in 1854, but also opened a second level known as Mine Slope workings. The Patent Nut & Bolt Company acquired Mine Slope in around 1879 and the final owners became Guest, Keen & Nettlefold in 1900.

With increased coal extraction, the need for suitable housing for the workers in the nearby drift mines - and their families - became essential. Hence the building of Incline Row, Mine Slope Cottages and, of course, The Square. The Square's rectangular layout was unusual for the middle of the 19th-century and supposedly based upon a Continental design: it first appeared on the tithe map published in 1840. The remnants of old quarry workings and the abundance of local freestone proved a convenient and durable material for the building of sturdy cottages in The Square and other homes and nearby farmsteads. Today, as of yesteryear, the hub of activity centres in and around The Square, a collection of neat rows of stepped, 'white-washed' terraced cottages.

The spoil from the coal workings was quite literally thrown down the mountainside. Conservation of the environment then was of little interest. With the passage of time, these waste tips have become completely overgrown with bracken and trees which gently blend into the reclaimed rural landscape; and where sheep now quietly ruminate.

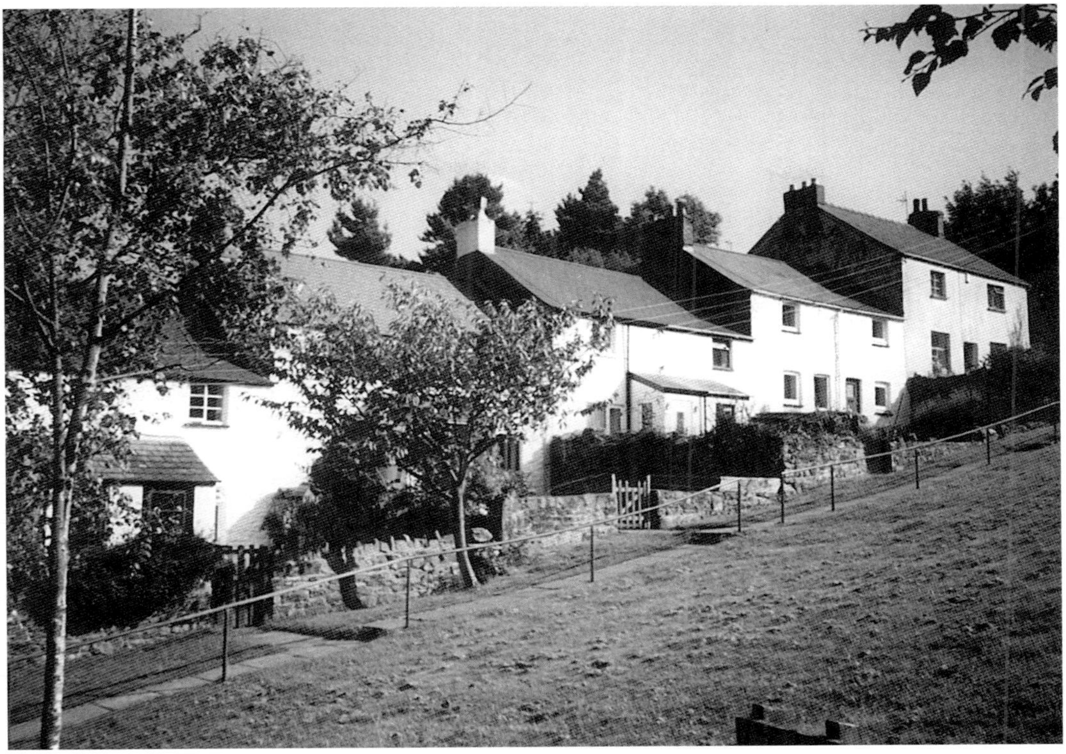

The Square as it is today.

Accidents were all too common in the damp and dangerous mine-workings and many a man or young lad died under a fall of rock or under a tram. Lighting conditions underground were primitive with workers toiling for 12 hours a day by candlelight. Because of the nature of drift-mining, gas explosions were surprisingly rare. Yet a few did happen. Nothing too serious. Just the odd death here and there, and an inconvenience to the owner of the workings. Such working practices would not be tolerated in this age, though it is increasingly hard to find a coal mine anymore. This will most likely change in the future.

On 26th April, 1866, three men were killed at Mine Slope when trams were derailed through travelling too fast and fracturing a steam pipe on a nearby boiler. Isaac Maynard, a mason aged 39 years, and with a wife and six children, was scalded to death. In the graveyard of Siloam Baptist Chapel his tombstone reads:

Death to me no warning gave but took me sudden to my grave,
To meet my Lord without delay for sudden death took me away.

The Victorians certainly had a way with words, a sense of passion and heartfelt emotion. His wife Jemima finally joined him on 28th October, 1891 aged 81 years. But who paid for the impressive headstone on the grave of a loving couple? Certainly not the mine-owners who cared little for the well-being of any of their workforce. Another headstone commemorates John Jones who died in 1871 at the age of 61 years: he had travelled the long journey by ship from Newburgh in Ohio, America, to visit old friends and relatives in the village. Upper Cwmbrân was destined to be his final place of rest.

Reputedly, near Mine Slope cottages (long gone) a tunnel was driven through the early mine-workings for several miles to Pontypool. Local women wishing to go to market and shop in the town regularly chose to ride through in the trams rather than make the arduous trek over the mountaintop. This has never been proven, yet the story remains another valuable part of local folklore.

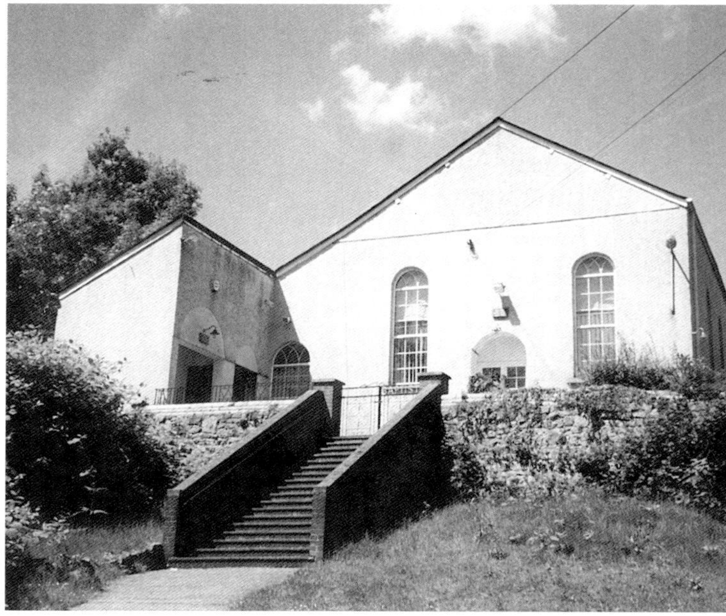

Siloam Baptist Chapel.

The community also had its own brickworks, lime kilns, woollen factory, shop, post office, several inns and chapels. (The latter exist still.) Rather surprising for such a small close-knit community. The brickworks was situated at the top of the incline and working in 1839 for Reginald Blewitt agreed to deliver fireclay there ***'unless prevented from doing so by faults, failure of clay or coal, or any general strike or combination among the Colliers or Miners'***. John Lawrence took the works over in 1845 when production had reportedly reached a staggering 100,000 firebricks per week and then in 1867 leased it to Henry Parfitt, a local builder, ***'with the Stoves, Kilns, Smith's shop and cottages'***. The woollen factory just below the present-day bus terminus was built in 1822 and powered by the waters of Nant Brân: it made flannel shirts for the local miners. It was still in production in the 1860s, but did not appear on the Ordnance Survey map of 1901. Cottages close by stood until May 1931 when a sudden storm and flood badly damaged them and they were demolished.

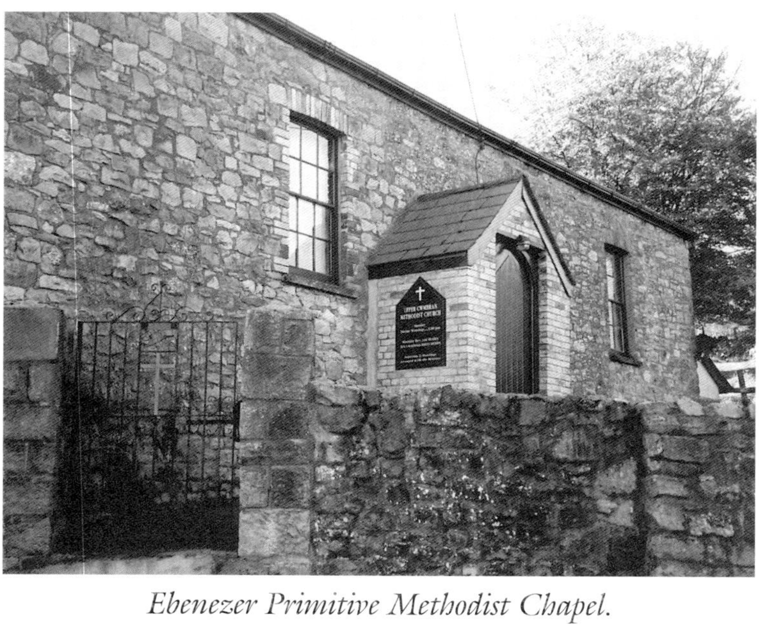

Ebenezer Primitive Methodist Chapel.

The influence of Nonconformity was growing fast as increasing numbers moved into the area seeking work in the colliery. So the faithful held regular meetings in each other's homes. Ebenezer Primitive Methodist Chapel was built in The Square during the 1840s and enlarged in 1865. Bethel Independent Chapel was established in 1837 (rebuilt 1869 and extended 1889) and Siloam Baptist Chapel in 1838, both directly below The Square. Initially, though, Bethel was intended to be a public house. Yes!! But a pious minister at New Inn Congregational Church strongly felt that a house of God was needed not another den of wickedness. He launched a public protest - and won the day. The owner of the building was forced to 'back down' and offered the property to the minister for the princely sum of £190. Thereafter, Bethel flourished as both a religious and a social centre. The chapel was not granted a marriage licence until 1948. The photograph of the first couple to wed there shows Arthur Mann with his bride Peggy

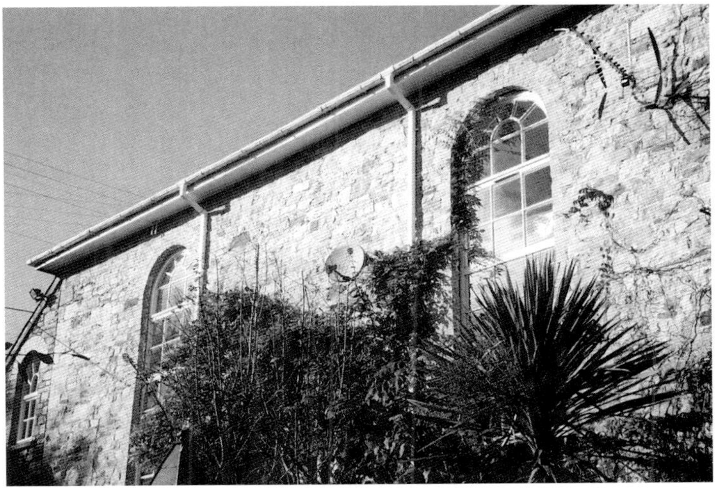

Bethel Independent Chapel.

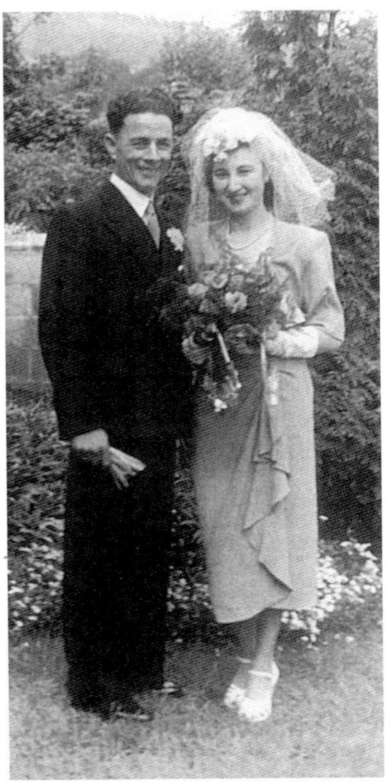

Arthur Mann with bride Peggy in 1948.

A headstone in the graveyard of Siloam recalls the death of brothers Llewellin and Thomas Williams who both died within 10 days of each other in February 1870 aged 2 and 7 years. To die so young was not uncommon. An inscription in Welsh is memorable:

NAC Y MFFROSTIA OR DYDD Y FORY: CANYS NI WYDDOST BETH A DDIGWYDD MEWN DIWRNOD.

Translated, this means:

'Do not boast of tomorrow because you do not know what will happen.'

A most perceptive sentiment.

With the start of iron-making on the valley floor, the need for coal was imperative. Coal from Porthmawr Colliery, Mine Slope was sent down the mountainside by trams along Porthmawr Tram Road to fire the furnaces. Likewise, the firebricks from the nearby works. This road passed the canal at Cwmbrân Village by the pub, The Half Way Inn, before continuing on to Ponthir and Caerleon. Strangely, the iron-workers considered themselves superior to the miners - and shunned them accordingly.

A school was established in 1852 by local people (with the approval and the assistance of the mine-owners) who wished to give their siblings an education to better themselves in life. During its heyday, over 100 children received a rudimentary schooling at The Square in a large upstairs room above the Squirrel Inn (long since in ruins). The first headmaster was Mr. Thomas Lewis of Goytre who had previously taught at Llandovery. He was followed in 1862 by Mr. David Morgan who recorded in the school's logbook of the perpetual noise from those drinking downstairs and of general truancy: moreover, of unhygienic and disciplinary problems due to serious overcrowding. He was genuinely concerned about so many young children under the age of 10 years old who did not attend school as they were working in the ***'coal-fields'*** to help support their parents' meagre existence. After many complaints to the relevant authorities which promised him a new school, he eventually despaired and resigned his position - a broken man with a passion for educating the future life-blood of a thriving community. Two years later a purpose-built school was built at the lower end of Upper Cwmbrân. On the 30th July, 1866, the foundation stone of the British School was laid by the much-respected dignitary John Lawrence who donated a gold sovereign towards the cost of its building. The school served the community well until the latter part of the 20th-century when a modern facility was erected alongside. Surprisingly, the Victorian building was not demolished and is in regular use as 'The Learning Zone' i.e. as a nursery school. The photograph (shown opposite) taken around 1917 of pupils at the school is fascinating as many children are wearing stout footwear, namely hob-nail boots, which were extremely expensive in those days. Their parents must surely have struggled to pay for them.

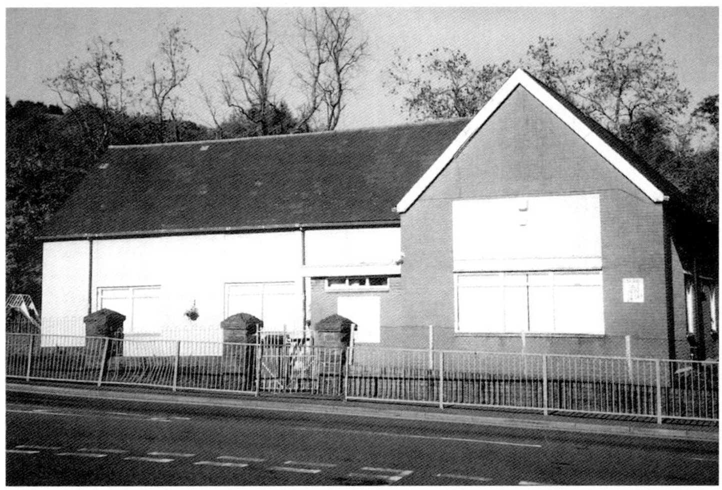

The Victorian British School - now 'The Learning Zone'.

The Squirrel Inn was a popular haunt of workers in the nearby firebrick works and Porthmawr coal works. And riotous behaviour was very much the order of the day. As an example it is recorded that in 1859 around 150 members of the fraternity of Oddfellows (Good Intent Lodge) enjoyed a lavish dinner. Of the Squirrel Inn there is little to see, only the end wall and its foundations. How did its demise come about?

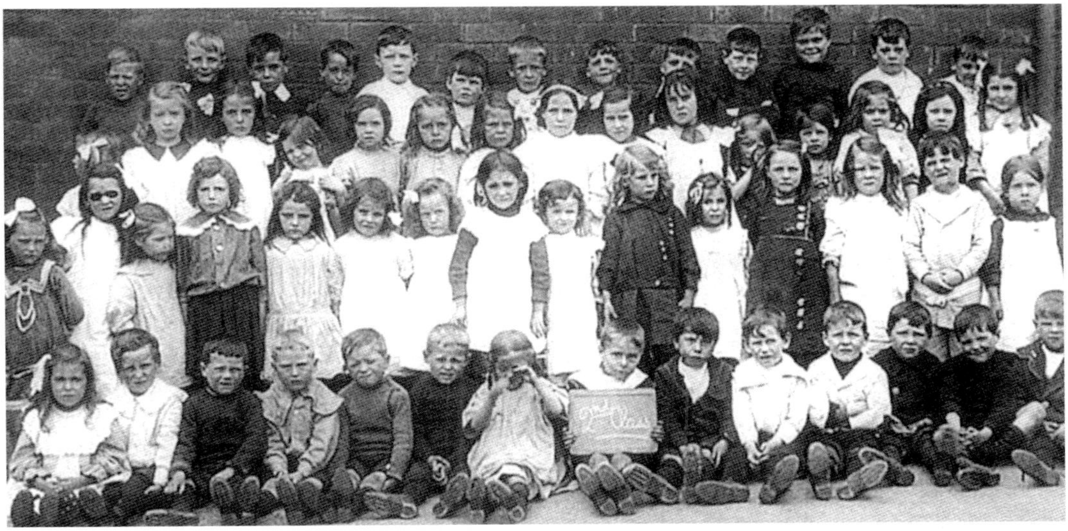

Grim-faced though well-shod pupils ca. 1917.

Following an exhausting day's toil at the coal-face, no doubt the weary miners looked forward to relaxation among friends and 'butties' at The Queen Inn, there to quaff a pint or two of foaming ale before returning home to their loved ones. In addition there were two other pubs in which locals could enjoy a tipple or two - The Crown and The Bush. Like the Squirrel, The Crown is long gone, but the other two situated below The Square remain ever-popular haunts for those desiring fine ales and convivial conversation. There used to be a saying: ***'The Queen lost The Crown in The Bush'***. Valley folk always seem to have had a saying for everything!

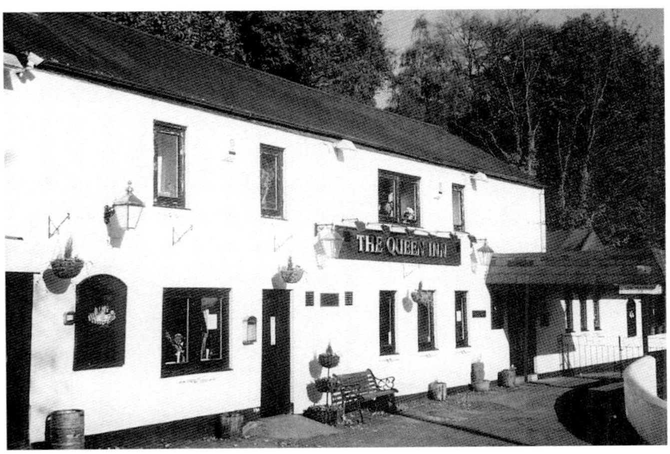

The Queen Inn.

For well over a century those living in The Square had lived a relatively contented and peaceful existence despite the many hardships they had endured. In January 1964 the community was threatened when the local council, intent upon eradicating the entire ancient settlement, began to implement a ***'slum clearance'*** policy and to demolish ***'unfit'*** individual houses and re-house occupants in nearby new council estates. Homes within The Square simply did not conform to the rigid standards set by modern regulations. And there was the issue of lack of proper drainage and sewage facilities which simply did not exist so far up the mountainside. Householders simply buried their sewage in their back gardens or deposited it elsewhere; some had septic tanks which discharged their effluent into an open brook lower down the hill.

However, the fiercely independent and proud community protested vehemently and with the overwhelming support of the general public from the New Town the council was eventually forced to back down. Councillor O.J.R. Pruden, the council's former public health inspector rebuffed claims that the cottages posed a threat to public health. He declared that ***'My memory of Upper Cwmbrân goes back 50 years and during that time there has never been an epidemic at The Square'...'the air (there) was like wine....and that the elderly community was held together by a spirit of neighbourliness all too rare in modern times'***. He certainly had a point and further maintained that ***'The aim should be to improve this attractive place, not to destroy it'***. Most praiseworthy sentiments. Nonetheless, despite all protestations a complete row of cottages was demolished leaving only two of the three original rows of dwellings standing. A costly social mistake by a misguided and intolerant planning department at the offices of Cwmbrân Development Corporation. Nevertheless, the hillside community clung on to its dignity and has since benefited from major improvement grants.

Until not many years ago the two Blaen Brân reservoirs nestled above The Square in the steep-sided blind valley surrounded with large aged beech trees. These were built to supply water to the communities of Llanfrechfa and Llantarnam. (At that time Upper Cwmbrân was in the parish of Upper Llanfrechfa.) The lower reservoir was constructed by Llanfrechfa Upper Local Board in 1884 on land owned by John Capel Hanbury. Its initial capacity was a mere 5 million gallons; this increased to over 11 million gallons when it was enlarged in 1930. The upper pool was built at the beginning of World War I. The larger reservoir proved an irresistible place for families to picnic and for youngsters to bathe in summertime although they failed to appreciate the perils of swimming in its deep and icy-cold waters. It has been drained of its water and little of its existence is evident. Nonetheless, the Nant Brân still journeys down the cwm, to spill its sparkling waters into the fast-flowing Afon Llwyd at Pontrhydyrun just as it has done since time immemorial.

Upper Cwmbrân's industrial past is just that - in the past. Nowadays, the residents of The Square and the vicinity tenaciously prize their independence and separate identity from modern urban growth lower down the mountainside. A visit and walk around The Square is quite an exhilarating experience for it truly feels like stepping back in time to the middle of the 19th-century. Indeed, the remoteness and beauty of the area is an important and invaluable link with our medieval and historical ancestry which should be treasured by all.

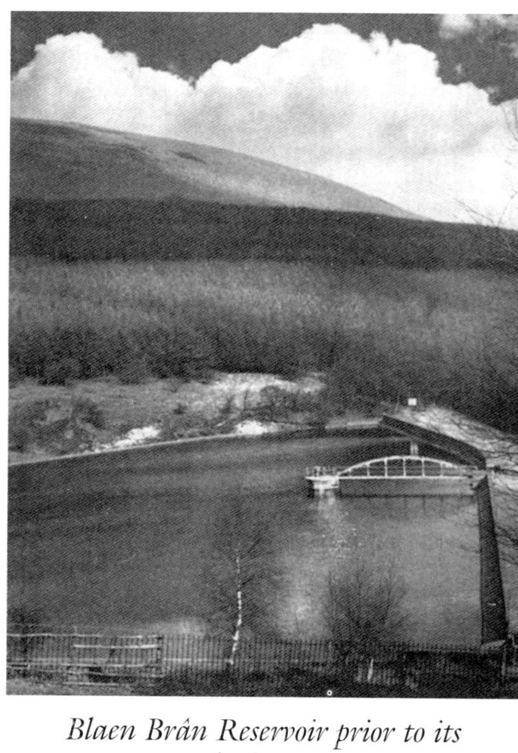

Blaen Brân Reservoir prior to its drainage.

Pontnewydd & Pontrhydyrun

Pontnewydd is an enigma. It may be many years since the former industrial village felt the wind of change with the development of nearby Cwmbrân New Town but, nonetheless, it has remained resilient against such change. There were real fears that its traditional way of life would disappear altogether. This has not happened. Somehow, this bustling village has kept both its sense of identity and its community spirit.

Its name simply means ***'new bridge'*** which spans the Afon Llwyd to the north of the New Town. Its close neighbour, Pontrhydyrun, is the ***'bridge near the ford where ash trees grow'*** i.e. ***'Ashford Bridge'***.

HOLY TRINITY CHURCH

Originally, All Saints Church at Llanfrechfa was the Mother Church of the Parish. With industrial expansion rapidly spreading along the valley floor and population growth there was a demand in Pontnewydd for 'interim rest' and further religious leadership. Advertisements were placed in the local press as early as February 1858 by the Church of England authorities ***'for persons wishing to tender for the building of a new church at Cwmbrân'***. On a rainy morning in June 1858 the stone laying ceremony took place in front of a very large gathering. Trinity Church was built on an acre of land just above the canal and opened in July 1860. This was designed and built by John Loughborough Pearson, architect of many churches of the Gothic revival in London and elsewhere. An extract from Elizabeth Mitchell's diary (wife of Frank Johnstone Mitchell of Llanfrechfa Grange) dated 17th July, 1860, reads: ***'All went to the opening of Cwmbran Church, built for £1,200; 400 people there. £43 collected. Bishop Oliphant of Llandaff preached an able and appropriate sermon.'*** An account in the ***Pontypool Free Press and Herald of the Hills*** stated: ***'It is a neat edifice, situated in the centre of a populous district... Over the entrance porch is inscribed, 'This is none other than the House of God and the gate of Heaven."***

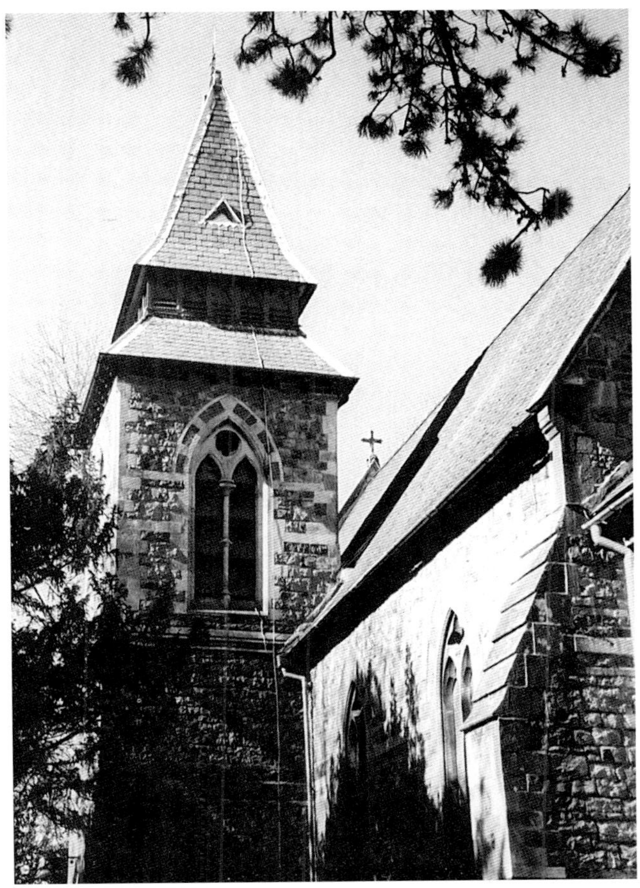

Holy Trinity Church.

The Reverend F. Bennett, B.A., was placed in charge but he was 'High Church' and introduced several changes in the service which caused offence to the Vicar of Llanfrechfa who complained to the Bishop of the Diocese of Monmouth. Upon an unexpected visit the Bishop found the chancel iron gates locked and entry barred. Despite protestations, in June 1885 the Chapelry of Llanfrechfa Upper became the Parish Church of the Holy Trinity.

The first vicar was the Reverend John Robert Phillips who continued his ministry for many years. With the ever increasing congregation crammed into the single nave the north aisle was added in 1889. The facial images on the pillars are reminders of bishop, vicar and churchwardens, Dr. R. Edmunds and Captain F. Wallace, both of whom served the church tirelessly. One incumbent, the Reverend Robert W. Sanderson was warmly welcomed by the parishioners, but didn't last very long after succumbing to pneumonia in 1899 after digging a grave in the churchyard himself! Perhaps his faith was not strong enough...

In the early 1900s the notable Alfred Pilliner and his wife of nearby Llanyrafon House and farm were staunch supporters of the church. A hand-carved oak screen is dedicated to the memory of his beloved wife.

A rather unusual memorial tablet reads:

The Electric Light was installed in the Church to the Glory of God and as a Memorial to the Men who gave their lives in the Great War 1914-1918 A.D.

For a century-and-a-half Holy Trinity has served the spiritual needs of a changing community. And, hopefully, will continue to do so throughout the 21st-century.

PONTNEWYDD SCHOOL

In its report for 1847 The Monmouth County Board of Education, while fostering interest in schools in the parishes, considered the needs of the industrial areas were paramount. They granted finance to build a Church School at Pontnewydd. This opened in October 1862 with a Mr. Barker as Headmaster. He gave instruction in *'pence, shillings, tables and weights and measures'*...and in compound and vulgar fractions. Commendable subjects of value in adult life. This remains applicable to this very day. Yet a highly unfavourable inspector's report for 1863 led to Mr. Barker's notice to leave... *'for faults of discipline and instructions...'* During April 1864 standard writing was taught and *'The first class began to read newspapers...'* Later, books were introduced and pupils encouraged to read them. Many children wished to take these books home and a 'Children's Home Reading Association' was formed: for one penny a month suitable periodicals were also available.

However, the children were largely unruly. A new master, Mr. Jacob, believed in strict discipline and stated in the school logbook of November 1865 *'I am determined to use the cane...'* He later noted *'Cautioned several with regard to playing in the churchyard and also against teasing Mr. Fraser's goat'*. Nowadays, this would appear petty in the extreme. After all, children are naturally mischievous.

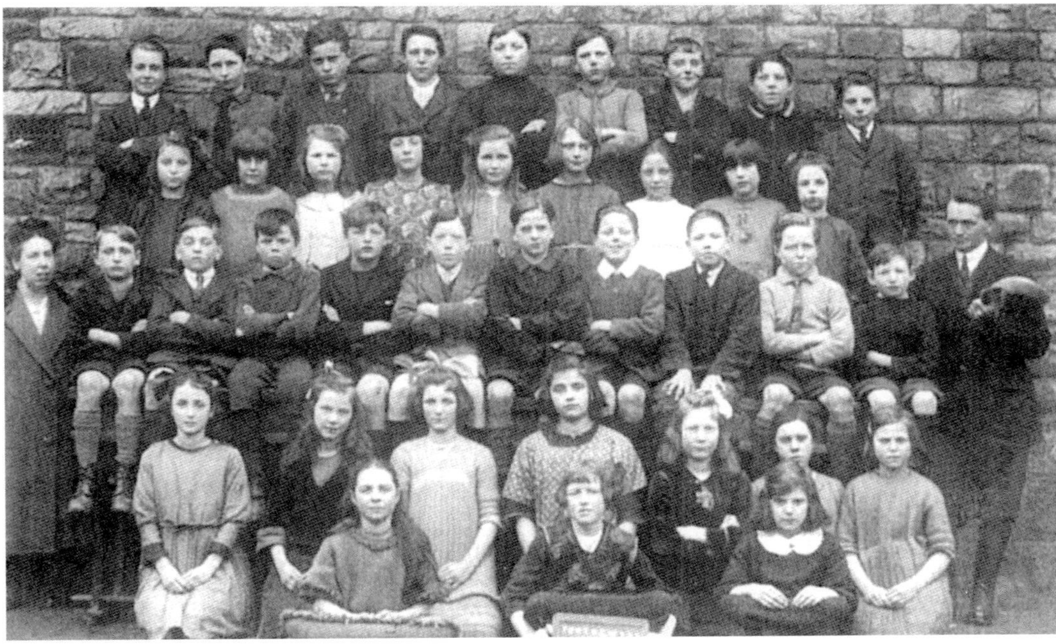

Pontnewydd Mixed School in the 1930s.

Attendance at the school was erratic with many children expected to help either on the land or work in the surrounding industrial works. In 1867 the National School logbook records ***'A great number of children of school age are allowed to work in the works of the neighbourhood'***. In 1866 ***'Several boys admitted for a short time while out of employment at Pontnewydd works'***. Pupils attended when there were stoppages at nearby Pontrhydyrun works. Again in 1893 ***'Many children are unable to attend from lack of clothing and shoes...'*** This pattern was repeated endlessly down the years much to the frustration of those who wished children to receive at least a rudimentary education and learn to read and write.

THE WHITE ROSE CINEMA

During the first half of the 20th-century work was hard, dirty and poorly paid. Even so, community spirit was manifest in all facets of relaxation and entertainment - all home grown. Apart from the churches and chapels which offered spiritual succour, the village had a male voice choir, brass band, theatre group and several sports clubs. These made the daily grind of life more bearable.

In 1914 the White Rose Cinema opened in Richmond Road and was run by the local families of Miller and Holloway. A cinema, The Palace, already existed just off Station Road, but being built of wood posed a fire risk and closed down in the 1920s. Thus the White Rose became the focal point for silent films up until the early 1930s. At the back of the auditorium rows of 'double seats' were much appreciated by courting couples. But did they actually watch the films? Then the first 'Talkie' starring Al Johnson in the ***'Jazz Singer'*** (1927) was shown. After a few technical problems with the sound the film thrilled and mesmerised the

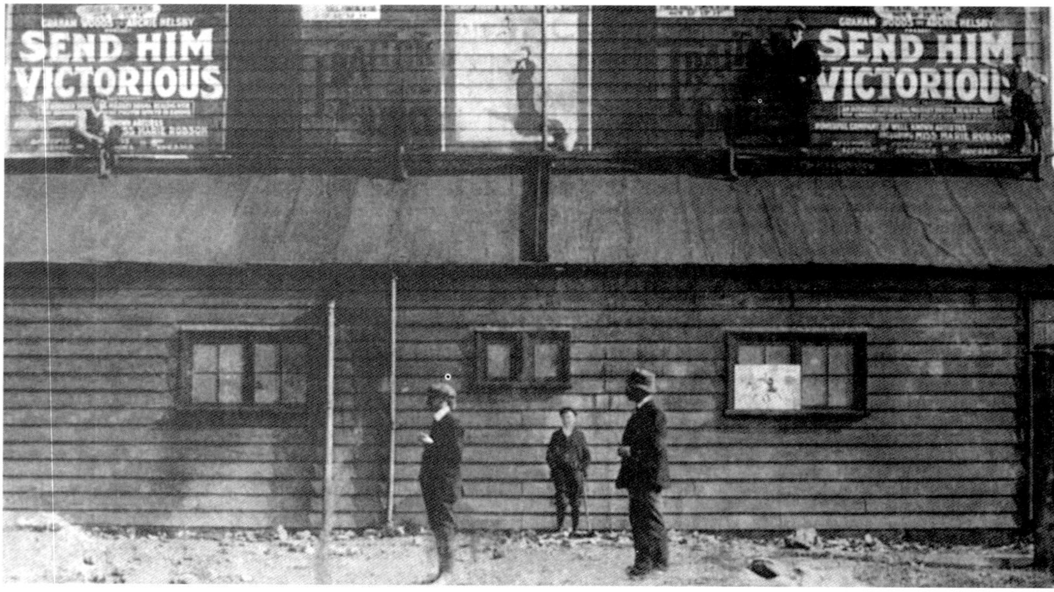

The Palace, a favourite haunt before The White Rose Cinema.

audience. A new era in cinematography had begun, much to the delight of film-goers eager to escape the harsh realities of the years of the Depression and World War II. And the Saturday matinée or 'penny rush' was a 'must' for impressionable youngsters.

However, with the arrival of mass television the White Rose, like cinemas elsewhere, suffered dwindling audiences and by the early 1960s was no longer viable. Instead it continued for some years as a Bingo Hall. The bill poster of 1954 gives a fascinating insight into human nature. For well over half a century later such films are still being screened on numerous television channels and enjoyed by present-day generations. What a turnaround!

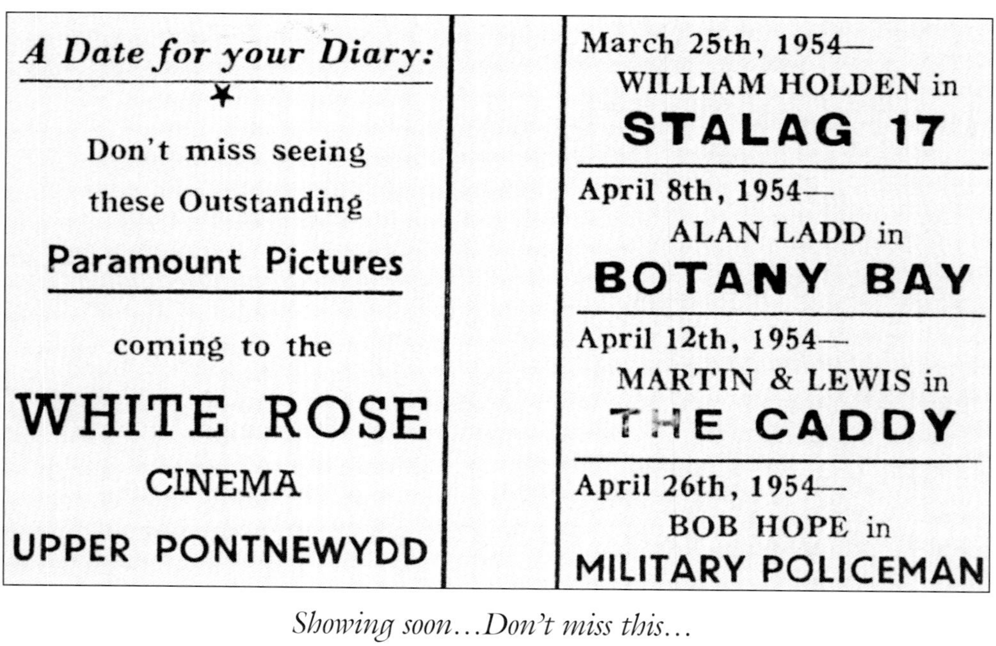

Showing soon... Don't miss this...

THE REAL WORLD

A reminder of childhood in Pontnewydd around the middle of the past century is captured in verse penned by the contemporary poetess Audrey Donoghue.

When we were young we had no restrictions,
Some things we did were beyond description.
We skated on the iced canal at Five Locks,
More often than not went home with wet socks.

At Church School break time we played many games,
Before 'political correctness' we all had nick names.
We played hop-scotch, skipping with glee, rounders,
We cheated and fell out, we really were bounders.

The White Rose Cinema was our Saturday treat,
A penny was all we paid for a seat.
As the cavalry charged we shouted and cheered,
The Indians may not be beaten we feared.

Sunday was the day we had to conform,
Washed and brushed up we tried to reform.
Off to Chapel or Church for afternoon School,
Welsh children were required to obey this rule.

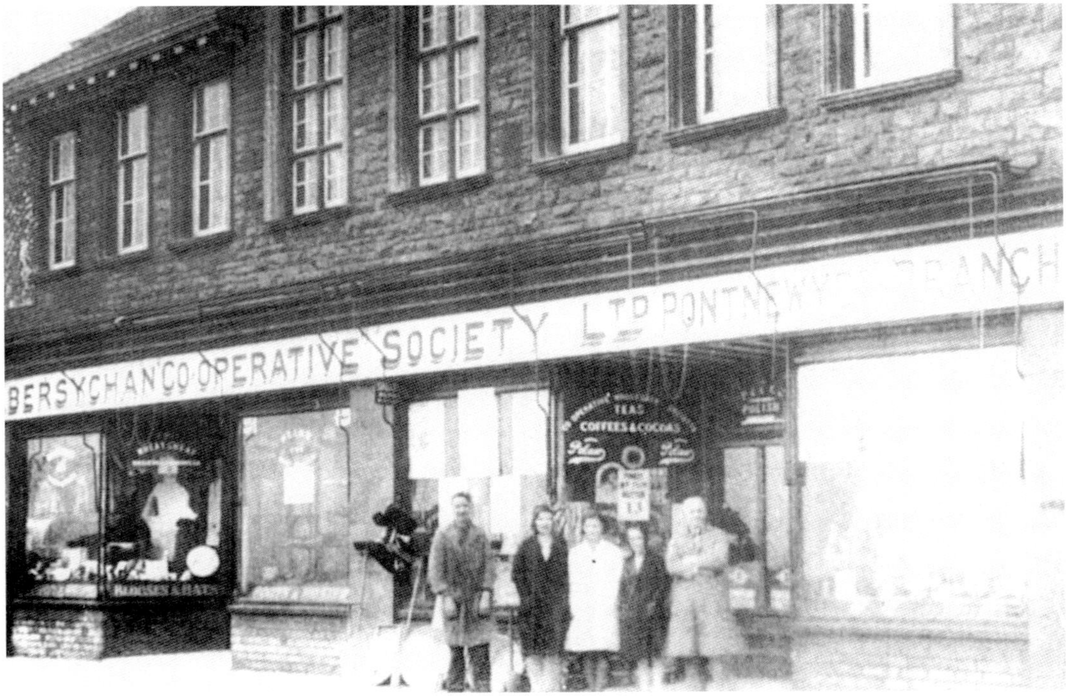

Store assistants at the Co-op store in Chapel Street during the 1930s.

The above sentiments will surely evoke fond memories for those able to remember such halcyon days. Her written description of life in the community is also worth recalling for it typifies a former way of valley life.

'From the butcher Mr. Poulton we purchased all our meat. We loved his faggots and peas which were served hot and had to be collected in our own jug. Jugs were also used for collecting beer from the Oddfellows public house...as children we shared a glass of shandy. We felt this was quite wicked - which made it all the more exciting!...close by was a bakehouse and it was always warm...in Winter it was lovely to put your hands on the wall heated by the large ovens inside. Mr. Price looked like a ghost as he was always covered in a dusting of white flour.'

But were they really halcyon days? For in the Summer of 1891 a lad called James Bowen had the option of doing 14 days in prison for stealing pears from W. Evans' orchard. Justice was harsh and utterly unfair. An anonymous account which appeared in *'A Living in Torfaen'* (1993) paints a very different picture of the reality of daily life for young girls 'forced' into domestic service.

'When the First World War was over I was 13 and I went into service in a house owned by a retired seaman in lower Pontnewydd by the Kings Head. I was a kitchen maid and I had to be there in the morning at 7 o'clock. It was hard work and it frightened me...I didn't like the mistress, but my mother told me to stay and have my meals at other tables because she could not afford to feed me.' Definitely 'food for thought'.

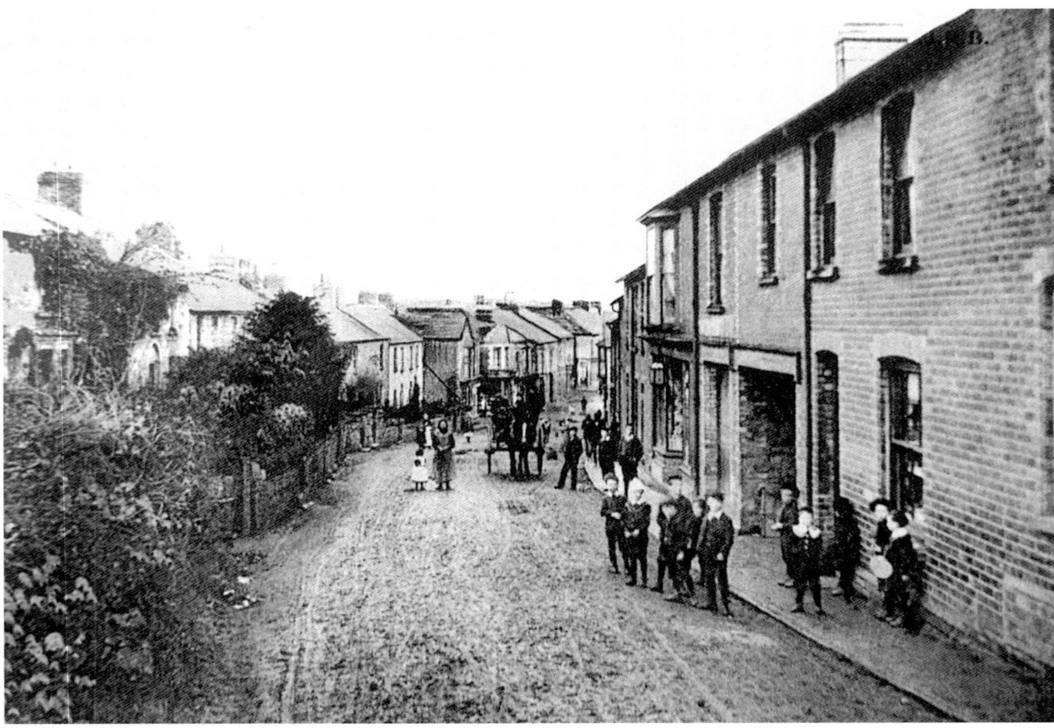

Commercial Street in the early 1900s.

CWMBRÂN GARDENS HOTEL

Despite the massive increase in the population of Cwmbrân over the years, the number of public houses and hotels has actually decreased compared with the early part of the 1900s. This may seem surprising or totally confusing and the outstanding and much frequented hotel in the area was Cwmbrân Gardens. Idyllically situated alongside the banks of the canal at Pontnewydd, its large ornamental grounds and Japanese gardens was a favourite playground for the more affluent young socialites of Cardiff. Here was a Mecca where people could relax and enjoy themselves as contemporary accounts readily support.

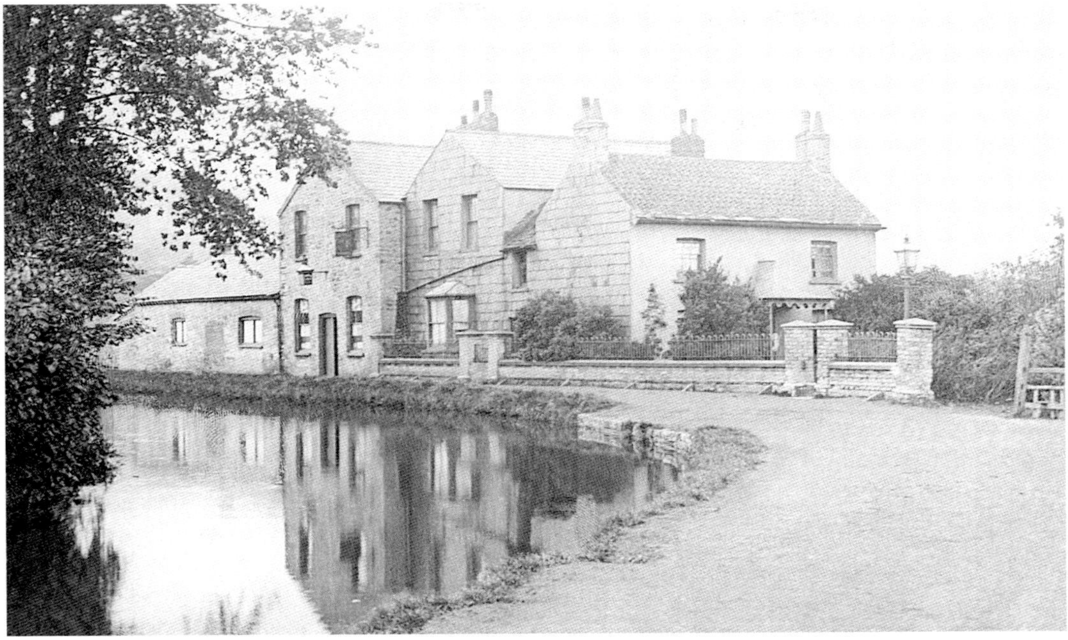

Cwmbrân Gardens Hotel.

In August 1877 the ***Free Press of Monmouthshire*** reported that in one day alone a staggering 1,500 visitors passed through the railway stations at Pontnewydd and Pontrhydyrun en route to partake of the many pleasures of Cwmbrân Gardens. The following account in the ***Monmouthshire Merlin*** on 5th September, 1884, shows the unselfish and courageous nature of an employee of a Cardiff firm of railway wagon builders.

'On Saturday last Messrs Andrews & Baly...gave their workmen the annual picnic. The party proceeded in brakes to Cwmbran Gardens and on arrival at the canal near the Patent Nut & Bolt Company's works, a cry was raised that a boy 8 years old, named Joseph Harrington, had fallen into the water between the locks, which was about 20 feet deep. One of the Cardiff men, named Henry Arthurs, immediately jumped into the water and brought up the insensible body, which was restored to consciousness. This is the 4th person he has rescued from drowning.'

In 1909 a runner from Roath Harriers won the 20-mile marathon from Cardiff to the Gardens in the remarkable time of just over 2 hours! And the ideal place to slake his thirst! (Or did he journey by tram or train?)

For many years it continued to be a popular venue for picnics and works outings whilst open-topped charabancs brought people in their droves from Cardiff for dancing. What a ball they must have had! Definitely the place to be -

if you could afford it. Which the ordinary penniless local family man or woman could not.

Inevitably, the haunt gained a reputation for outrageous behaviour and revelry. After well over a century it suffered severe structural damage due to its very proximity next to the waterway: it closed in the early 1950s and was subsequently demolished. There is nothing left nowadays to suggest the excitement and infamy of those heady days. Nevertheless, the Gardens Hotel will long be remembered as playing an important role in the social fabric of Pontnewydd.

A FESTIVE TIPPLE TOO MANY...

Reports about over indulgence at Christmastide abound throughout the press over centuries. The following report in the ***South Wales Argus*** on Saturday, 7th January, 1911, typifies this.

Apparently, William Nicholas, landlord of the Cross Keys Inn, was summoned at Pontypool Court for selling intoxicating liquor during prohibited hours on Christmas Day. Two friends, Ivor Morgan and John Hibbs, both local colliers, were also accused of being on the premises and drunk at the time of the offence. The three defendants pleaded not guilty. The local constable P.C. Hughes stated that ***'at around 10 a.m. he visited the pub but initially received little response but heard a commotion inside'***. When Nicholas finally opened the door he spotted the other two sitting by the side of the kitchen table with glasses half full of beer and empty bottles beside. When questioned as to why they were on licensed premises at that time of day Nicholas maintained that the two were being entertained as ***'guests'***. The landlord further added: ***'It is a simple affair and I hope you won't make anything of it.'***

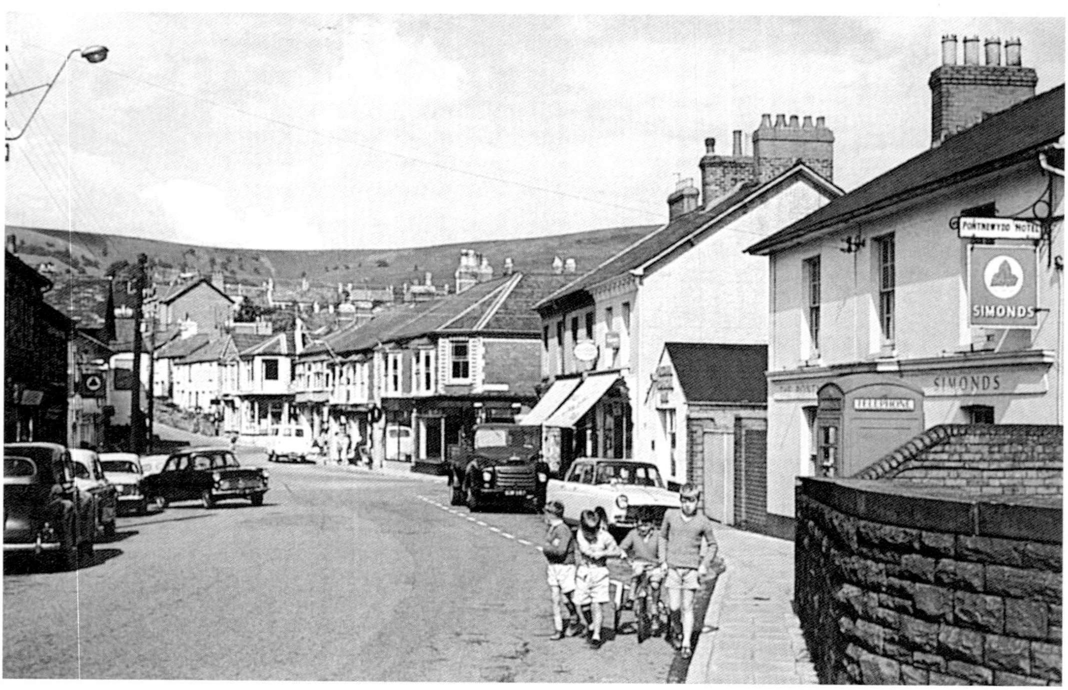

Young and free in Commercial Street during the 1960s.

Needless to say the belligerent police officer would not agree and insisted upon pressing charges. In court the defendants' solicitor, Mr. W.J. Everett, addressed the Bench stating that this was not a case ***'where a conviction should be recorded'***. Nicholas, on oath, maintained that his ***'friends'*** stayed at his house until ***'stop-tap'*** on Christmas Eve. They then left but returned shortly afterwards ***'to sing some Christmas Carols'***. Sounds plausible enough. Upon being invited back in they were given copious quantities of ginger brandy and lemonade. In court Morgan and Hibbs remained adamant that they had received no intoxicating liquor on Christmas morning.

To the sound of laughter within the court, the defendants both gave similar evidence that they ***'only tried to sing carols'***. Which may well have been true in their presumably drunken stupor. A Mr. E. What asked whether they had sung ***'While Shepherds Watched'*** or ***'While Policemen Watched?'*** More raucous laughter from those present in court, including a wry smile from the presiding magistrate. The constable who had clearly made a complete fool of himself muttered: ***'While Policemen Watched would be more appropriate.'*** Further laughter. Anyhow, the Bench fined each of the accused 20 shillings. The lesson to be learned is that tippling ***'Carol Singers'*** beware - at your cost! A wonderful story.

HOPE METHODIST CHURCH

Another religious house was needed in the village for nonconformists who were weary of the arduous trek up the mountainside to Ebenezer Chapel at The Square, Upper Cwmbrân. On 2nd April, 1866, the trustees of the Pontnewydd Primitive Methodists paid Miss Leah Jones the princely sum of £10 for meadow land fronting the parish road leading to the railway station. In September 1866 a devotional service was held with the laying of the foundation stone by Mr. F.G. Grice of the Patent Nut & Bolt Company. The church opened the following year without ceremony and since has been 'a rock' within the community. In 1966 Hope Methodist Church celebrated its centenary and continues to remain a fine place of worship.

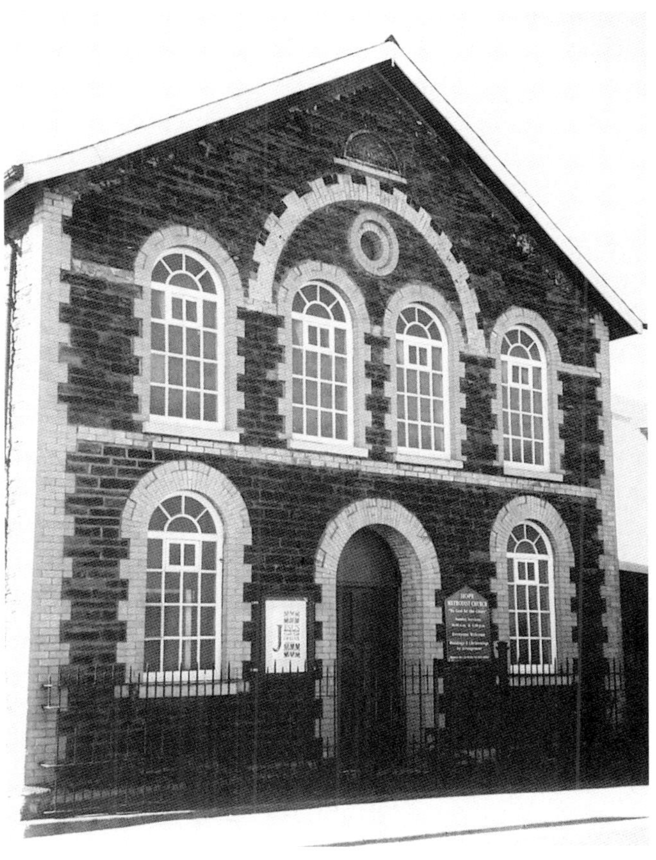

Hope Methodist Church.

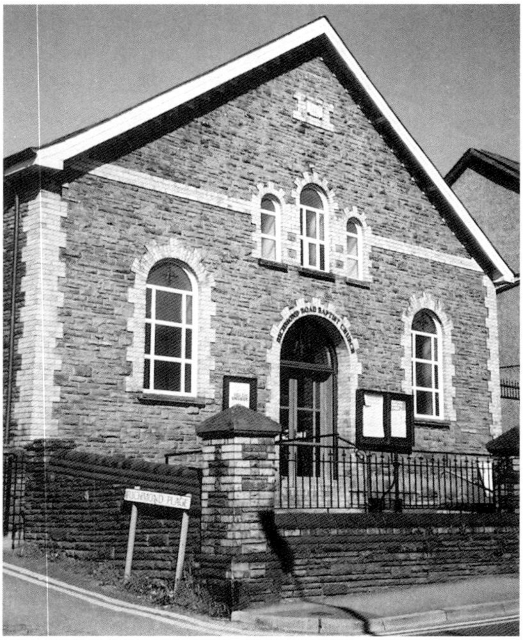

Richmond Road Baptist Chapel.

THE BAPTIST CHAPEL

Situated directly opposite the former White Rose cinema in Richmond Road is the Baptist Chapel. This was built in 1880 primarily for workers of the Baptist faith at the Tynewydd Iron & Tinplate Company. Land fronting Richmond Road was purchased for £55. The chapel opened its doors on Sunday, 27th August, 1882. As well as worship, this was another important centre of recreation and culture for the inhabitants of the village. An amusing entry in the minute book of 1877 states: ***'That any member of this church visiting Cwmbran Gardens for pleasure be brought under church discipline.'*** Clearly, The Gardens were regarded as a 'den of iniquity' by staunch believers of the faith. No doubt, though, many strayed with the lure of pleasure so close. In 1934 it held the 'first annual Pontnewydd Eisteddfod' with considerable success. The war years, inevitably, took their toll and the event ceased. The chapel continues to flourish where others have long fallen by the wayside.

THE CENOTAPH

Pontnewydd cenotaph is a lasting legacy of remembrance for the communities of Pontnewydd, Cwmbrân and Croesyceiliog to celebrate the heroism and sacrifice made by those fallen in two World Wars. The memorial built in 1925 stands in front of the former Pontnewydd council offices. During 2006 the granite façade, much weathered by the passing years, was given a much-needed facelift thanks to the generosity of the local branch of the Royal British Legion and Torfaen Council. At the foot of the cenotaph, in identical stonework, is a 'Book of Remembrance'. This bears the names of the 26 men of the area who lost their lives during the Great War and the 41 men who perished during World War II. The re-dedication and unveiling of the refurbished war memorial took place on Sunday, 1st October, 2006, amidst much ceremonial attended by local dignitaries, the Welsh Piping Society, a detachment of the Royal Monmouthshire Royal Engineers (Militia) and veterans organisations. A fitting if belated tribute to the folly of human conflict.

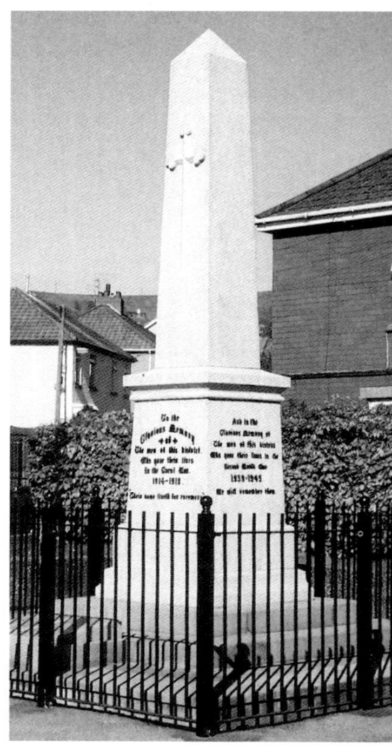

A Fitting Tribute to Warriors Past.

THE MALE VOICE CHOIR

Most entertainments were home-grown. This choir began life as Upper Cwmbrân United Male Voice Party, only later to become Pontnewydd Male Voice Choir. It got off to an enthusiastic start in 1905, but encountered difficulties during periods of industrial unrest. Notably, following the closure of Cwmbrân Colliery in 1927 when the choir lost nearly half its men in what founder member Will Evans described as ***'a wave of indifference produced by bad industrial and economic conditions'***. Throughout the 1930s the group had difficulty keeping officers who suffered financial insecurity at home. Yet members of the public willingly contributed towards travelling expenses of unemployed men eager to take part in performances outside the area. During the 1920s and 30s when unemployment was rife, there was a grim determination within the community 'to soldier on' whatever the adversity.

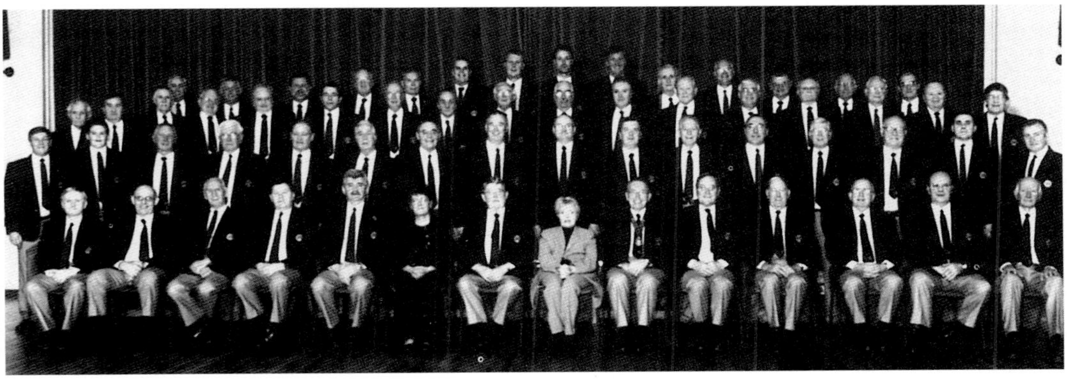

Pontnewydd Male Voice Choir - 2004.
Fourth row: Jim Branigan, Martin Jones, Graeme Jones, John Walding, Terry Westcott, Mark Homan, Geoff Durham, Martin Curwood, Dave Moyle, Gerry Ray, John Carpenter, Ernst van Eijkern, Lawrence Crowley, Carl Robins.
Third row: Fred May, Alwyn Nutland, Graham Parry, Alan Dunn, Trevor Owen, Dan Spanswick, John Davies, Ron Jones, Arthur Wood, George Docherty, Emlyn Stokes, Geoff Potts, Roy Fisher, Phyl Evans, Reg Seal, Graham Roberts, Bernard Morgan.
Second row: Terry Hole, Ben Powell, Bernard Dyer, Ray Ewins, Frank Gardner, Idris Howells, Clive Parton, Mike Willis, Robert Powell, Jeff Williams, Roy Williams, Alan Jones, Mel Flowers, Ernie Spokes, Neil Dixon, Bert Williams.
First row: Paul Wellington, Robert Ford, Blandford Durham, Keith Jones, Lyn Birch, Annette Williams (acc.) Walford Hutchings (M.D.), Pauline Carey (acc.), Lionel Boughay (Chairman), Roy Dixon (Secretary), Derek Parry (Treasurer), Dave Wilks, Brian C. Davies, Tom Crowley.

Inevitably, times change and following the Second World War the choir slowly saw its rebirth as a musical culture the envy of other choirs throughout the valley. The past twenty years have seen it prove ever popular and excel. The 100-year-old choir celebrated its centenary during 2005. What a success story! The above photograph is a worthy tribute to its success and longevity.

PONTRHYDYRUN

Pontrhydyrun had been little more than a hamlet beside the Afon Llywd for centuries. By the early part of the 20th-century it had been eclipsed by the development of neighbouring Pontnewydd with its influx of migrant workers, mostly Irish, seeking employment in the nearby tin-plate and industrial works.

TIN-PLATE WORKS IN THE AREA

The first tin-plate works were built at Lower Pontnewydd on the side of the fast-flowing Afon Llwyd in 1802 by George Conway. Four years later, in 1806, the Edlogan Tinplating Works were established higher up the valley at the bottom of Chapel Lane, Pontrhydyrun, by his son John. During the early years, pig-iron was brought by canal barges to Pontnewydd from Pontypool and carried by mules to the Conways' works. A tramway constructed between Pontnewydd and Ponthir carried goods from the tin-plate works to the wharf alongside the Hanbury Arms Hotel in Caerleon close to the bridge over the River Usk.

By the early 1820s it had been realised that tinplate was an ideal metal for packaging and preserving foodstuff as it was not only strong but light, did not rust, was non-toxic and, importantly, was very cheap to produce.

The works at Pontnewydd and Pontrhydyrun together produced a staggering third of the County's tin-plate output. These were golden years for the industry. Between 1839-50 profits exceeded £3,000; annual production was upwards of 2,000 boxes which found markets as far away as France, Germany and Spain. In 1870, the Edlogan Works were still operating two mills.

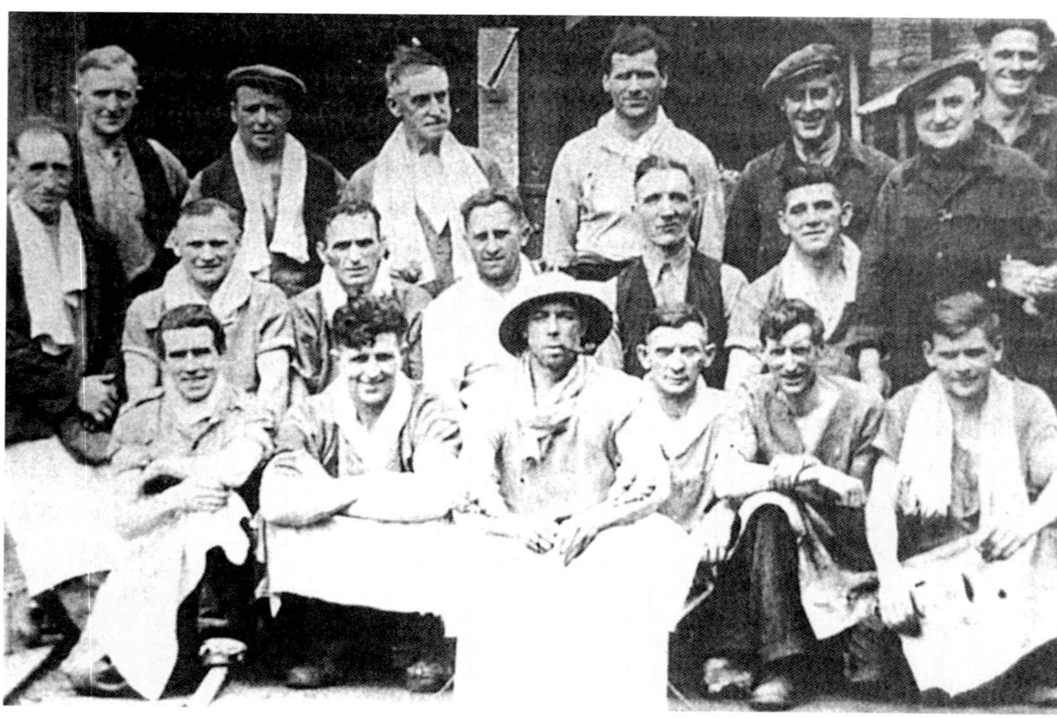

Tin-plate workers ca. 1947.

Though the workers were mainly men, a number of children were employed at both works. A Government report into the employment of children during 1841 presents a fascinating and contradictory insight into the thoughts of youngsters at the plants. Phoebe Conway, aged 8 years: '*...I have not been long at the works...my work is not hard; I would rather work than go to school; I have been to school a little, and go on Sunday to chapel school; I can't read, I am spelling; I am going to school again next week.*' Thomas Evans, aged 12 years: '*I am dusting plates with sawdust; I work 11 hours; I have an hour for dinner;...I was at school for 3 years, and I attend Sunday-school; I can read; I would rather go to school than work; I don't know how much I get; my father receives my money.*'

Competition for such a lucrative market led to the opening of Tynewydd Tinworks by Charles Roberts in 1874 near Pontnewydd railway station along with that of H.D. Griffiths on the opposite side of the river. So by 1877 four separate tin-plate works were operating and competing with each other for a seemingly inexhaustible and lucrative market. Yet the Edlogan Works was one of the last mills reliant on water from the river: during dry summers there was often insufficient water to power the wheel. The latter was taken over in 1894 by the Avondale Company. In 1908 these works were purchased by Richard Thomas & Co Ltd and ceased to trade as a separate company. In 1942 the premises were requisitioned by the Ministry of Supply for storage of 'general goods'. In 1946 three of the mills were dismantled as being redundant to the nation's needs. The old Edlogan Works were dismantled in 1946 but the site has been used for small businesses to the present day.

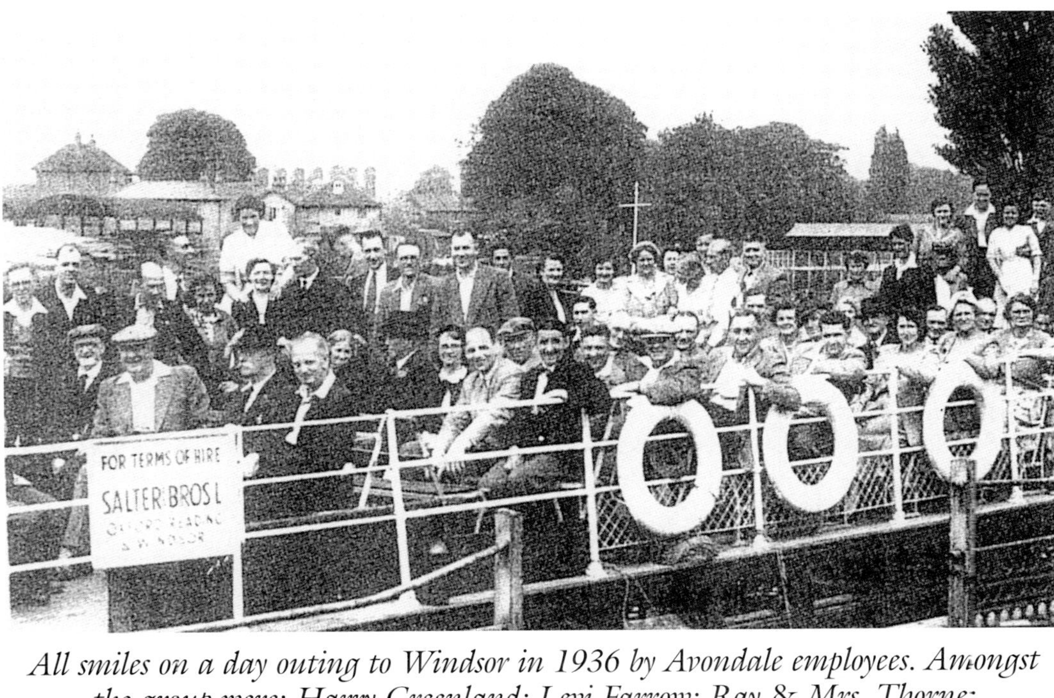

All smiles on a day outing to Windsor in 1936 by Avondale employees. Amongst the group were: Harry Greenland; Levi Farrow; Ray & Mrs. Thorne; Jack Murphy; Billy May; Fred May & wife Joan; Geth Williams; Arthur Cook; Mr. & Mrs. Farley; Percy Evans & wife; and the tenor Archie Filer much renowned for his singing and radio broadcasts.

The Pontnewydd operation owned by the Conway family ceased trading in 1885 due to out-dated industrial practices and lack of inward investment. The tin-plating industry was temporarily in crisis largely due to over-production throughout the British market. The Edlogan Works at Pontrhydyrun, continued to manufacture tin-plate well into the late 1920s.

Tynewydd Works was owned by various firms until bought out completely by the Redbrook Tin-plate Company Ltd in 1898 and in 1904 the first electrically-driven hot and cold tin-plate mills were installed. The Company gained the enviable reputation for the sheer excellence of the finest and thinnest tin-plate available in the world. In 1947 the Tynewydd Works became the first in the valley to operate oil-fired mills. A photograph (on page 66) of tin-plate workers at the plant shows a seemingly content group and a central figure with clay pipe in mouth.

Another photograph (on page 67) presents a different picture with employees of Avondale Tinplate Company enjoying a rare outing to Windsor in 1936 and taking advantage of a boat trip on the River Thames. The works later closed down in 1957 following a shortage of orders after almost 70 years in production. The Redbrook Tin-plate Company went the same way in 1961 for similar reasons.

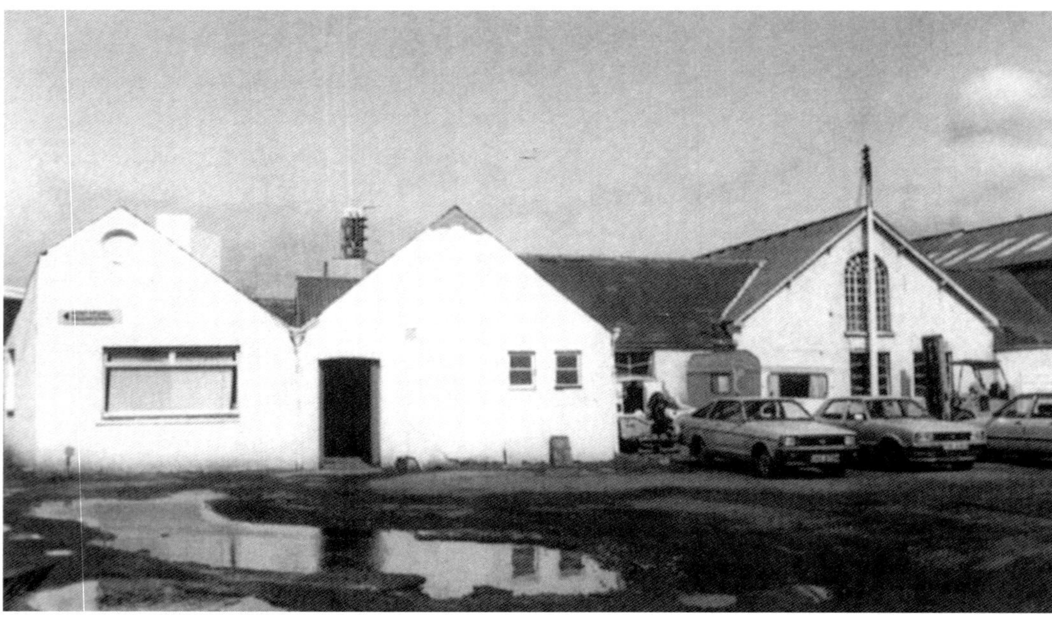

Edlogan Works in a more modern era.

The Conway family were deeply religious and held a sense of public duty towards their workers and their families. They lived in Pontrhydyrun House adjacent to the site of Edlogan Works. A room at the works was set aside to provide a Sunday School for children. This quickly proved too small, so a Baptist Chapel was built at the top of Chapel Lane on Pontrhydyrun and opened in 1807. (See Chapter on Croesyceiliog.) They constructed a row of terraced houses for domestic staff and works foremen, aptly named Conway Terrace, which still stands today; also, Garw Cottages, known as Lower Row, for their workers.

A BRIDGE TOO FAR

The former railway bridge in Pontrhydyrun is remembered mostly for the wrong reasons. Built well over a century ago, it was not a high bridge and the narrow roadway underneath was certainly not designed for modern traffic. Children used to play happily on the old line over it. (Are children today any different in risking serious injury?) But there were regular accidents involving vehicles at what became a notorious 'black-spot'. Buses, vans and lorries regularly became wedged under it and had to be hauled out.

During the 1940s a Weston's Biscuit lorry (now Burtons) had its top ripped off scattering biscuits and tins all over the road. The children of the village had enough biscuits to last them a week or more! Of far greater concern was a double-decker bus in 1982 that took a wrong turn at Pontrhydyrun Road and crashed headlong into the bridge. The top of the bus was virtually sliced off thus causing a number of fatal injuries to those passengers upstairs. This was Cwmbrân's worst road accident in recent times. Trains had ceased to run over the 'metals' of the bridge some years earlier, but British Rail had allowed the bridge to stand. Why? Whatever, though, it was demolished shortly after and the site later became part of Cwmbrân Drive.

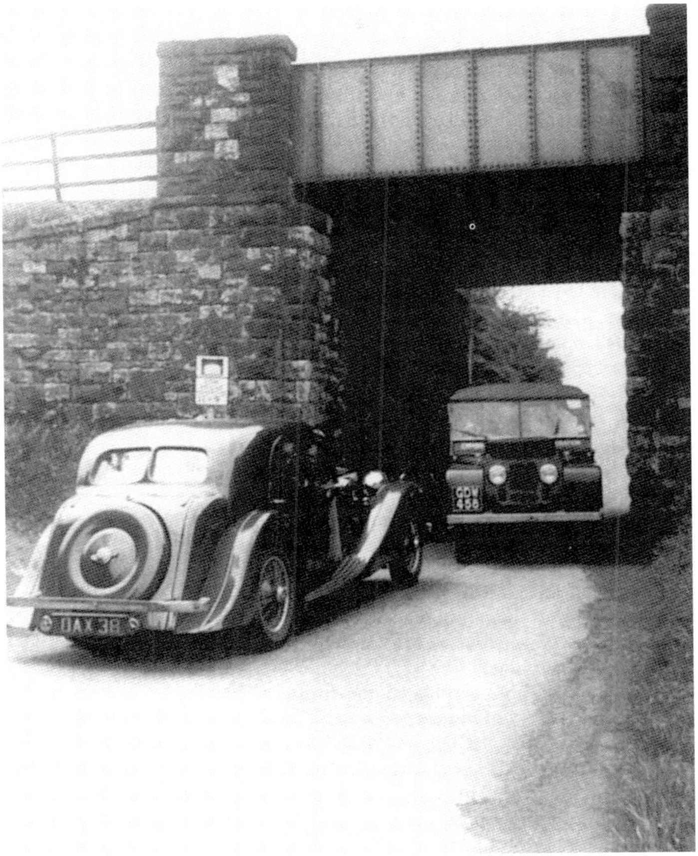

Congestion at Pontrhydyrun Bridge.

Today, Pontnewydd offers all manner of shopping experiences and with a great deal more customer-user friendly service than can be found in its more prestigious and larger neighbour. Long may the valley village and its community continue to prosper. And Pontrhydyrun remains a part of Pontnewydd - more than just a mere appendage.

Llanfrechfa

The picturesque village of Llanfrechfa lies on rising ground and bridges the eastern side of the valley of the Afon Llwyd and the neighbouring Vale of Usk. It probably derives its name from the Welsh ***'Brechfa'*** meaning ***'the church in a spotted or speckled place'*** and reflects the profusion of quartz conglomerate pebbles and boulders of red sandstone in the surrounding fields, although most are scarcely visible to the casual eye. Ancient records show that Llanfrechfa belonged in the Lordship of Usk and, in particular, to the Manor of Edlogan.

LLANFRECHFA CHURCH

Llanfrechfa's focal point, naturally, is the Parish Church, for centuries a place of Christian worship. Set a little way from the main highway to Caerleon-upon-Usk, it stands proudly on the hilltop among a cluster of trees and affords splendid views over the surrounding countryside.

A church has stood on this site since the 9th-century, possibly much earlier. The south porch dates from around this time and retains a number of sound ancient timbers; the stately Perpendicular embattled western tower with its projecting stair-turret and carved roof from the 14th-century. However, the main body of the original church burned down in the early part of the 19th-century and was largely rebuilt or restored during 1873-74 with over £4,000 raised for the work. The renovated church was re-consecrated on 1st September, 1874, by Bishop Olivant of Llandaff and dedicated to All Saints.

But why such an unusual dedication? The Griffith family resided in the Manor House at Llanyravon (long since gone) and were both land and property owners in the parish. One particular member of the family, Walter Griffith, in his Will dated 20th November, 1629, stipulated that he wished to be buried in the church of Llanfrechfa. The connection between Llanyrafon and Llanfrechfa may seem tenuous, but did he and his family regularly worship at the holy seat? Presumably so, though there is little record to verify this. Furthermore, amongst his various bequests he gave instruction to make payment ***'forever, yearly to the churchwardens of Llanfrechfa and Llantarnam the sum of £10 to be distributed among the poor, not being pensioners, at the feast of All Saints and the Nativity of our Lord God'***. The church records in existence during 1873-74 almost certainly recorded this dedication.

The Griffith Will also bequeathed money ***'to the repair of the church at Llanfrechfa'*** which suggests that the building had become somewhat neglected and crumbling. Surely, evidence that much of the church originated from Norman times.

Following the disastrous fire, the church records were retrieved, placed in a safe and transferred to the nearby vicarage (also rebuilt in 1874). Thus, they were supposedly preserved for posterity. But even the most well-intentioned plans sometimes go awry. When the then bachelor incumbent Thomas Reynolds died in July 1918, and having no known relatives, it fell to his solicitors to settle his estate. With the heaviest of hand, the safe was prised open and the papers contained therein regarding church affairs destroyed - lost irrevocably, robbing future generations of valuable historical information.

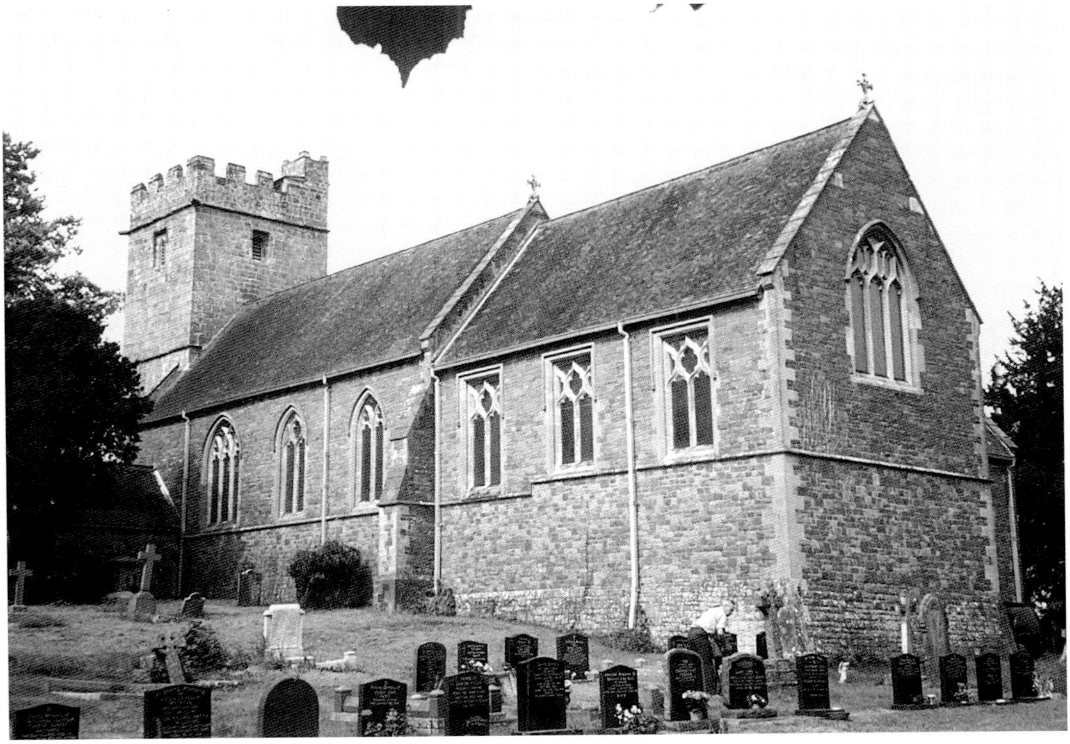

The Church of All Saints.

The tower bears a sundial on its south side, while a stone carved with the lower part of a Maltese Cross appears on its west face some 8 feet from the ground. The belfry houses eight bells. Of these, six were cast in Birmingham in 1873 and are inscribed with Latin verses taken from the 14th-century hymn ***'Salutatio Jesui'*** beginning:

Salve Jesu noster honos
Fac videre dies bonus,
and ending
Salve Jesu vox sonora
Juve nos in mortis hora.

The two other bells are later additions. One was cast with the inscription ***'King Edward VIII. Coronation 1937'***. But before it could be hung this was swiftly chiselled out following the monarch's Abdication and the name of his younger brother George substituted. The eighth bell marks the ***'coming of age'*** of Hopton Addams Williams of Llys Brechfa House and donated by the generosity of his wealthy parents.

The spacious chancel contains an ornamental marble screen (a reredos) above the back of the altar. Designed by James Redfern in 1873, this impressive large-scale relief depicts in fine detail Jesus celebrating the Last Supper and blessing the Holy Chalice - and the five wounds of Christ. The Caen stone was brought from Normandy.

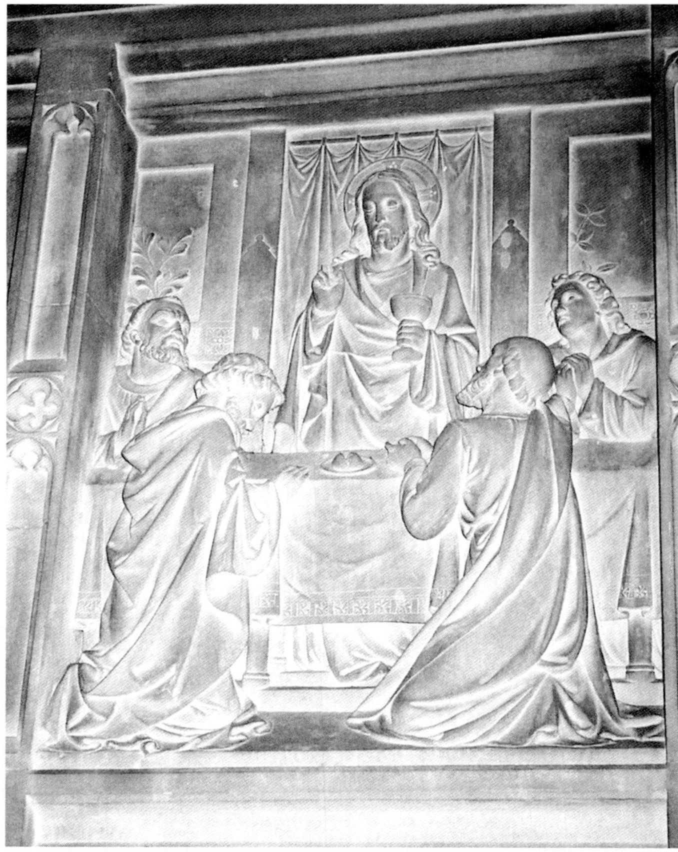

Marble screen showing Christ celebrating the Last Supper.

Other curiosities within the church include an ancient piscina to the right of the altar (a simple stone basin or sink for draining water used in rinsing the sacred vessels after the celebration of the Eucharist); a sedilia (three stone seats in the south wall for priests) and a carved wooden screen below the chancel arch with small figures of the Saviour, the Virgin Mary and St. John - representing the Holy Family. An arcading of four bays divides the nave from the north aisle which has an unusually conspicuous baptistery (dated 1873) **above** floor level where, presumably, the ordinance of baptism by immersion has long been performed. Shields on the front depict the Ark, the Fish and the unmistakable ancient Christian symbol - the Chi-Rho. The baptistery is covered by a heavy oak top. The church registers date from 1727.

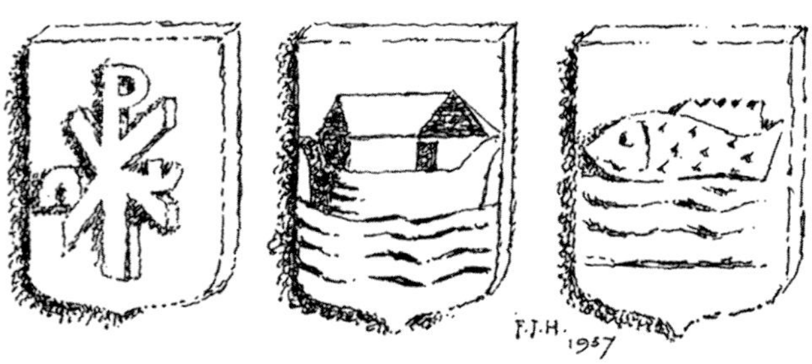

Carved shields on the baptistery. (Drawn by F.J. Hando)

The walls of the interior display several memorial tablets, several of them surely taken from the earlier building. The oldest, dated 1696, is dedicated to the memory of Charles Griffith of Llanyrafon Farm. Another is to the memory of Mordecai Jones and dated 1720. Others are well worn and hardly decipherable. The north wall remembers several of the landed gentry of the 18th-century and their wives.

Inevitably, many of the monuments within the church and tombstones in the churchyard were casualties of the major rebuilding programme. Most of these were afterwards remembered by small lozenge-shaped brasses set into the chancel floor.

A plaque on the inside west wall of the tower commemorates Frank Johnstone Mitchell, Justice of the Peace and Deputy-Lieutenant for the Shire, who died on 11th October, 1913, aged 89 years. Also, his wife Elizabeth (nee Rolls) on 16th September, 1910, aged 76 years. Interestingly, Elizabeth was the aunt of Charles Stewart Rolls, pioneer aviator and co-founder of the prestigious firm of Rolls-Royce motor cars.

The churchyard itself holds much of interest. The largest of all the yews, now a lowly but impressive stump, has a girth of some 16 feet and is probably well over 400 years old. Incredible. An upright headstone near the south porch remembers Gwenllian, wife of John Jones, Yeoman, who died on 1st June, 1772, aged 31 years. (Did she die during childbirth? This was not uncommon in those days.) The couple were reunited in the afterlife upon John's death on 19th April, 1807, aged 68 years.

The churchyard cross is relatively modern and bears the following inscription:

TO THE GLORY OF GOD
and the beloved memory of John
Etherington Welch Rolls of ye Hendre
and Elizabeth Mary Rolls his wife
this Cross was rebuilt by Frank
Johnstone Mitchell of Llanfrechfa
Grange and Elizabeth Harcourt
Mitchell his wife daughter of the
above A.D. mdccclxxx

The industrial expansion of the valley floor inevitably saw a huge surge in population growth. To cope with the added demand for 'interim' rest, All Saints Chapel of Ease was built in 1860 at the village of Pontnewydd in Upper Llanfrechfa. During 1885 it became a vicarage dedicated to the Holy Trinity.

The parish has long boasted numerous incumbents befitting the affluence of this rural part of the former village area of Cwmbrân. One such member of the clergy was Francis Forster, M.A., Queen's College, Oxford, who was appointed in 1875 by the Llandaff Chapter and served ***'his flock'*** faithfully until his retirement in 1899. He died 16th July, 1916, aged 88 years and lies buried at Llanfrechfa. So, too, is his successor, Thomas Reynolds.

Coming to the present day, a stained glass window remembers the bravery of Corporal Dave E. Denbury, a member of the Special Air Services who was awarded the Military Medal and the Queen's Gallantry Medal. He died in action during the Gulf War on 21st February, 1991, aged 26 years. At the time his parents kept The Star Inn, Ponthir.

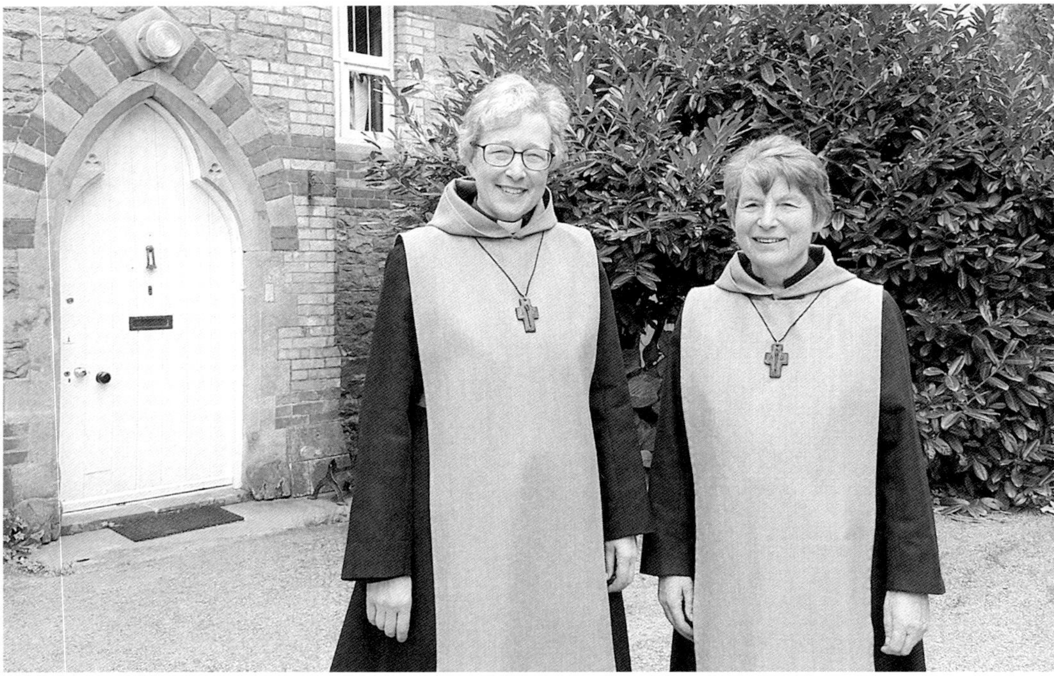

Sister Anita and Sister Enid outside the vicarage 2006.

It is often forgotten that in the past not everyone was entitled to a Christian burial as a matter of right, as the following tale vividly illustrates. Wil Wyth Tiwn (Will Eight Tunes) was an itinerant musician who lived at the foot of Mynydd Maen, Cwmbrân, and so nicknamed because he could play just eight tunes on his fiddle. He earned his meagre and precarious living playing outside public houses and was a well-known character throughout the neighbourhood. He performed at local festivals such as the ***'mabsant'***, an annual Welsh patronal festival (***'gwyl mabsant'***) held in June or July which, like many festivities today, had already become debased and to the consternation of ***'righteous folk'*** were ***'nothing else but sin'***. When he grew old and fell on hard times, he apparently did away with himself. As a suicide, the parish authorities resolutely refused burial in the consecrated ground of the churchyard. But why was this? Since time immemorial, suicides were believed to be the work of the Devil who had possessed the minds of the ungodly. Without timely exorcism their souls were damned for eternity. What utter nonsense!

According to the custom of the day, his friends duly buried Will at night at the crossroads at Lower Llanfrechfa. But rumours quickly spread that the area was haunted by the spirit of Will of the eight tunes; farmers maintained their horses shivered when approaching the crossroads. Eventually, they dug up his body in the dead of night and reburied it well away from any road, near the isolated Mountain Air Inn, Pen-yr-Hoel. Even as late as 4th January, 1937, a report in the ***South Wales Argus*** described how the older people of the district supposed that a strange formation of stones marked the grave of Wil Wyth Tiwn. Whether the above is true or gleaned from the realms of folklore really matters little, for it accurately reflects the attitudes and ingrained beliefs of our forefathers who were, essentially, of sturdy but humble country stock.

About half a mile to the east of the church on the brink of Candwr Brook (meaning ***'the singing waters'***) and close to the parish boundary is Coed-y-Caerau, an Iron Age hill-fort reputedly used by the Roman garrison at Caerleon as a temporary place of safety on higher ground for their families during times of danger. They possibly built the first wooden bridge over the Candwr which runs into the Afon Llwyd in its lower reaches near Ponthir. Apparently, a wooden structure was in place in 1600 when a Llanfrechfa yeoman left the princely sum of ***'three shillings and fourpence'*** in his will for its repair. The hill camp is easily approached from Candwr Lane.

LLANFRECHFA GRANGE

The original manor house was built in the grounds of a much older estate whose history is inextricably linked with that of Llantarnam Abbey prior to the Act of Supremacy in 1534 and the subsequent Dissolution of the Monasteries ca. 1536. Evidence suggests that this former manor (in reality a farmhouse) stood behind the doubled-fronted house known as Whitehall, visible from the junction of the Pontypool, Newport and Caerleon roads.

In 1835 Charles Prothero, Clerk of the Peace to the County of Monmouthshire, and 3rd son of Thomas Prothero of Malpas bought the property and lands. The present Llanfrechfa Grange, designed by local architect F.H. Langdon, was built around 1848 in the style of the Elizabethan period; the 140 acres of surrounding fields were landscaped as attractive parkland with fine trees and wonderful views on all sides. Unlike other substantial houses in the area, it was residential and its influence purely local.

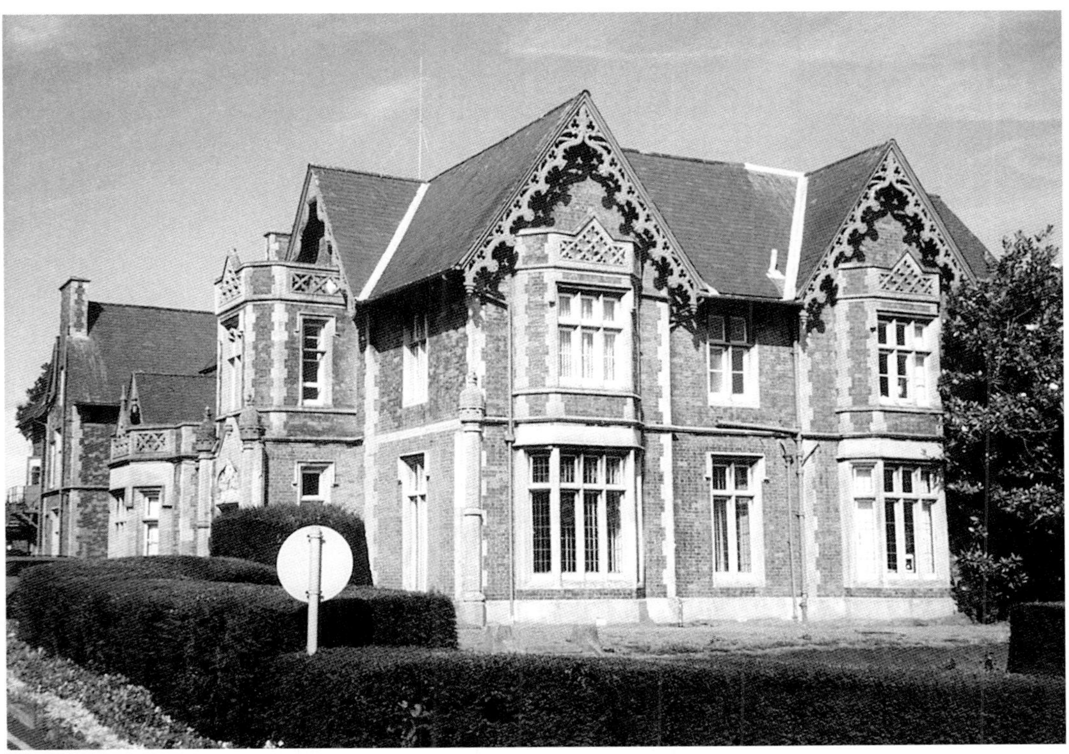

Llanfrechfa Grange.

An extract from *The Monmouthshire Merlin*, 2nd January, 1858, notes the generosity of the Prothero household towards the villagers of Llanfrechfa Lower at Christmas:

> ***On Christmas Eve...'not less than thirty families in the parish were supplied...with a plentiful supply of beef for Christmas Day. Many hearts rejoiced on the occasion, particularly under the present depression. On Christmas day Mrs. Prothero, with her usual benevolence presented (at the Grange Mansion) mince pies to the church Sunday School children, each countenance expressing a warm sense of gratitude to their benefactors for their kind marks of attention.'***

In around 1860 Francis (Frank) Johnstone Mitchell acquired the house. Both he and his wife, Elizabeth, travelled widely and upon returning from a visit to the Holy Land added a small but beautiful chapel to the east side of the house to catch the rising sun.

The splendour of the house was recorded in typically florid contemporary Victorian tones. ***'The front door opened into a large hall and to this was added a conservatory where ferns and flowers were always to be seen...The library was filled with old and interesting books...The dining room and staircase were made of oak and the furniture made to harmonise with the woodwork...The drawing room had a lovely Adam fireplace, whilst the ceiling was of moulded plaster picked out of gilt...And a large hall behind the servants' quarters was used for all festivities and celebrations in the parish, such as those connected with jubilees, coronations and harvest festival suppers.'*** Opulence personified and a world apart from those less privileged who had to strive for a daily crust just to survive.

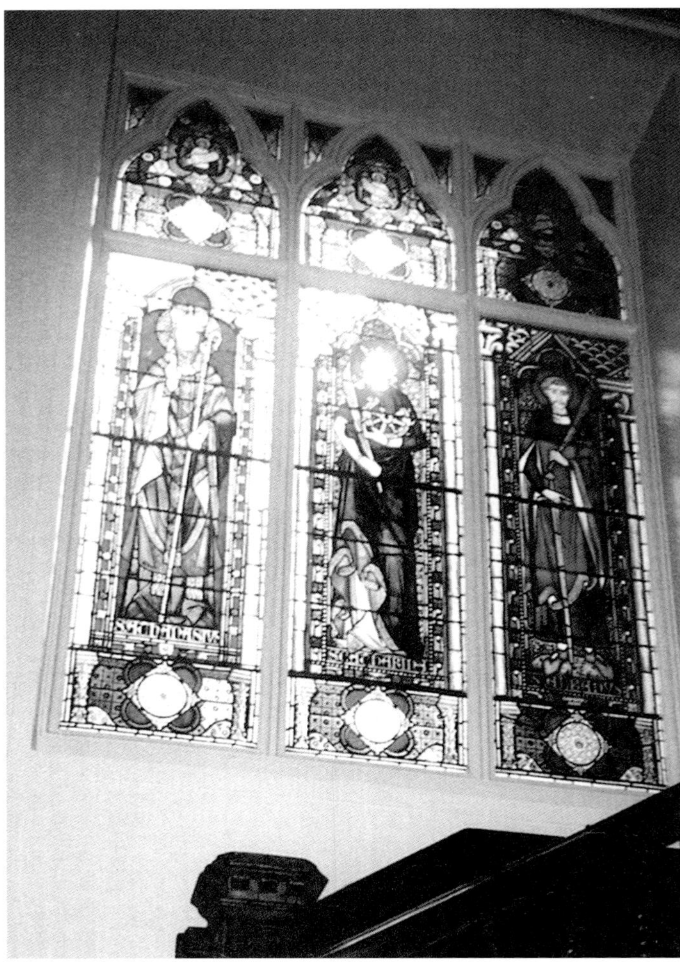

Stained glass window on the main staircase of the house was brought from London in the early 1860s.

The account continued: ***'The chapel has a carved wooden altar...and beautiful handmade frontals. A beam had been especially erected...with figures of Christ on the Cross, John and Mary.'*** Although brought from Southern Europe, probably Oberammergau, and intended for the local church, the authorities shunned the work. Thus, for a brief spell the artwork languished in the estate's chapel before a welcome was found within the parish church. The religious significance of the craftsmanship was seemingly belittled.

The stained glass window on the main stairs of the house is something of an enigma. Commissioned for the like-named Church of All Saints, Margaret Street, London, it was aptly designed by the Victorian architect William Butterfield. The glass was fashioned by Alfred Gerente of Paris in 1857, but for some strange reason it was removed from its intended English home in the early 1860s and replaced, only to be brought to Llanfrechfa Grange. Most puzzling.

The imposing entrance gates to the estate were of wrought iron mounted on stone pillars from the Parish Church following its rebuilding in 1874. The photograph taken ca. 1910 shows the main entrance to the house and lodge with its neatly manicured front garden.

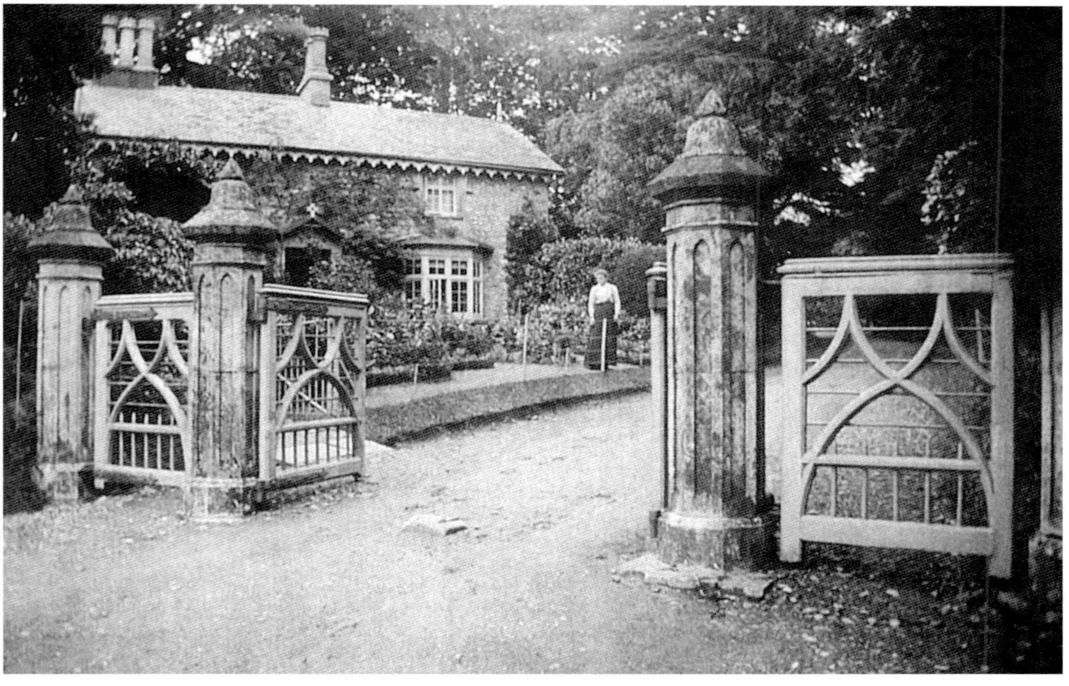

The main entrance to the house and lodge around 1910.

There were formerly several cottages on the estate, notably Park Cottage, Gardener's Cottage, Cowman's Cottage and the front Lodge. Mr. Mitchell installed a pound for cattle and sheep which strayed on to his land until reclaimed by their owner. For a fee? Probably.

The landowner also bought the licence of the Crown Inn situated at the top of Crown Lane and promptly closed it down. Was he a teetotaller, or did he merely object to revelry and ribald behaviour by those in his employment? The reason is unclear, but no doubt his action proved unpopular among the locals. Mr. Mitchell then erected a ***'handsome fountain'*** close by as a sop to weary travellers for the loss of the inn; also, to refresh horses after hauling heavy loads up the steep slopes of Crown Lane. It also provided a source of water for the neighbouring homes and farmsteads. An inscription read: ***'The Fount of the Lord is the Fountain of Life.'*** How very true. But the fountain is no more…

Following Frank Mitchell's death in 1915 the Grange passed to his daughter and family, then to Sir John Cecil Davies who after a stay of only 2 years sold it in 1924 to Baronet Sir Leonard Llewellyn who died in October of that year. Thereafter, the house remained empty for some time languishing in relative obscurity, but with a sense of notoriety.

MURDER MOST FOUL

The headline in ***The Free Press of Monmouthshire***, Friday, 29th April, 1921. Followed by ***'Old Man Battered to Death at Llanfrechfa Lower'***. The lengthy account of the gruesome murder begins ***'Monmouthshire is fast gaining an unenviable reputation for the terrible crime of murder. On Sunday the quiet agricultural district of Llanfrechfa Lower was startled by the discovery of the brutal murder of an old man, aged 74, named William Richards who resided alone in Park Cottage on the estate of Major-General W.F. Cleeve, C.B., J.P.'*** The cottage, nestling among trees was but some 30 yards from the main road and looking down directly upon Cwmbrân.

William Richards was Church Warden for many years and highly respected within the local community. For more than 50 years he had worked as a check-weigher in the employment of Messrs. Guest, Keen & Nettlefold at their steelworks in Cwmbrân. On the previous Wednesday he was busy at his usual work. Yet, for whatever reason, he was absent on the Thursday, fuelling speculation as to his whereabouts on the following day. The unfortunate fellow was born in the very cottage which became the scene of his tragic demise.

William was a widower who lived alone and kept poultry in his garden. His body was discovered on the Sunday morning by Mr. Frank Purkiss, a railwayman who lived at the Lodge with his parents, none of whom had seen him for several days. Being the victim's nearest neighbours, they tried their best to help the lonely man. But on this particular occasion there was no sign of him. On entering an outhouse Frank made the grisly find. The victim lay partly covered in hay with his head battered in a pool of blood. The police at Croesyceiliog were immediately informed. A further search of the shed established the murder weapon as a blood-stained garden spade.

Richards was fully dressed when found and had a considerable sum of money on him which was untouched. Clearly, robbery did not appear to be the motive. The post-mortem revealed that he had been dead for at least 2 days. Two women came forward to state that they had gone to Park Cottage on the Friday evening to do some household cleaning but they got no reply. The police initially assumed that after hearing a knock on his front door ***'Mr. Richards…went to the door to receive***

his visitor; and on the threshold of his cottage, he fell, the victim of a foul and unexpected blow. Blood spurted from his wounds and spattered the walls. Lifeless, or nearly so, he was carried, or dragged to the rear of the house. A trail of blood indicates the route of his last journey...To cover up the deed, the front door was again locked, the key taken away...'

As the inquest into his death opened at Cwmbrân police station on the Tuesday amid much sensational coverage in the local press, ***'hundreds of curious sightseers again visited the vicinity of Park Cottage...and lined the road for a distance of about 100 yards, sitting on the roadside discussing the murder'***. Why do so many people hold a morbid fascination with death and disaster? It's human nature after all.

So who committed the heinous crime? And for what motive? The police finally came to the conclusion ***'some person or persons had attempted to steal Mr. Richards' poultry and the cackling of the fowls alerted Richards who went to investigate and upon entering the yard encountered the person or persons who abandoned the contemplated theft for the graver crime'***.

Certain evidence supported this theory. Several strangers had been seen in the vicinity for some time previously, noticed by many in the close-knit community. A neighbour of Mr. Richards had experienced a scruffy man unexpectedly barge his way into his home demanding food and money with menaces. When he refused and picked up a poker from the hearth to threaten the intruder, the stranger fled empty-handed. And there were similar tales to lend credence to the police theory. Sadly, William Richards' murderer was never caught and brought to the justice of the hangman's noose.

The Church Warden's funeral was attended by several hundred people and the body interred in the churchyard of All Saints Church. Such was the respect for the deceased. The breast plate on the unpolished oak coffin bore the simple inscription: 'William Richards died 22nd April, 1921, aged 74.' It must be remembered that violent attacks on the frail and elderly, though exceedingly rare, continue to haunt society to this very day.

A NEW LEASE OF LIFE

In May 1936 the Boy Scouts' Association took over Llanfrechfa Grange, changing its character completely as it became a centre for young boys from disadvantaged areas: they underwent training to become 'below-stairs' domestic servants, waiters, etc. A few weeks prior to his abdication the rightful but doomed heir to the throne, Edward VIII, visited Llanfrechfa Grange in November 1936 to witness for himself and encourage the praiseworthy work in transforming wayward youngsters into becoming useful future citizens of the Kingdom. He instinctively held out a compassionate hand and in doing so (like elsewhere in the South Wales Valleys) earned the respect of all he met. Yet ultimately, and perhaps this was his destiny, he failed the people he purported to love and support. Hindsight proves that Time is a hard taskmaster.

In May 1947 Monmouthshire County Council purchased the house and grounds and used it as a maternity hospital for expectant mothers evacuated from the heavily-bombed areas of England and to cope with an anticipated soaring birth rate following the end of World War II.

But strange happenings went on, most summarily dismissed by doctors and staff as being the wild imagination and ramblings of pregnant women and young mothers. In one instance a youthful Mrs. Irene Hole had just given birth and was asleep in a corner of the ward. Suddenly, she was awakened by ***'something with icy cold hands'*** tugging at her bed clothes as if trying to pull her bodily out of the bed. Sounds very much like a scene from a horror movie! Though badly shaken by the experience, Irene remained adamant about the ***'icy cold feeling'***. Perhaps the Grange has a far darker past than is generally supposed and holds other equally terrifying tales...

During 1953 its use changed again to care for the mentally ill and subsequently the psychiatric hospital was greatly enlarged to cater for some 400 long-stay patients.

Clearly, Llanfrechfa Grange Hospital has had a chequered history. Recent years have seen its facilities deliberately run down as the local Health Authority's policy has been to resettle patients and those with learning difficulties in specially-built residences within communities throughout the County. While commendable in theory, such ideology has proved impractical: society's most vulnerable people have become sacrificial lambs on the altar of bureaucratic 'statism'.

With closure imminent the land, designated officially as a 'brown-field site' will no doubt be sold in part to a property developer. Not generally known is that the former Cwmbrân Development Corporation had seriously considered expanding the housing stock into Llanfrechfa, but this never really came to fruition. This now seems likely to change and another sprawling housing estate in a semi-rural area lacking in everyday main conveniences seems inevitable. Whatever happens to the parkland, at least the house is a listed building and likely to remain. But in what capacity? It has been suggested that the buildings themselves become the location for a new specialist and critical care centre to treat Gwent's most seriously ill patients. This could prove a key element in the modernisation of hospital services in the County. Time alone will decide its future use.

THE GATE INN

Not far from the church, beside the main highway to Caerleon, stood The Gate public house. Like many of yesteryear, it tried to entice customers by a simple rhyme on its colourful inn sign:

This gate hangs high and hinders none,
Refresh and pay and follow on.

Sometime later, a Eugene Stratton added another couplet on the back of the sign which read:

Come into the Gate and taste of the tap.
Drink and be merry but keep off the strap.

The message is clear. All are welcome to partake of good ale but, to use modern parlance, ***'Pay as you Go!'*** Have times really changed that much down the years? The answer requires little explanation.

The photograph of the Gate Inn taken ca. 1923 shows members of the Challenger family who owned and ran the popular establishment until 1934. The inn sign is just discernible at the top left of the picture.

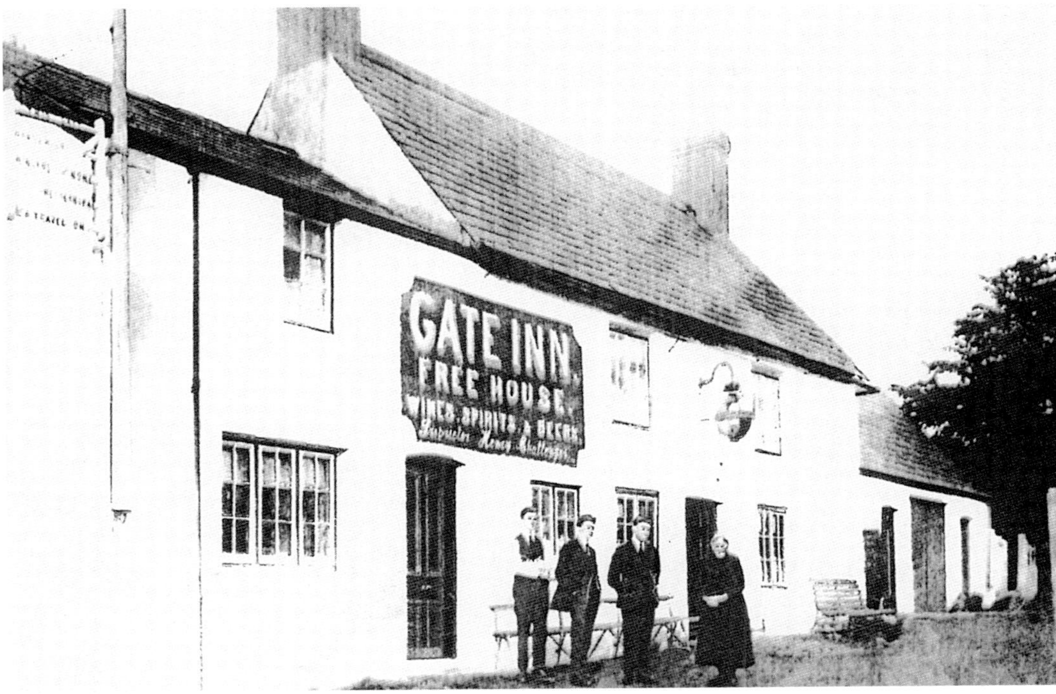

The Gate Inn circa 1923.
Left to right: Barman, Levi Challenger, Percy Challenger, Mrs. Challenger, wife of Henry Challenger, Landlord.

An amusing anecdote recalls such halcyon days. Two men of substance, Noel T. James and Mark Howell were returning from a day's hunting at Llangibby and paused at the hostelry to partake of a tipple or two and enjoy good cheer. Noel boasted that his horse could jump any gate in the county. A bold assertion which did not go unchallenged by his companion who retorted ***'OK, jump that one'***, pointing to the pub sign - a real gate suspended some 12 feet in the air!

The Gate was on the old tram road carrying iron from Blaenafon down the valley and across the eastern ridge to the barges moored at the former bustling port of Caerleon for export to the smelting works along the coast and across the Severn to Bristol. (There was no dock at Newport at the time.) The hostelry afforded refreshment and a welcome break for those plying the route. Remarkably, there were some eight inns in about a mile running from The Crown to the Ponthir Inn. Almost all of these have since reverted to private dwellings. Evidence of tram lanes through the village still exists.

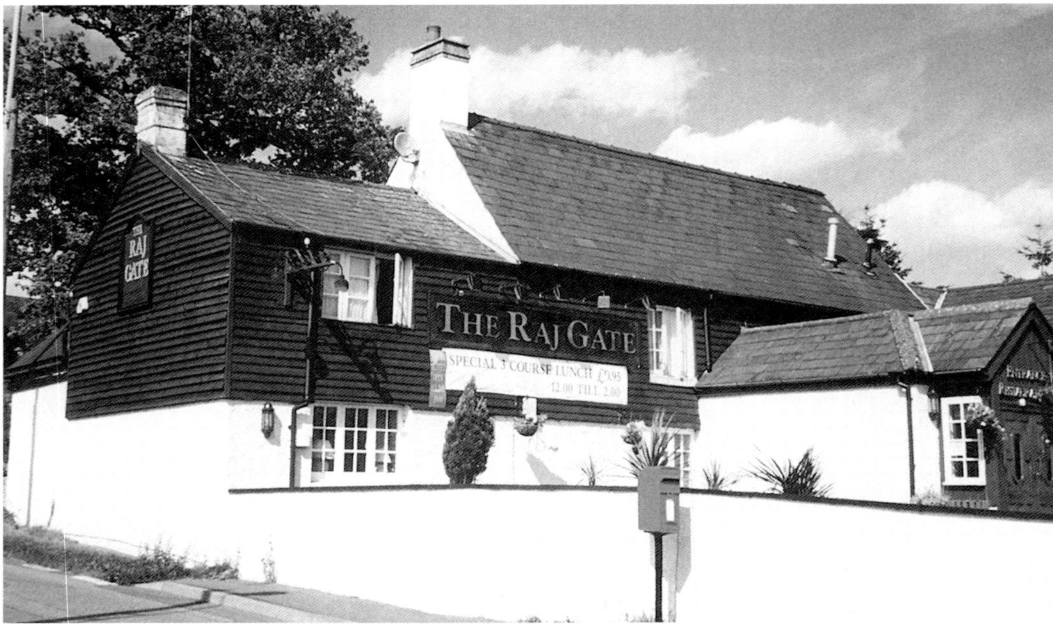

The Gate today, renamed The Raj Gate.

In modern times, The Gate was bought by Whitbread's Beefeater chain of pub-restaurants and turned into yet another 'eating house', thereby losing its traditional pub character and atmosphere. Very recently, it has again changed ownership to become The Raj Gate, a tastefully appointed restaurant offering the finest of authentic yet contemporary Indian cuisine.

LLANFRECHFA SCHOOL

The local school used to be situated close to the junction of Tram Lane and Caerleon Road, opposite the former Gate Inn. Some years ago the Lower National Church School established on 5th September, 1864, proved no longer viable and finally closed its doors in 1975. Thus was the heart and soul of the village all but snuffed out.

Even so, the school log books provide a fascinating insight into a former era when poverty and hardship were rife. Notwithstanding that, many of the children attending were from outside the parish boundary, notably Llanfrechfa Upper (i.e. Pontnewydd), Llantarnam and Panteg. This prompted fears of overcrowding; the daily running of the school proved difficult with serious sanitary problems contributing to the continual spread of illness and disease - an ongoing source of disquiet.

Various teaching methods were employed to discipline and educate the unruly young charges and a variety of subjects taught. For instance, in 1873, the Headmaster, Mr. Hillean, began instructing pupils in the metric system (whatever for?), whilst infants were given regular ***'object'*** lessons which included learning about such things as ***'bread, turnips, thimbles, wheat, tea, cotton, sugar, tin, the square and the triangle'***. Hardly the essentials for contemporary everyday valley life! His successor, Mr. Plessey, took over the mantle in July

1887 and knew *'how to keep children interested by constant questioning'*. A valid teaching tool equally relevant today.

Discipline was all important. Misdemeanours were dealt with severely. Again, the school log of 9th April, 1877, describes the punishments meted out: ***'Punished...for drawing figures on his slate and showing it to the girls...when told to hold out his hand, he at first refused but obeyed after being well shaken...'*** Such was the order of the day. Though this changed somewhat in September 1904 when Monmouthshire Education Committee issued the ***'Corporal Punishment Regulations'*** which instructed all headmasters throughout the County to refrain from all forms of punishment, ***'save for grave moral offences until other methods have been tried and failed...Every occurrence of corporal punishment shall at once be entered into the punishment book'***.

The school records from 1904 to 1952 show the difference in attitudes of successive headmasters. Similar 'offences' were not necessarily treated with the same degree of tolerance. For instance, the new headmaster of 1925 gave a young boy four strokes of the cane for ***'refusing to sit up and then refusing to open his hand...'*** Another lad was given six strokes for ***'Mumbling persistently...'*** Perhaps, after all, the severity of education has moved with the times. But for the better?

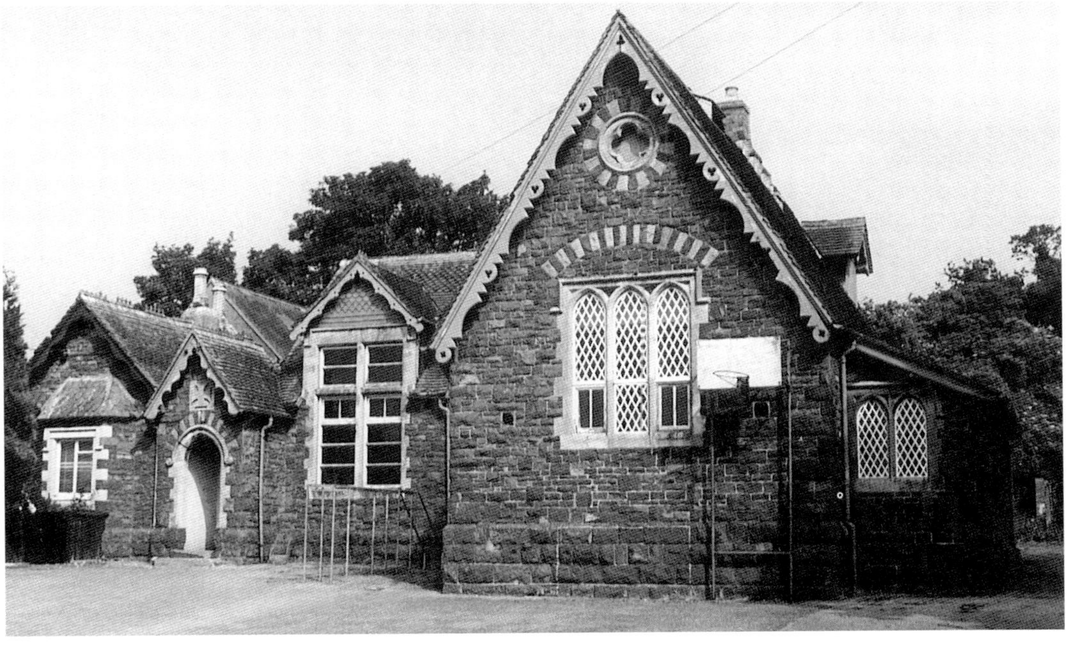

The Victorian school during the 1960s and shortly before its closure and demolition.

Following its closure, the old school was temporarily used as a Special Needs Centre for slow learners - and then demolished. Another link with the past gone. The School House and land has become a private dwelling.

The original school was replaced by a modern church school built on a pleasant green-field site in nearby Ponthir. This appeared under threat itself due to dwindling numbers, but following a massive lobbying campaign of Torfaen

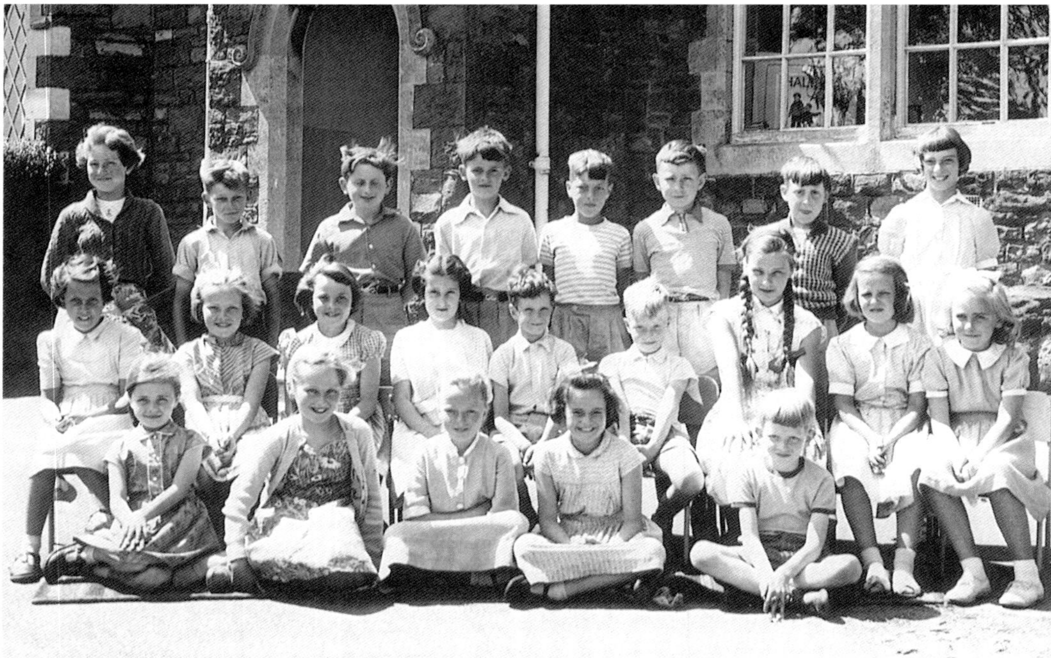

A class of smiling pupils taken in the 1960s with their teacher.

Council and the Welsh Assembly, in 2006 the school was granted Voluntary Aided status and is now under the control of the Church in Wales.

RIFLE RANGE

A rifle range in Llanfrechfa? Sounds highly unlikely. Yet in 1905 a range was built to the south-west of the railway line by volunteers using materials donated by a wealthy local gentleman on land rented from a farmer for the annual sum of two shillings and sixpence. The club was affiliated to the Welsh Rifle Club and for many years enjoyed considerable success, winning gold and silver medals throughout the country. Unfortunately, the building was severely damaged by heavy storms in 1923 which led to the club's eventual demise. And that was that. To commemorate its existence a stone plaque dated 1909 was set into the wall at the site of the former school by the entrance to Tram Lane.

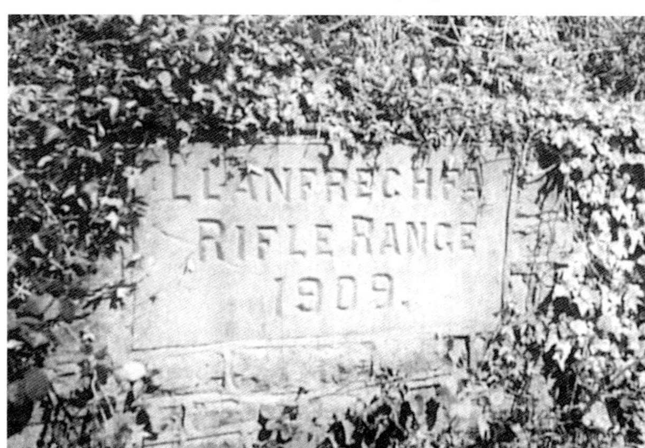

A blast from the past!

Nowadays, Llanfrechfa still remains a largely rural village set among an expanse of rolling fields untouched by the hand of Time; and where in summer sheep and cattle safely graze in pastures green under azure skies. It offers a welcome respite from the hustle and bustle of everyday suburbia.

Llanyrafon & Croesyceiliog

Llanyrafon is a pleasant and thriving suburb of Cwmbrân. Situated on the eastern bank of the Afon Llwyd, it is not too far from the hustle and bustle of everyday town life and has several features of interest.

LLANYRAFON FARM

Llanyrafon was the chief estate and manor house of the widespread parish of Llanfrechfa for many centuries and is the principal survivor from the pre-industrial landscape which would so heavily blight the entire lower valley. The earliest known owner was the attorney Walter Griffith, who acquired it in 1616. Records state that he purchased: ***'One mansion house, one barn, four gardens, one orchard, one barton and four parcels of land on the road from Croesyceiliog to Caerleon.'***

Successive members of the Griffith family acted as stewards of the ancient manor of Edlogan (a name which survives in Croesyceiliog still) until 1886. The gradual enlargement of the house and outbuildings down the years reflects the growth in the family's wealth and social status.

The present name ***'Llan-yr-Afon'*** was adopted during the early 1950s when the planners of the proposed new town of Cwmbrân decided to create a 'housing village' between Croesyceiliog and Llantarnam. Prior to this the area was rural. The original name of the grey Elizabethan farmhouse was probably ***'Glanyrafon'***, implying the house ***'on the bank of the river'*** - the Afon Llwyd.

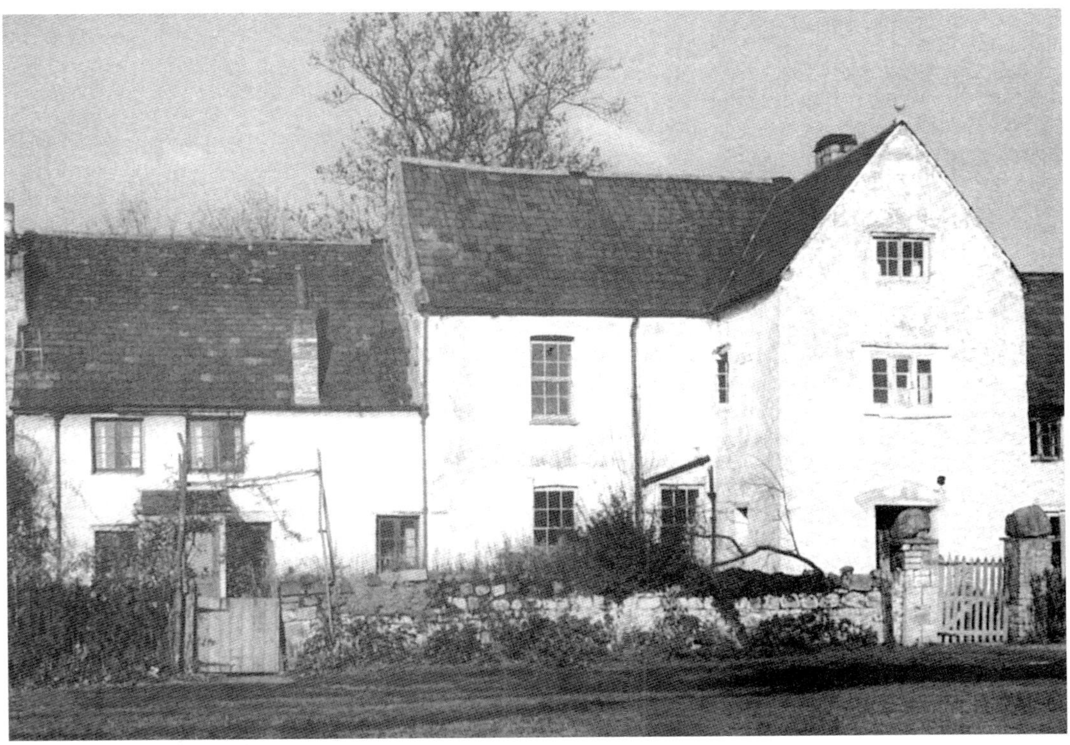

Llanyrafon Farm during the late 1940s.

Today, the house is known as Llanyrafon Farm. During the 1890s the distinguished antiquarian, Sir Joseph Bradney, frequented the County and described the house as the most important mansion in the parish (of Llanfrechfa) and the seat of the Griffith family. The last of the line was Charles Griffith, steward of the manor of Edlogan. Upon his death, his widow married Mordecai Jones, the steward of Tregrug. The couple did not share a harmonious relationship for when Mordecai died in 1719 his will stated: *'...to my most unkind and unnatural wife £20 on condition that she do not imbezell any of my money, goods, papers, etc., or molest my executors.'* Most telling!

The origins of the house date from the late 16th-century, probably between 1550-1610. It is likely though, that a building stood on this site from the Middle Ages and belonged to the Cistercian monks of Llantarnam. The oldest part with its mullioned stone windows is the east wing; this has a parlour and hall separated by an oak post and panel partition bearing the initials 'CG' referring to one of the several Charles Griffith that resided here. The central body was constructed by 1616. Inside, remnants of its Elizabethan splendour are long gone and has become somewhat austere in appearance.

Around 1800 William Griffith, a successful solicitor, moved to Gloucester where 'pickings' were richer, but he returned regularly to Llanyrafon to manage his valuable estate. He died in 1831 and his lengthy obituary appeared on 27th August in ***The Monmouthshire Merlin***: *'...in the 74th year of his age, William Griffith, of Gloucester and of Llanyrafon...the excellence of whose public and private worth will long remain an exemplary instance of one who in his generation, has not died in vain.'* In life he held the respect of family, friends and business associates alike.

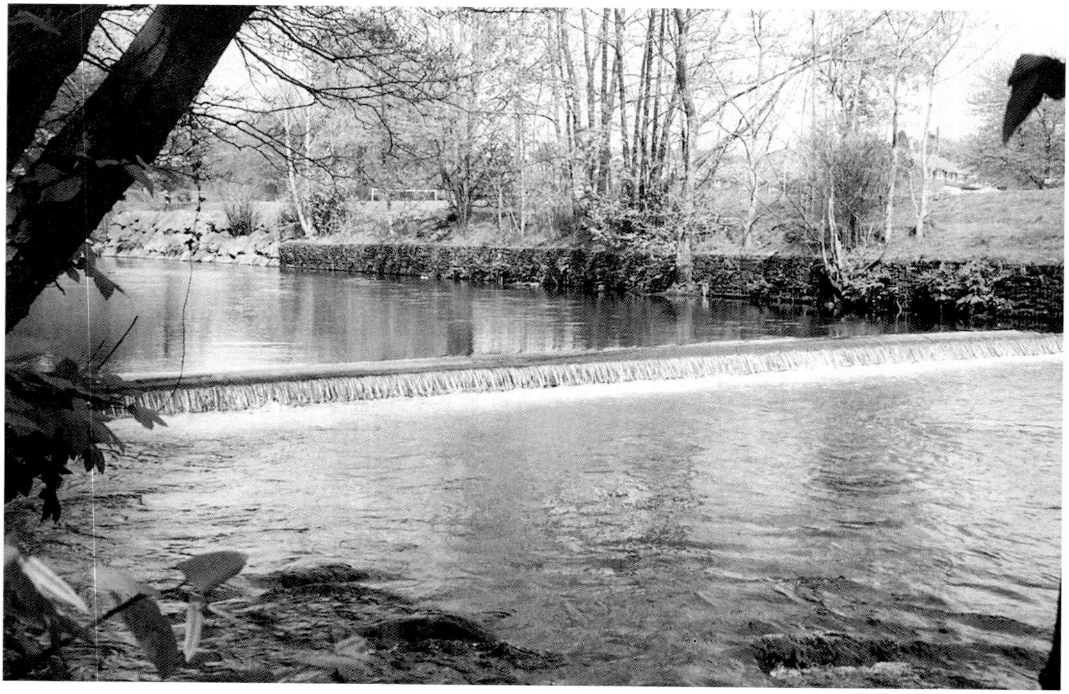

The Afon Llwyd close to Llanyrafon Farm.

Llanyrafon Farm passed to his son, another Charles Griffith, who died without issue. His sister Florence, gained possession and she died a spinster in 1886, thus ending the domination of the Griffith family over 200 years.

In 1892 the estate was broken up and sold. Richard Laybourne of Malpas bought the farm and house as a wedding present for his daughter upon her marriage to Mr. Alfred Massey Pilliner (son of A.C. Pilliner, J.P., of Llantarnam Grange and managing director of Oakfield Wire Works). Farming continued as before. But in the 1900s the newly-weds moved to nearby Llanyrafon House, a new red-brick villa, ***'a modern mansion in Gothic style'***. A highly artistic woman, the new Mrs. Pilliner designed the tile surround of the huge fireplace in William Morris style and had the original staircase removed from the old farm to the new house.

Alfred Pilliner divided the farmhouse into three separate houses. Originally a cider cellar and granary, the west wing was converted into a cottage. So too, the central section. Both were occupied by workers on the farm. The north wing was turned into bachelor quarters for single workers, a shrewd move as their sometimes rowdy behaviour could be readily observed.

Prior to the First World War, Alfred's son, Rupert, made plans to install electricity but, sadly, he was killed in action. A hero of the retreat from Mons, he

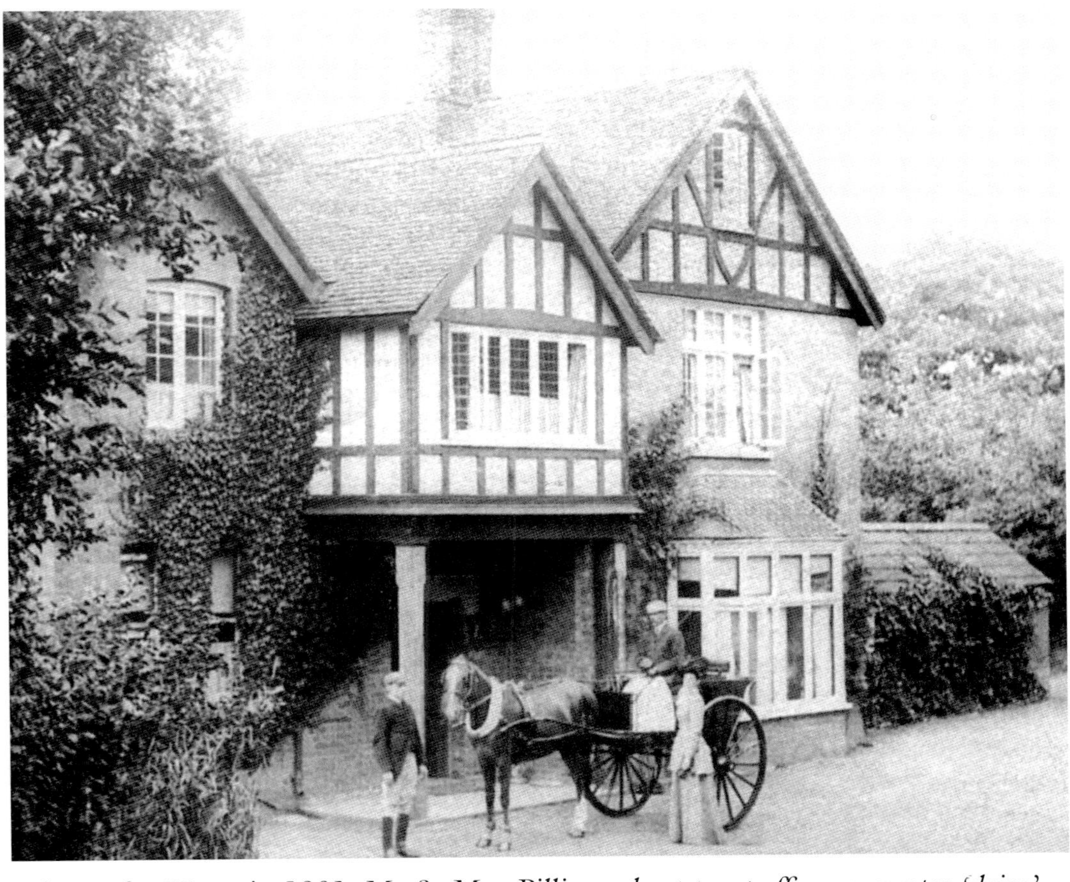

Llanyrafon House in 1901. Mr. & Mrs. Pilliner about to set off on a country 'drive'...

was recommended for gallantry and the notable Legion of Honour of France. A brass plate in Llanfrechfa Church honours his death.

The farm was always an extremely busy agricultural concern. During harvesting, cider was given freely to a grateful workforce to quench their insatiable thirst.

The Pilliner family owned the farm until the 1950s when the estate comprising some 1,000 acres was sold to the Cwmbrân Development Corporation for expansion of its housing stock. Llanyrafon House, in later years a home for the Stirrup Cup Club, was subsequently demolished for the building of the first large-scale popular hotel in Cwmbrân, the Commodore Hotel, set back off Llanfrechfa Way and now enveloped by housing.

But what to do with the farmhouse itself? No-one had any real idea - apart from demolishing it! It lay empty, vulnerable to the elements and open to vandalism. Fortunately, it was decided that this ancient Grade II listed building should 'live' again and become a tourist asset to the area. The enterprising Torfaen Museum Trust took full responsibility for it in 1980 and restoration work commenced. It was intended to be developed as a museum of rural history charting the life of a typical late Victorian valley farm with livestock and farm gardens. A year or so later the house opened to the public on weekends from April to September.

But this initial success was to be short-lived. Due to structural problems and safety concerns for the public, the farmhouse closed in 2001. But the wider issue was that the Trust could not find the estimated £2 million needed for restoration and repair. A spokeswoman for Torfaen Council admitted in December 2002 that the Trust was ***'focusing activities in Pontypool and has suggested they shouldn't be involved in Llanyrafon Farm'***. Her arrogant dismissal of this sector of Cwmbrân's heritage was reprehensible - and indeed somewhat short-sighted.

At present, this historic 17th-century farmhouse remains in limbo. When restoration is eventually completed Llanyrafon Farm should begin a new chapter in its compelling history and become one of the County's finest tourist attractions. If ever...

LLANYRAFON MILL

Llanyrafon Mill stands silent in a dilapidated state, just a short distance from Llanyrafon Farm. A shame really, for this formidable stone building has stood beside the waters of the Afon Llwyd for many centuries. Water-mills were a common enough sight during the 17th-century, but with the arrival of the Industrial Revolution most had outlived their usefulness and became redundant and derelict.

Documentary evidence proves that a mill was in operation here in 1632. Yet there is good reason to believe that the mill dates back a few centuries earlier. On his map of 14th-century South Wales and The Borders, the cartographer William Rees plots a ***'Mill on Avon'*** - surely Llanyrafon Mill.

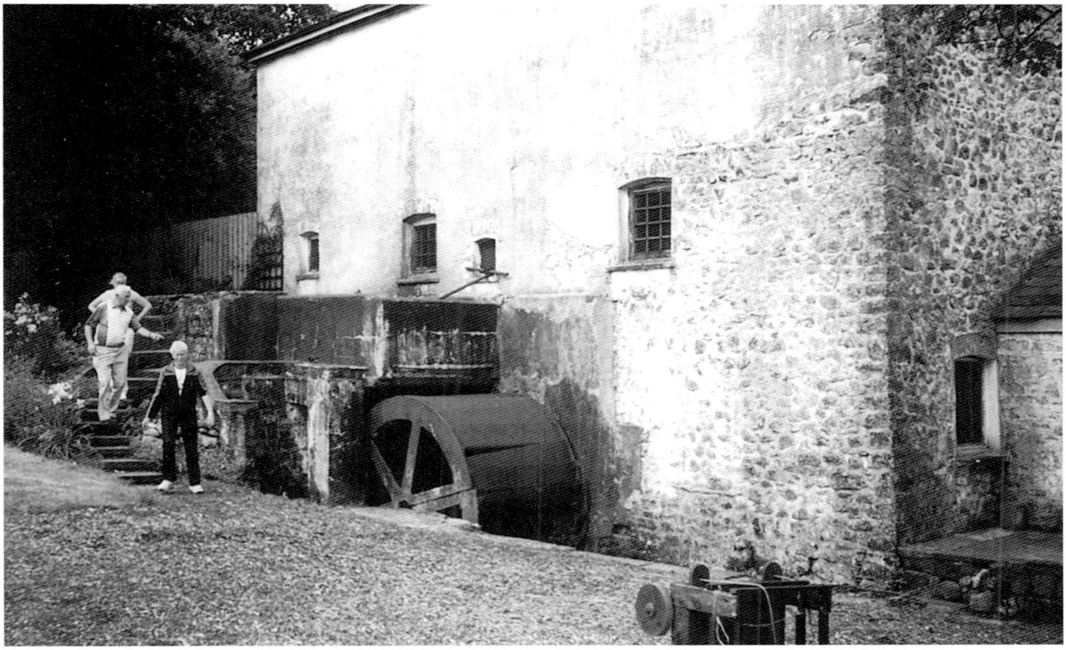

Llanyrafon Mill as it appears today.

The mill belonged to the ancient Manor of Edlogan which was owned by the Griffith family from the 1660s until 1892. Thereafter followed a succession of owners and different millers. Throughout its working life the mill served a wide-ranging area; also, it provided the flour for several notable houses including Tredegar House, Newport, the home of the Morgan family. During its heyday the mill was an essential and integral part of rural life.

Originally a three-storey corn mill powered by an enormous waterwheel of the overshot type, the mill is unusual as it should really be named Llanyrafon Mills. For unlike the majority of mills found elsewhere which have one set of grinding stones, Llanyrafon possesses ***three*** sets of such stones connected to a complicated mechanical gear.

Water is the 'life-blood' of any water-mill. This was drawn from the nearby Afon Llwyd about half a mile upstream and carried along a narrow, fast-flowing feeder stream or 'leat' at the correct height to power and drive the huge iron waterwheel. The path of the old 'race' is still evident along Miller's Ride on the present-day Llanyrafon estate. The miller controlled the water level to the wheel by use of a lever which opened and closed the sluice gate in the trough. The existing trough replaced an earlier wooden one around 1920.

Like mills everywhere, it was customary for the miller to let water trickle constantly over the wooden blades of the wheel even when no milling was in progress. This prevented the wood drying out and splintering, thereby ensuring its longevity. The present metal blades are badly affected by years of corrosion.

Despite alteration and modification down the years, the basic structure of the mill remains much as when first constructed. Sacks of harvested grain were hoisted

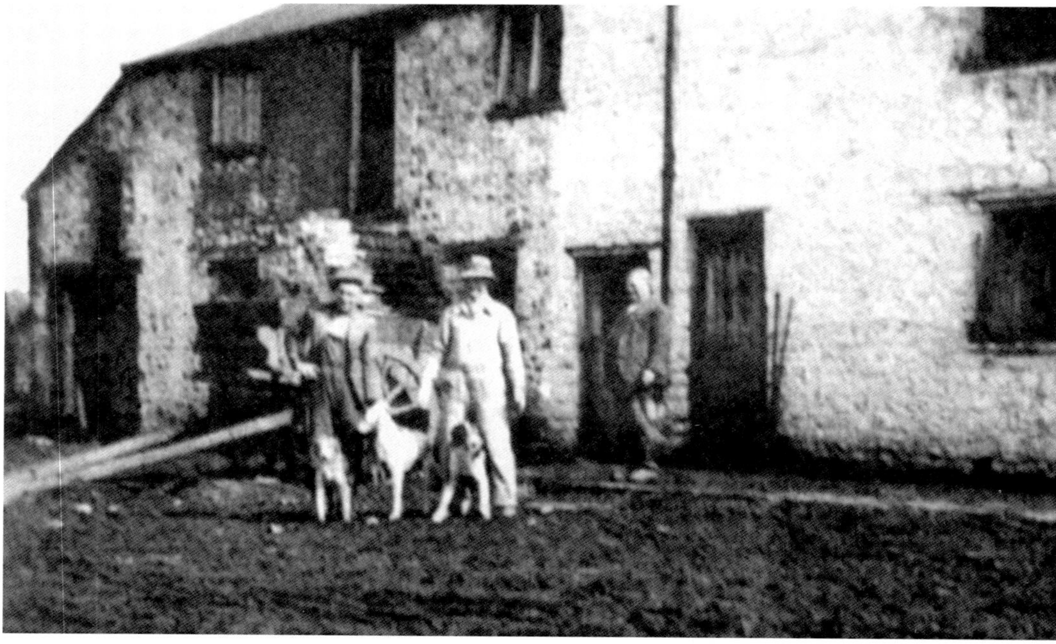

Farm workers at the mill in the 1930s. Is the 'jolly miller' Tom Wait in the background?

to the top floor and stored in large bins, or hoppers. Chutes led down to the grinding stones on the first floor, massive stones of hard-wearing French burr. Following milling, the flour or 'meal' passed downward to the ground floor where it was bagged ready for despatch to the customer.

Thomas Wait took up the tenancy of the mill in 1916 and lived in the nearby house. Highly respected, Tom later purchased the property and became the first owner in its history to actually carry out the milling himself. Tom was quite a character. In fact, he was the typical 'jolly miller'. Regularly, he'd visit the Corn Exchange in Newport to purchase a load of corn which was brought by rail to Llantarnam Station where it was transferred to a horse and cart for the short journey to the mill.

Throughout the First World War the mill ground vast amounts of flour. Thereafter, it was mostly used for preparing animal feed. During 1945 an electric grinder was installed and used until the mill ceased operating in 1951 and abandoned. No-one seemed to care.

When the author Fred J. Hando visited the defunct mill in January 1954, Tom, then 73 years of age and still sporting ripe-faced apple cheeks and a wide smile to match, pointed out the following inscription on the wooden framework penned by a Mr. W.J. Hope in 1879:

'If your lips you'd keep from slips
Five things have you beware:
Of when you speak,
To whom you speak,
And how and when and where.'

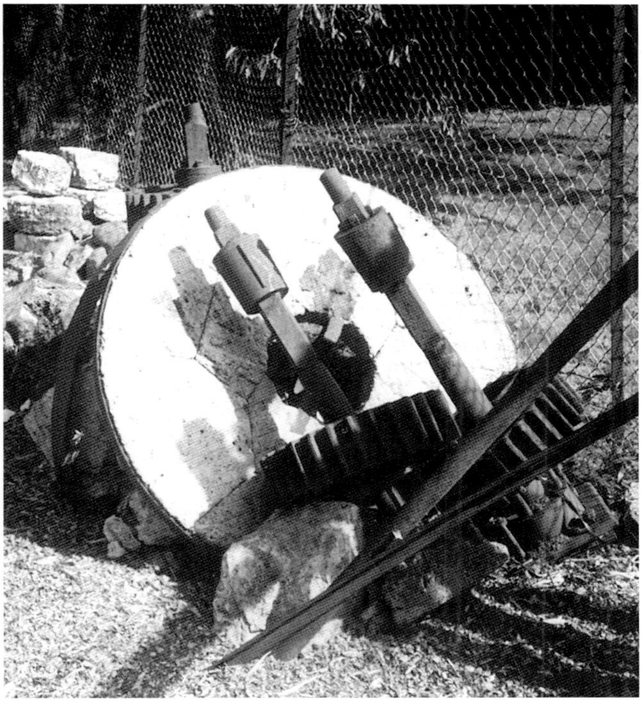

Part of the disused grinding gear.

The lines were written by a philosopher for they encapsulate a basic human weakness, i.e. to know where and when 'to keep your mouth shut'.

In 1967 the mill was acquired by the Cwmbrân Development Corporation - and thereafter ignored. During April 1971 a serious fire ravaged the redundant building destroying the entire roof structure. The end of a historic building. Not so. Government money became available in 1977 for unemployed people to contribute useful work to their community. The fabric of the building was completely renovated.

Then in December 1995 'The Friends of Llanyrafon Mill' was formed consisting of people eager to preserve a small part of the heritage of the locality. The mill then passed into the ownership of Torfaen County Borough Council and has become a Grade II listed building of historical importance. But will it ever be restored to a working facility? Remember an old proverb: ***'A mill grinds no corn with water that has passed.'***

Only when the waterwheel turns incessantly will the building come alive again, alive to the rumbling of the cogs and the lively chattering of the damsels, and the syncopated sound of water falling on to the wheel's broad blades - sounds of man attuned to nature and his environment. Then, and only then, will future generations be able to gain an enlightening glimpse of an almost forgotten way of rural life.

PUSHING THE BOAT OUT!

A boating lake close to the centre of Cwmbrân! Who'd have thought it? But the planners of Cwmbrân Urban District Council certainly did - along with suitable recreational facilities. This ambitious project was designed by the Council's Engineer, R.O. Hann. Funding for the work amounted to some £60,000. Work began in April 1971 and was completed in May 1972. This included a boat house, café and public toilets, and a well-frequented children's playground and other amenities.

Her Royal Highness, Princess Anne, recognised the significance of the facilities and was only too willing to officially open the premises on Friday, 12th

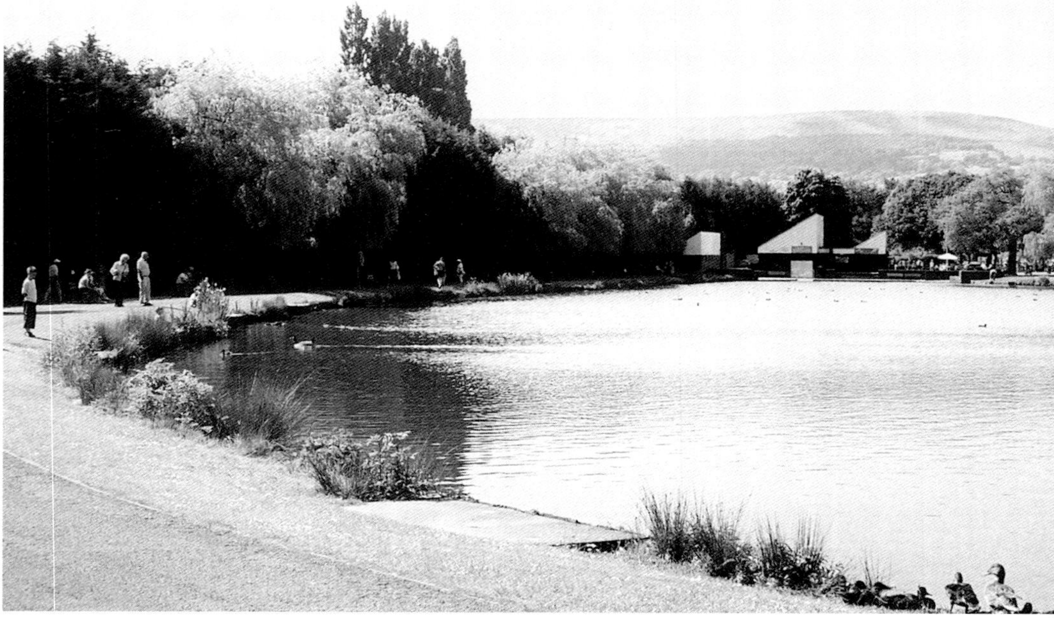

The boating lake set against the expanse of Mynydd Maen.

November, 1971, and unveil a commemorative plaque at the head of the lake. Afterwards, she was introduced to local dignitaries by the Lord-Lieutenant for Monmouthshire, Colonel (Edward) Roderick Hill, before being entertained to a canoeing display by a group of local children. Surely, this must have brought back fond memories of her childhood and later escapades.

The boating lake covers over 4.5 acres and has a capacity of approximately 4.25 million gallons. Water is fed to the lake from Cwmbrân Brook at its northern end and introduced via two concrete stilling ponds to remove carried silt, algae and ensure pristine water quality.

Canadian geese frequent the lake along with swans and ducks. What better sight is there to see than cygnets and ducklings following their parents in formation or Indian file? Wonderful. Anglers can enjoy the relaxation of coarse fishing and dream of catching 'the big one'. Altogether an oasis of sheer pleasure, fun and frivolity for all the family!

Set in delightful surroundings, the boating lake and amenities remain a valuable resource for the people of Cwmbrân and its environs. It offers facilities for picnicking, barbecues, and much more beside. May it long continue to give pleasure to those who wish to escape from the constrictions of mundane urban life.

Close by is a publicly-owned riverside nine-hole golf course which is ideal for golfers of all abilities, whether novices or more experienced players. Significantly, no membership fee is required: it is run on a 'pay as you go' basis. No wonder it proves so popular with all ages the year round.

Just opposite Llanyrafon Farm **The Crows Nest** is a comfortable and popular licensed establishment - but primarily an 'eating house'. Hardly haute cuisine but, nonetheless, still offering fine fayre at an affordable price. Its most attractive feature stands outside, a superb metal artwork depicting a jet-black crow perched on the edge of its nest with wings spread wide and holding in its beak the final twig to complete the structure. But how many who frequent this establishment actually pause to appreciate this compelling work?

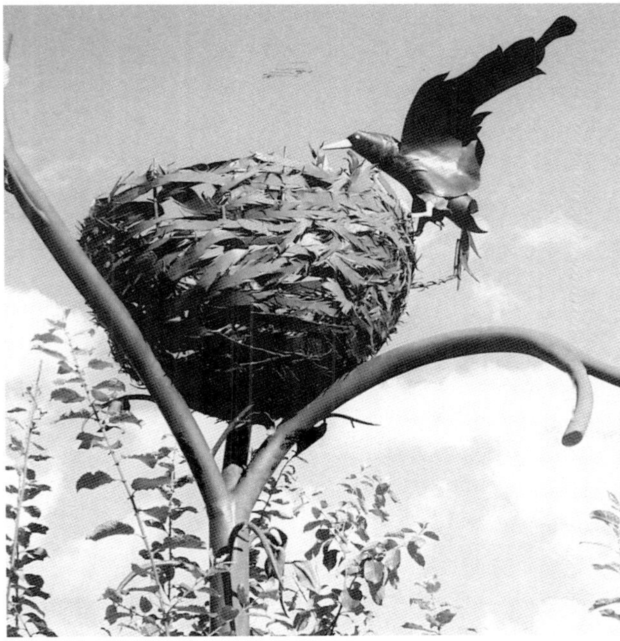

A compelling crow's nest.

FAITH IS THE FUTURE

Whereas church attendances have fallen steadily in the past 50 years or so, a handful of new churches have successfully been established in the Cwmbrân area. **Llanyrafon Methodist Church** is testimony to this. Worshippers wanted a local church of their own and set about raising sufficient funds to erect one on land acquired at the top of Llanyrafon Way. The photograph taken in July 1960 shows Sunday School pupils participating in the bricklaying ceremony at the start of construction. The name of each chosen youngster was etched into the brickwork. The scene displays an inherent and aspiring Christian brotherhood to delight future congregations.

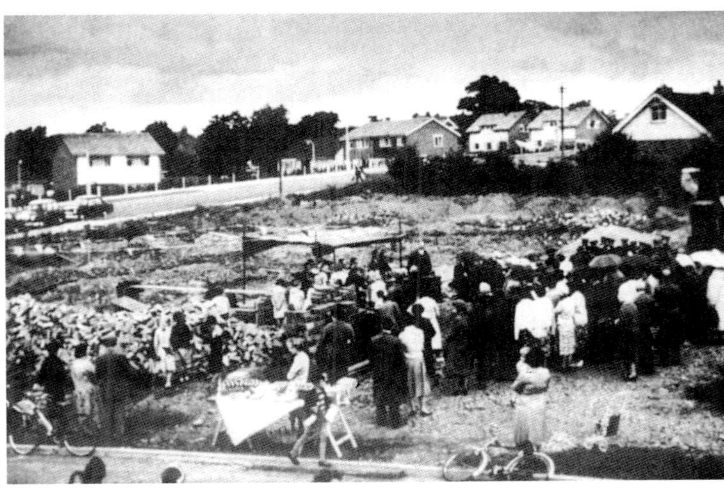

Local children laying foundation bricks in 1960.

Since its opening in 1961 the church has flourished and continues to prove a big hit with the local community. The religious side apart, it is the home to a variety of groups, including Scouts, Brownies and even a ballet club. Presently, the building is used by some 500 people every week. During 2006 the church secured a £200,000 Welsh Assembly grant to improve and enlarge the building and improve its facilities. This remodelling should reach completion within a few years. Truly, here is a church that is ***'reaching out to the community and making a difference'***.

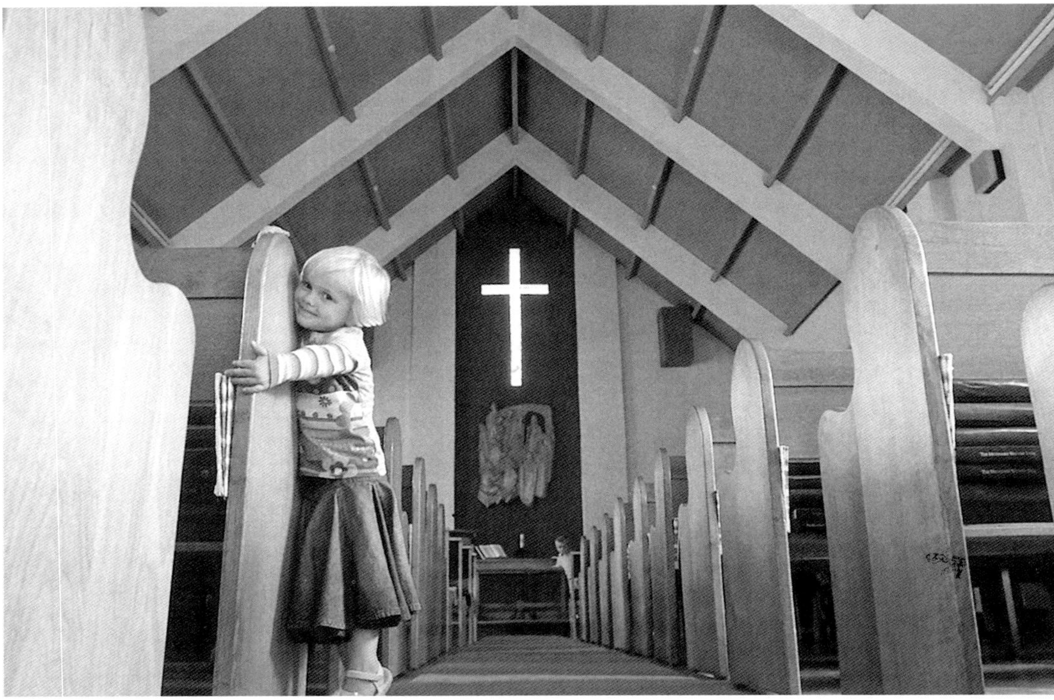

A very young Madeleine Vowles glimpses a brighter future.

By courtesy of South Wales Argus

CROESYCEILIOG

The village of Croesyceiliog on the rising north-eastern slope of the valley was incorporated within the designated site of Cwmbrân New Town in 1949. Very much an urban sprawl, it has few features of its past remaining.

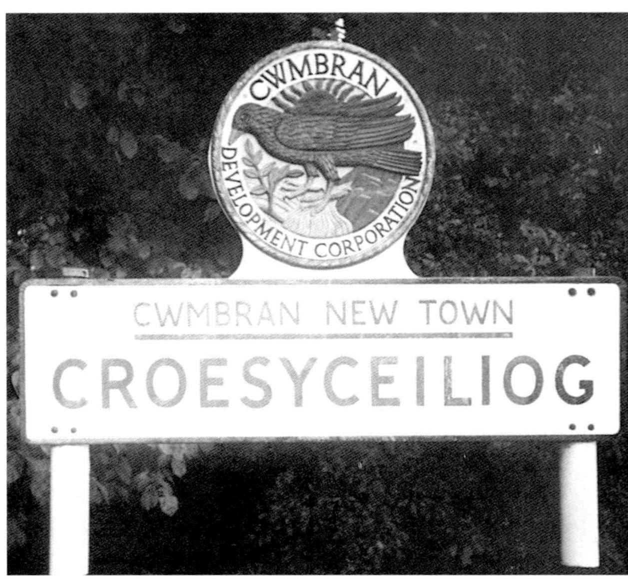

A sign of things to come.

Its Welsh name means ***'Cross-Roads or Cross of the Cock'***. The latter is said to come from a large sculptured crowing cock with out-stretched wings on a hillock in a field near the Upper Cock inn: this, supposedly, was a medieval reminder of St. Peter's denial of Christ. By its side was a stone Celtic preaching cross reputedly erected by St. Ceiliog some time during the Dark Ages and where villagers gathered when the priest conducted open air services. Both have long since vanished without trace, attributed to a band of Cromwell's Roundheads in 1646 who ransacked the neighbourhood on their way to the siege of Raglan Castle ***'breaking all tendencies to superstition and pious monuments'***. Surely, another instance of wanton vandalism under the guise of religious dogma.

THE UPPER COCK INN

This ancient hostelry stands at the crossroads of The Garw and The Highway. It once had a sign of a painted cockerel with a rhyme in Welsh on one side and English on the other, both extolling the good beer inside.

Dyma dafarn Croes y Ceiliog
Groesaw i bob un am ei geiniog
Cwrw da i bawb trwy dalu
Dewch i mewn, chwi gewch ei brofi.

Translated, this means:

Here is a tavern, the Cross of the Cock
A welcome to each one for his penny,
Good ale to all for payment
Come in, you can taste it.

In November 1839 the Chartist's Eastern Valley contingent led by William Jones paused here late at night for refreshment en route from Blaenafon and Abersychan through Pontypool to its fateful meeting outside the Westgate Hotel, Newport, on the following day. Predictably, they demanded ale and proceeded to drink the Upper Cock dry! After marching down the valley in wet weather their gunpowder was damp - so they dried it in the pub's oven. Sounds implausible and

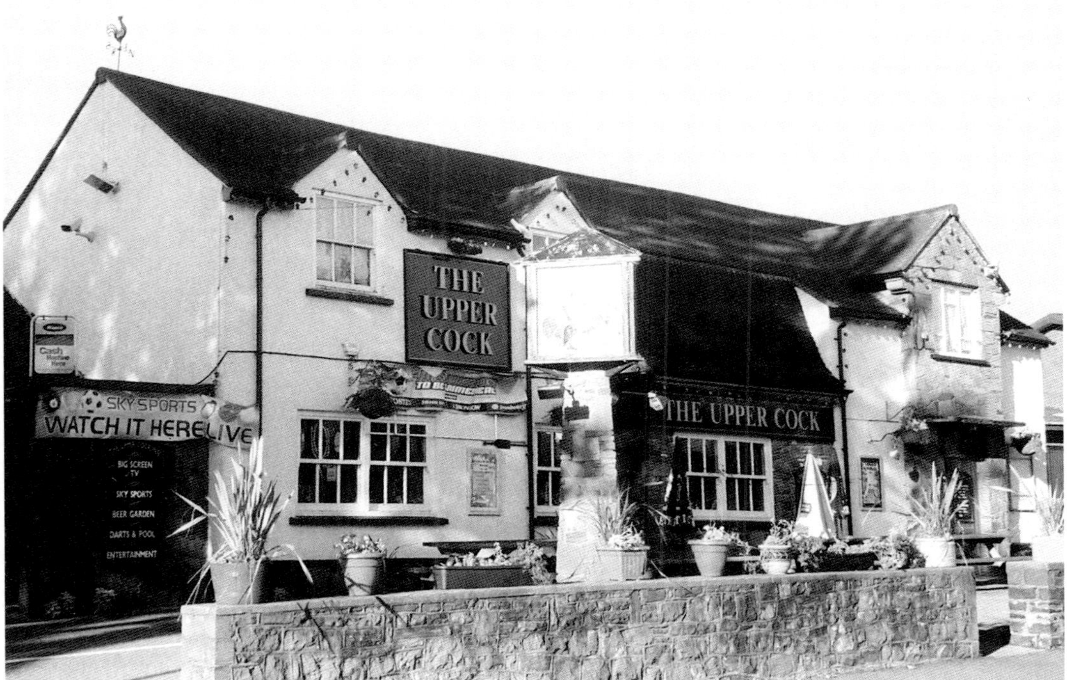

The Upper Cock Inn.

potentially highly dangerous! The innkeeper very sensibly left them to it and sought refuge in the nearest wood.

The Chartists were desperate men hard as nails and no respecters of property nor the law. They barged their way into a thatched cottage at the junction of The Highway with Turnpike Road where a John Lewis, a mere baby only three days old, was being nursed in his mother's arms. Exhausted following the boy's birth, she held the baby aloft and with contempt said: ***'Here's the only man in the house; take him with pleasure!'*** The young father was so terrified of being pressed to swell their ranks that he fled under the cover of darkness and cowered under a yew tree. John Lewis grew up to become the miller at Llanyrafon Mill. He became renowned as 'Lewis the runner'. Local tradition avers that this remarkable athlete even won a 100 yards race against younger competition approaching 70 years of age!!!

The inn has been modernised and welcomes those seeking refreshment and good quality fayre. A reminder of the old sign is carved in stone on a triangular plinth supporting a stained glass lamp. A veritable treasure for the folklorist.

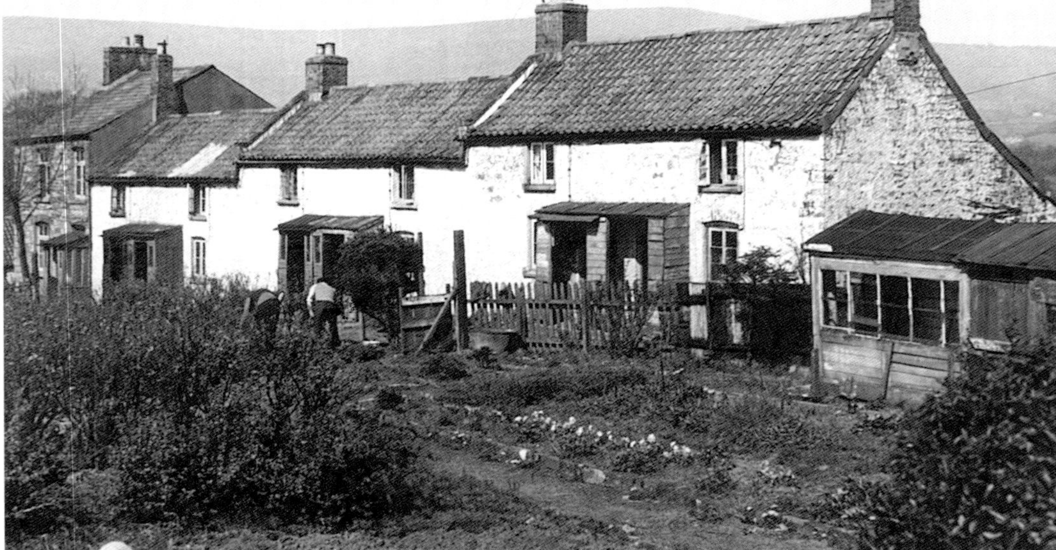

Top Row in 1965 before proposed demolition.

Just to the west of the Upper Cock Inn is Garw Row. The Row has fifteen cottages dating from the 1880s built to house workers in the nearby tin-plate works. The Row had the unusual nickname of 'Bull Panch'. These cottages had flagstone floors and a small water-pump serving all the residents. Toilet facilities were outside and raw sewage went directly into a nearby stream and straight down the hill into the Afon Llwyd. Although remnants of the former industrial era, the semi-detached dwellings were modernised by imaginatively and cleverly interlocked kitchen extensions with bedrooms above. This in no way detracts from the essential character of the original homes. For such endeavours, in 1978 Cwmbrân Development Corporation was justifiably awarded a Welsh Office Design In Housing Medal.

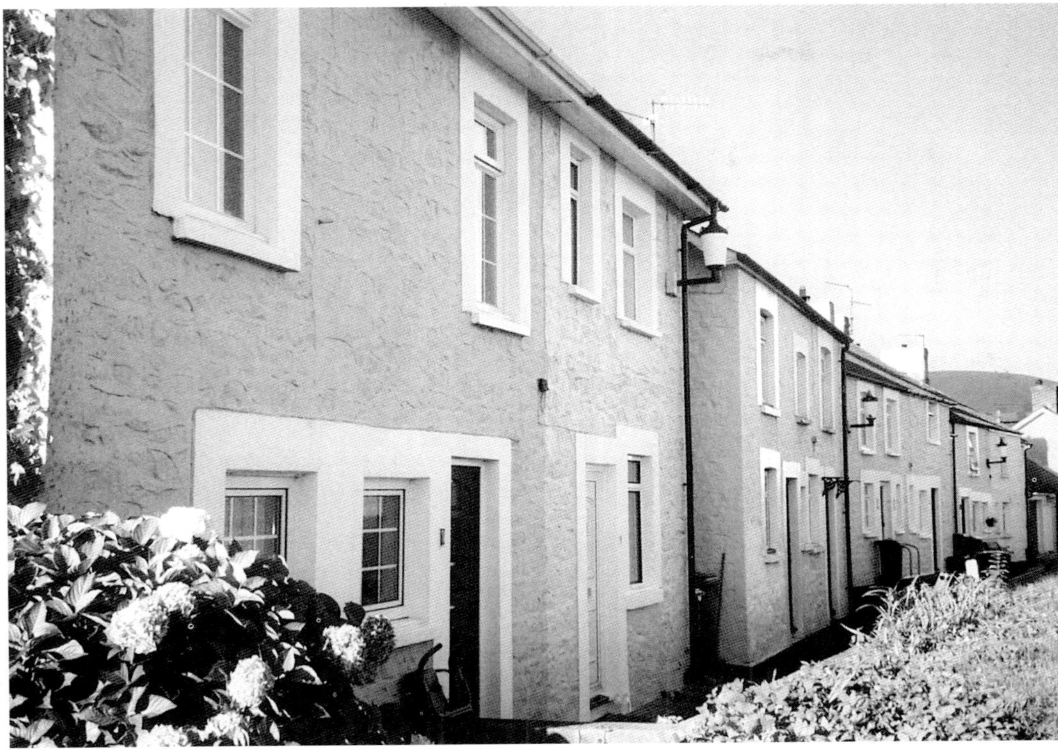

A rejuvenated Garw Row in 2006.

JIM CROW'S COTTAGE

A curious 19th-century home is Jim Crow's Cottage which possesses an unusual and particularly fascinating front façade. No doubt it caught the eyes of travellers about to ascend The Highway. Benjamin Evans, a man of many parts - schoolmaster, postmaster and shopkeeper - rented the cottage from Squire Capel Hanbury Leigh of Pontypool. So why is it called Jim Crow's Cottage? Ben's great friend, Jim Crow, ***'a seafaring man out of England'***, lodged there with the family during the 1840s. When the itinerant mariner died, Ben and his wife Temperance decided to call the cottage, field and wood after him. This is recorded in the 1851 National Census.

In ***Out And About In Monmouthshire (1958)***, Fred J. Hando wrote:

> ***'With its pretty symmetry, its decorated barge-boards, its hood mouldings and mock Tudor windows, and its general air of a cottage out of Never-never Land, designed by Puck and erected by Lewis Carroll, it smiles serenely on our matter-of-fact world, ready at any moment to be swept up on the wings of a cloud and transported to fairyland.'***

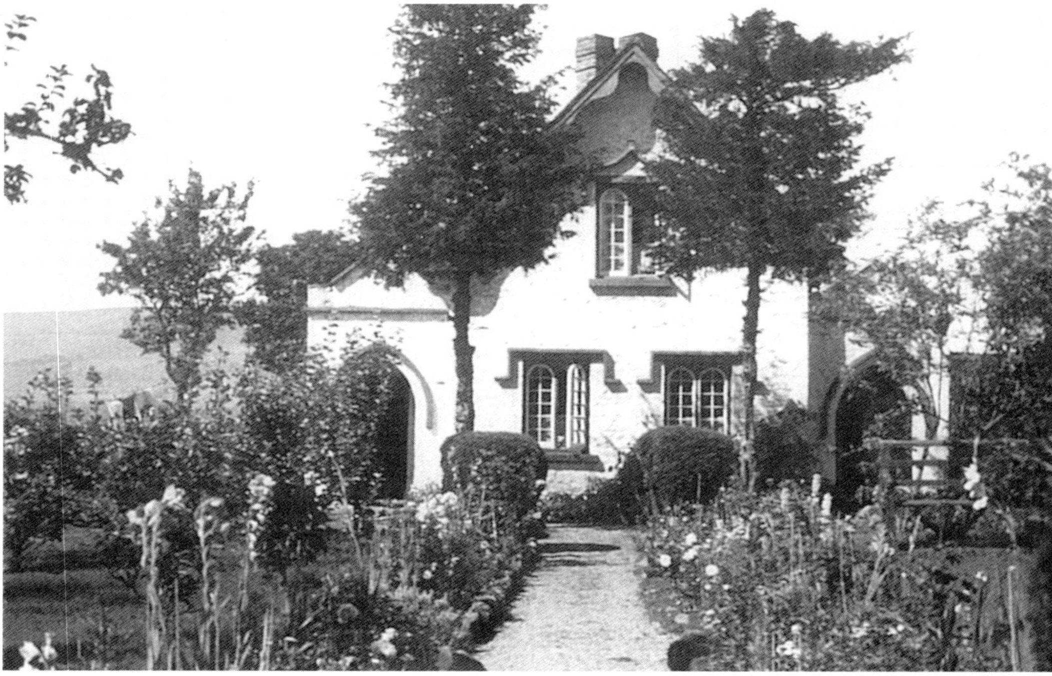

Jim Crow's Cottage in splendid isolation before urbanisation. Probably taken in the 1940s.

The distinguished author rarely struggled for a colourful 'turn of phrase'. The cottage is the only surviving example of this particular style of Gothic revival architecture in the locality. A modern-day photograph can no longer do justice to this unique little building as its frontage is all but obscured by a giant yew tree ablaze with the bright-red cups which protect the yew seeds. Yet one taken before 'urbanisation' is wholly delightful.

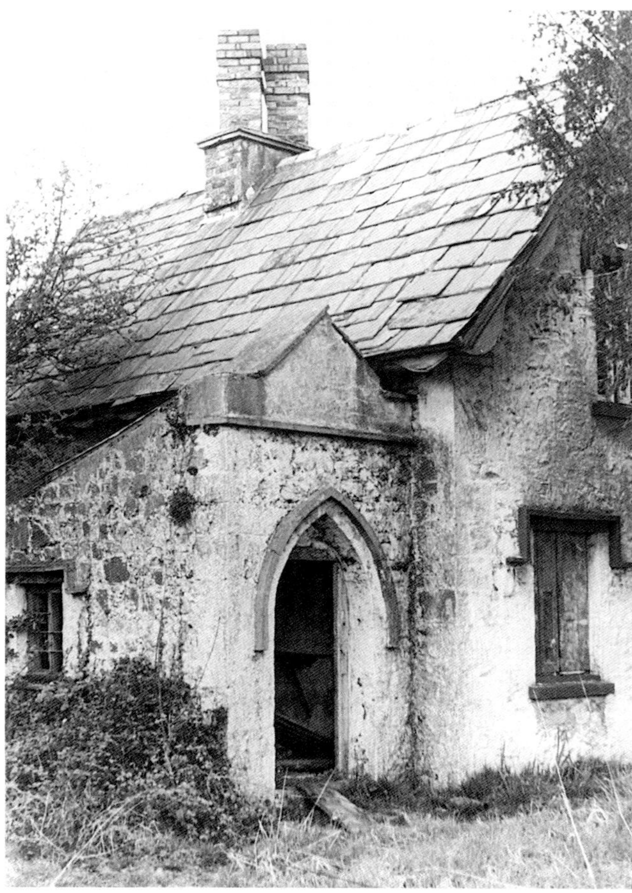

Jim Crow's Cottage fallen upon hard times.

Cwmbrân Development Corporation purchased the cottage and surrounding land in the 1950s with the intention of demolishing it. Yet they had not reckoned with a groundswell of affection to save the cottage. And duly relented. A prime example, if needed, of 'power to the people'. The cottage was renovated and set in a landscaped garden. It is now engulfed within a morass of dwellings. Jim Crow's cottage is certainly incongruous in its present environment - and was equally so in its former isolated setting.

PONTRHYDYRUN BAPTIST CHURCH

The church stands in Chapel Lane on a parcel of land at the top of Pontrhydyrun Hill donated by William Conway, the eldest son of George Conway, owner of the tin-plate works at Pontnewydd. George had come to the area from Melin-Griffith in Glamorganshire some time around 1770 to make his fortune. The foundation stone was laid on 13th May, 1815. Like his father, William was a deeply religious man with staunch Baptist beliefs. He wished a chapel to be built for the benefit of his workers and their families. Prior to this a room in the Edlogan tin-plate works at the bottom of Chapel Lane was used from 1807 as a Sunday School for children. The new centre for worship costing £600 was opened on 15th November of that year.

However, this chapel soon proved far too small for the swelling congregation of around one hundred. In 1836 it was pulled down and a much larger, impressive edifice based on ancient Greek influence and again financed by the wealthy Conway family erected in its place at a cost of £2,000: it opened for worship on 16th August, 1837. Later additions in 1905 included a large hall and classrooms.

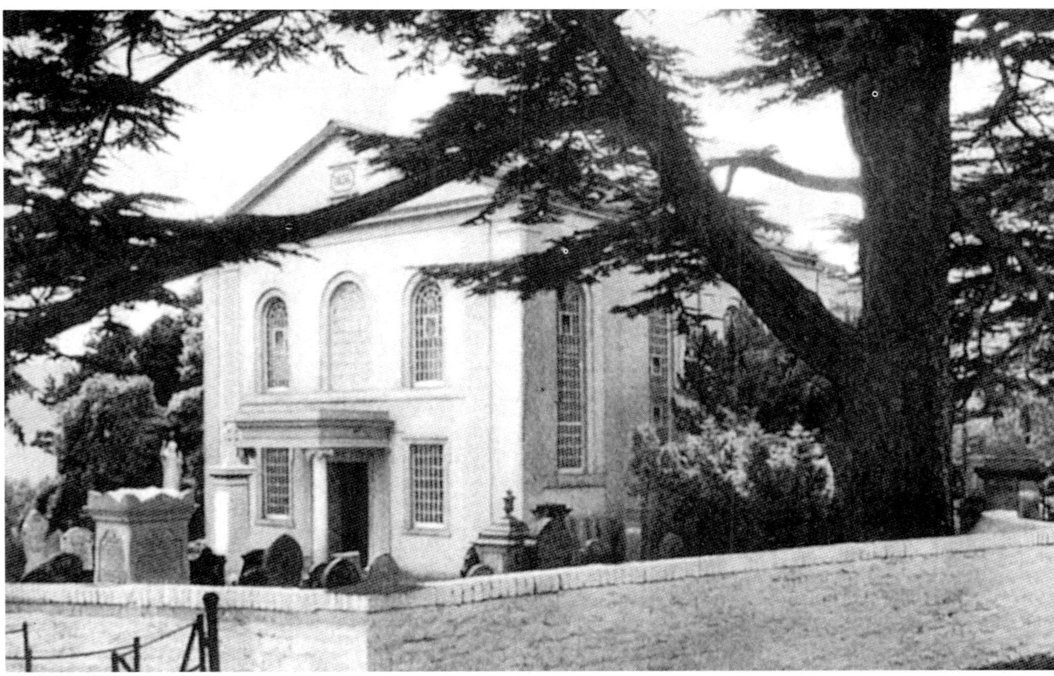

Pontrhydyrun Baptist Church.

The Conway family settled at Pontrhydyrun House, a commodious dwelling situated at the bottom of Chapel Lane next to the site of the Edlogan works at Pontrhydyrun (*'the bridge of the ash-tree ford'*) which William founded in 1806. George Conway died on 4th July, 1822, and is buried in the chapel's churchyard in a large family plot affectionately known as 'Conway Yard'. Members of the family married and lived in various large houses at the junction of Edlogan Way and Station Road. A complex of modern flats now dominates the site. A row of terraced houses was occupied by domestic staff and the works foremen; Conway Terrace still stands.

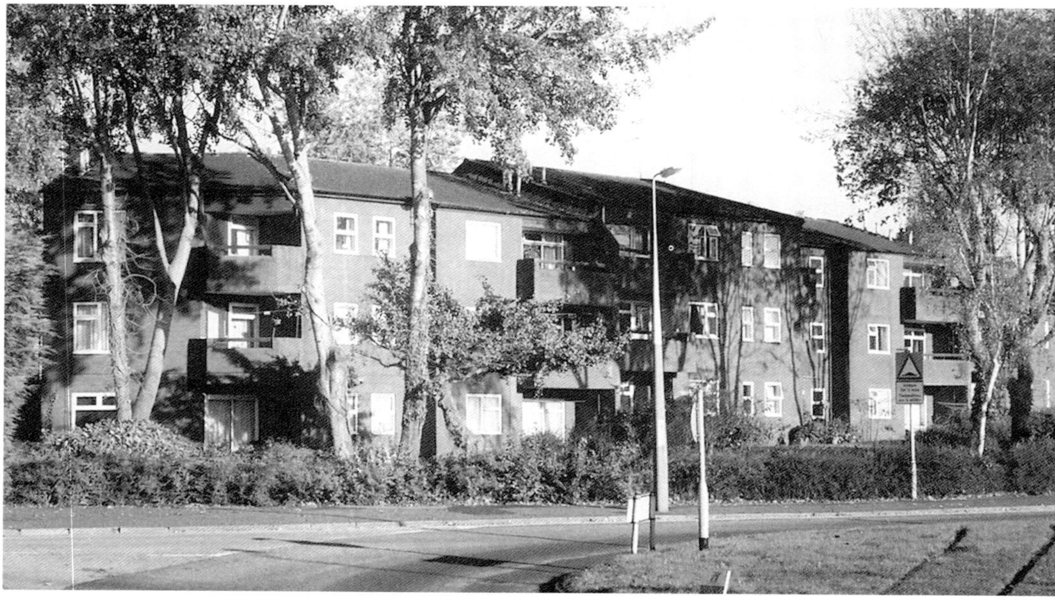

Modern flats at the bottom of Edlogan Way.

The burial ground was much enlarged and on three corners Cedars of Lebanon planted; these were brought back by a member of the Conway family who had been on a pilgrimage to the Holy Land. The trees flourished for years and the ***'Cedars of Lebanon'*** became renowned throughout the district. However, two of these handsome trees were uprooted during a raging storm in November 1928 and only one survived. This giant Lebanese cedar stands at the entrance gates to the chapel and its huge branches form a canopy for those seeking shelter from inclement weather.

An elderly lady from Oakfield, now in her 90s, recalls how as a youngster she witnessed the devastation caused by the storm: several large branches were ripped from the trunk of the remaining cedar demolishing a stone boundary wall and exposing the skeletons of those long buried. Apparently, the incident was not generally made public for fear of being the work of the Devil.

At the bottom of the graveyard horses were stabled to help weary travellers make the steep ascent up Chapel Lane. A 'stepping' or 'ripping stone' on the grass verge outside the main gate to the chapel helped fashionable ladies mount their horses. The local blacksmith thrived while this mode of transport lasted. An old wives tale claimed that warts would disappear if the hand was dipped into the water 'Johnny' the smithy used to quench the steel.

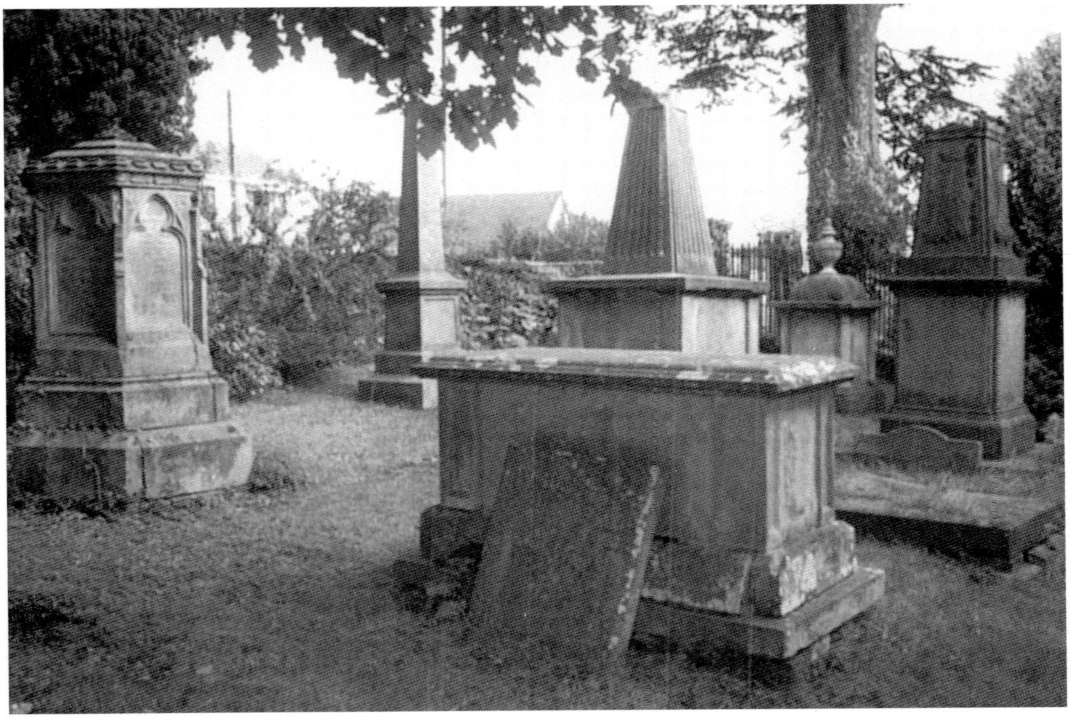

The Conway Yard burial ground.

During December 1940 and at the height of World War II a German plane dropped a bomb which badly damaged Pontrhydyrun Chapel. It was assumed that the pilot had mistaken the chapel for part of the not-so-far-away weapons factory at Glascoed. Feasible, yes, unless he was being pursued by a British spitfire and simply off-loaded his last bomb to ensure a safe return home. After all, this was fairly commonplace throughout the industrialised valleys of South East Wales in wartime. Anyhow, the bomb exploded in the woods at the near end of the graveyard leaving a crater some 60 feet wide and 20 feet deep; the explosion brought down the vestibule ceiling and shattered windows in the west wall.

Following further renovations and extensions in 1951, this fine religious edifice was designated as of special historical interest. Pontrhydyrun Baptist Church continues to flourish in an age of disenchantment, of declining moral values and outright materialism. Yet it is a fitting tribute to the benevolence of the Conway family. And the ***'Cedar of Lebanon'*** still stands as a lone sentinel guarding this much-loved portal to heavenly grace.

CROESYCEILIOG BOARD SCHOOL

By the late 1870s, due to an influx of those seeking employment in the nearby tin-plate works at Pontnewydd, the population of Croesyceiliog had increased greatly and a school was needed for the workers' young families. A Board School was duly built alongside The Highway for infants and juniors. The headmaster appointed was Mr. D.M. Evans and Mrs. Mary Evans as infants' mistress. In 1893 the school was enlarged, but sanitary arrangements were a constant source of concern. The Chief School Inspector believed the village cesspool was too close to the school for the children's well-being. Moreover, he considered that the playground was too small for the boys' physical well-being. A strange point of view considering the welcoming freedom of the surrounding hillside.

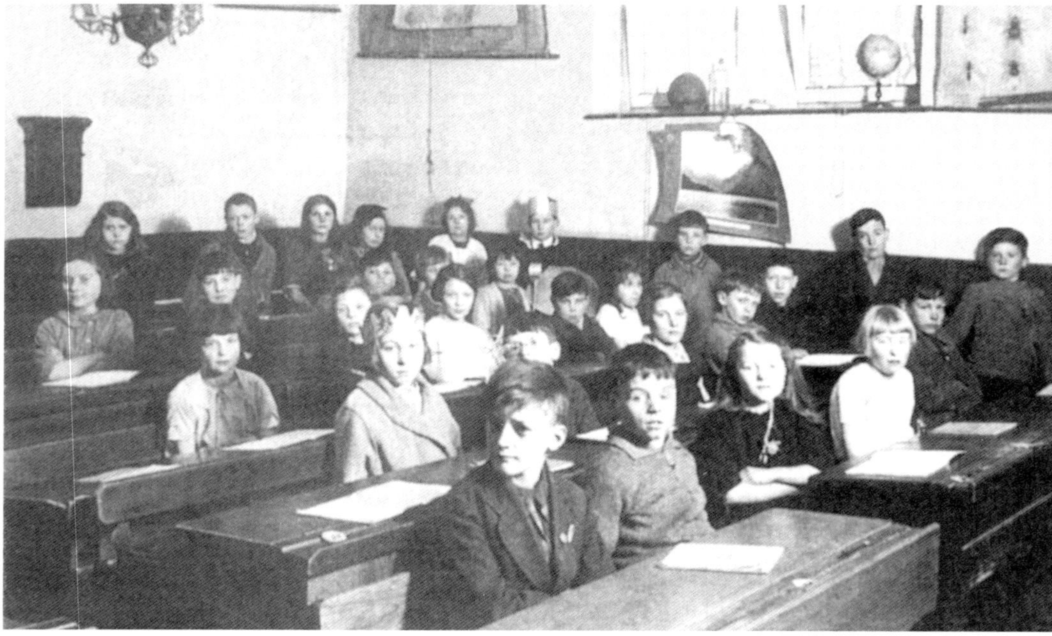

Youngsters at their desks ca. 1925.

A photograph taken around the mid 1920s shows a class of junior pupils clearly bemused by the novelty of the camera. But where stands their teacher? Notice the globe of the world, the wallchart of insects, and the pendant oil burner at the top left of the scene (electricity had yet to arrive in the vicinity).

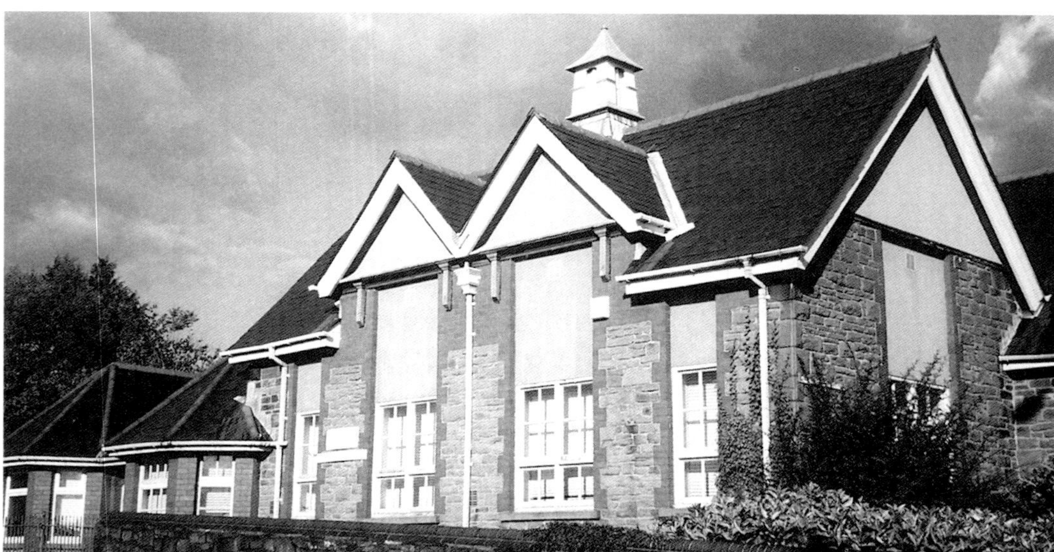

The old Board School now used by Gwent Probation Service.

The infant's school closed in 1955, but briefly reopened in 1959 to ease the pressure on places brought about by the expansion of the New Town housing policy. When a new school was built in the mid 1970s, North Road Junior and Infants, the old school, was boarded up until its present use by Gwent Probation Service.

CROESYCEILIOG COMPREHENSIVE SCHOOL

This stands on 'Jim Crow's Fields' and fronts Woodland Road. It was opened on Wednesday, 3rd February, 1960, as a County Grammar School by the Director of Education for Monmouthshire, the much respected Mr. T.M. Morgan. It became renowned as a centre of academic excellence and was dubbed the ***'Crystal Palace of Culture'***. Which was true. The school motto exemplifies this: ***'Learning, Tolerance, Service'***. Today, it is a comprehensive school.

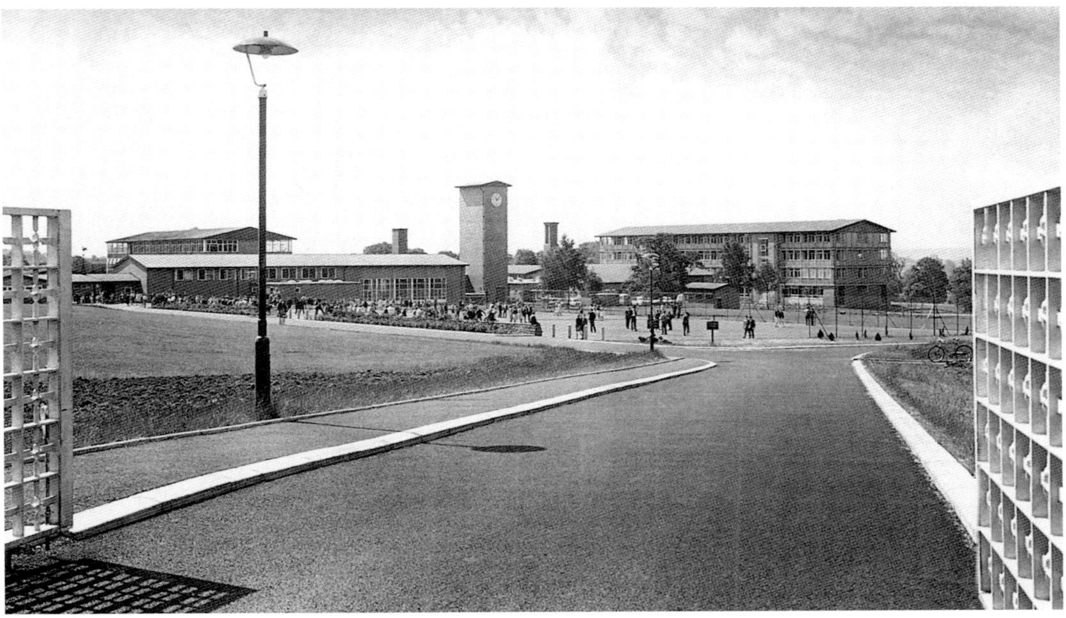

Croesyceiliog County Grammar and Secondary Modern Schools share the same 'campus' in 1965.

Looking across from The Highway stood the village's first Post Office (shown around 1911 on the following page). A Mrs. Emily Evans was the sub-postmistress at that time and she knew virtually everyone in the community. A new Post Office was later established on The Highway itself in 1938 with Mr. & Mrs. Millwater in charge. How Mr. Millwater coped with the demands of such a responsible position is unclear as he had previously lost both his hands in an accident at the local tin-plate works. The office was later held by a Mr. A.G. Wait followed by a Mrs. Crum who single-handedly ran both the Post Office and a grocery shop within the same premises for some 22 years (1967-89). And, nowadays, bureaucrats maintain that Post Offices should diversify or face closure. Laughable. Sadly, Croesyceiliog's Post Office closed in 2003 under the guise of rationalisation.

With a growing population in need of religious succour, St. Mary's church was established in 1903. This daughter church of St. Michael's, Llanfrechfa, began

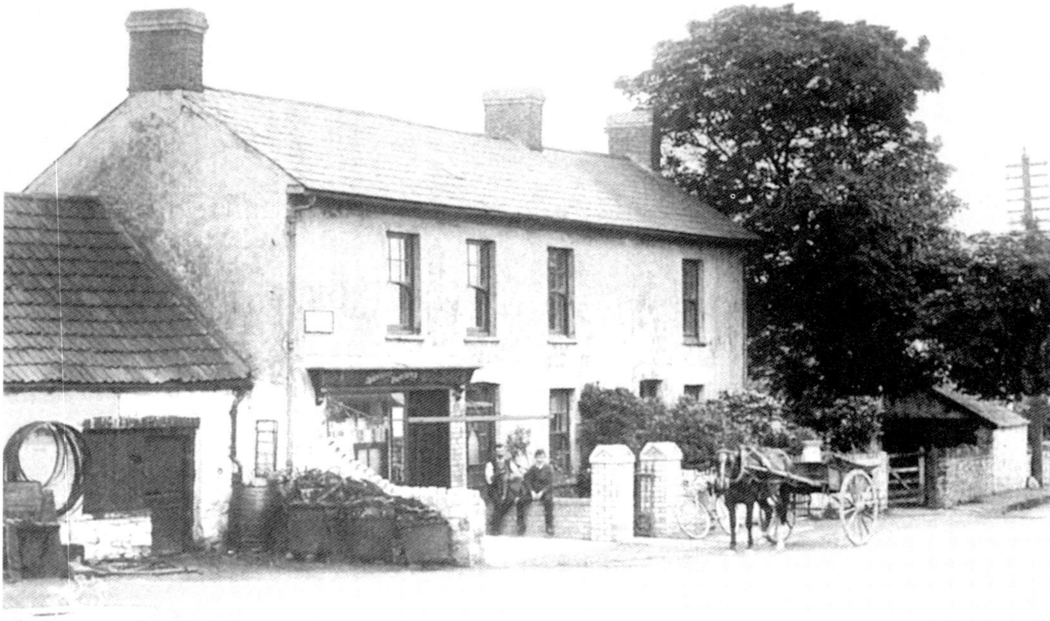

Croesyceiliog village Post Office around 1911.

life as a galvanised hall, but donations and monies collected soon realised a substantial stone building. During 2003 it celebrated its centenary. Strangely, it was not licensed for weddings until April 1971 when it broke free from the clutches of its parent church: the first wedding was held there in October 1971.

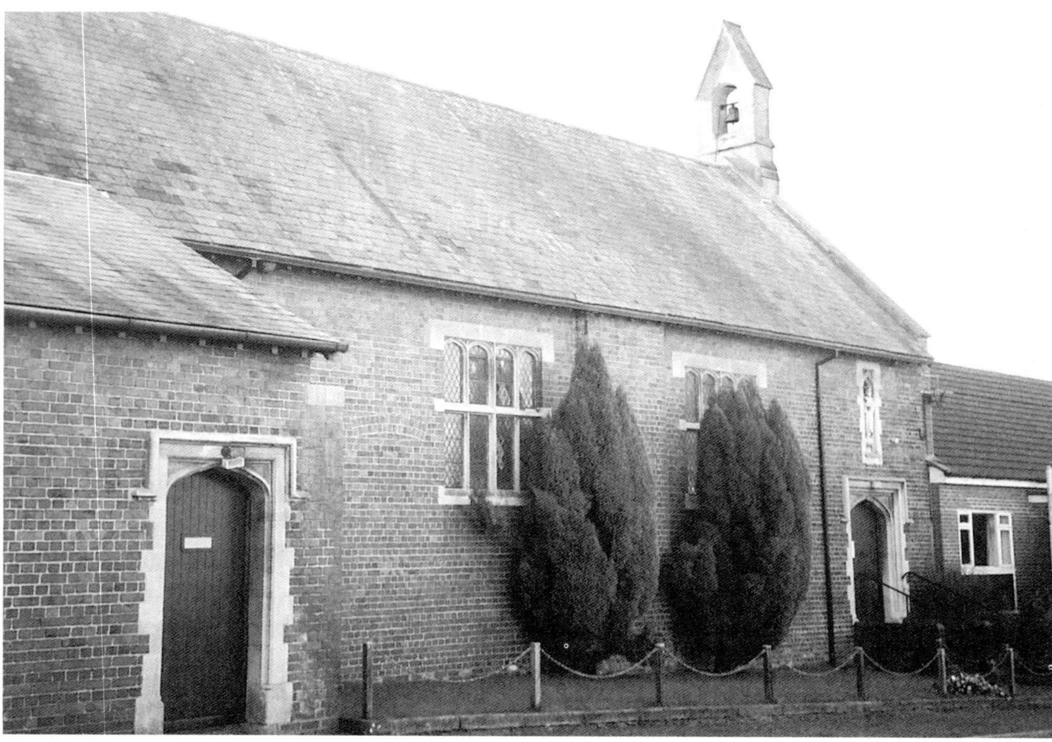

St. Mary's Church.

Croesyceiliog swiftly lost its rural charm as major building projects relating to the development of the New Town came to fruition and transformed the hilltop landscape altogether. During the 1970s Gwent County Council moved from its traditional home at Pentonville, Newport, to the geographical centre of the County - Cwmbrân. The seven-storey building was constructed between 1969-77 and is less than memorable in its design, let alone its creeper-hung balconies. Worse still is Gwent Police Headquarters relocated here from Abergavenny and which was officially opened on Friday, 12th November, 1971, by Princess Anne. Monmouthshire County Council offices also share the same building as County Hall. Where is the sense of this for it is well outside the boundary of the County Borough which it purports to represent? Notwithstanding, both buildings typify architectural design of the latter years of the 20th-century - functional, unattractive and suffering from the modern phenomenon of 'concrete cancer' or 'spalling'. Their future is predictable. Demolition - what else? Our forefathers would surely have been aghast at such shoddy and downright ugly constructions.

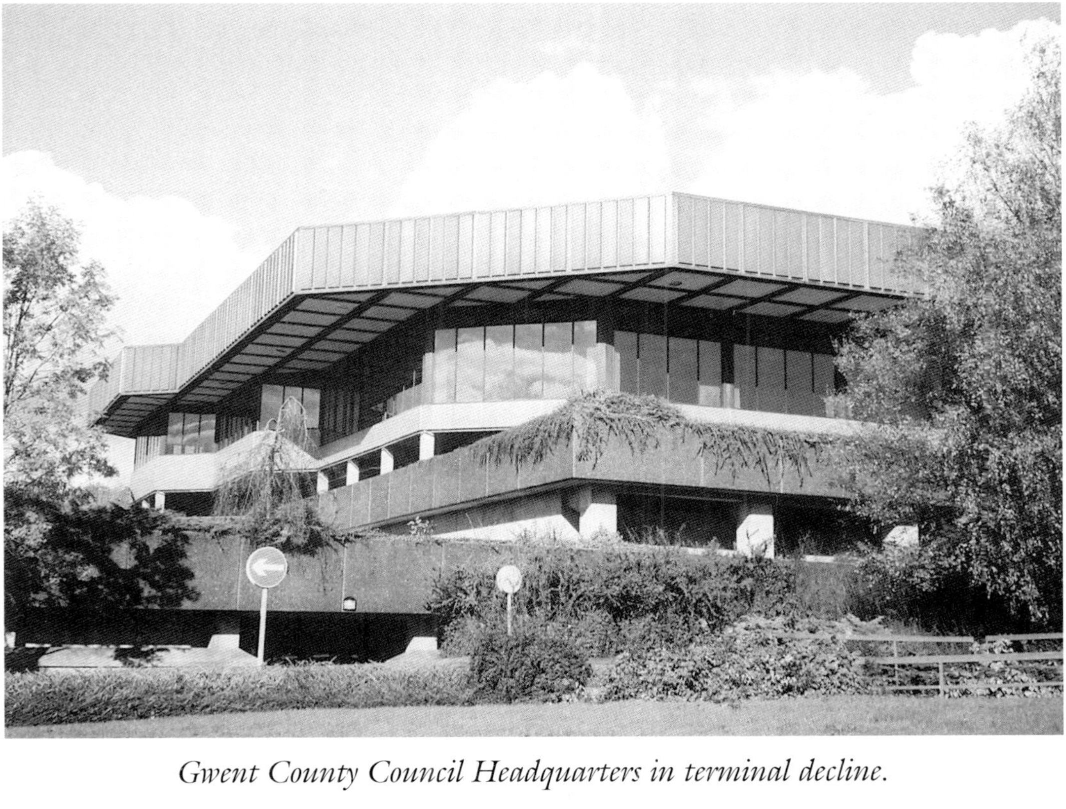

Gwent County Council Headquarters in terminal decline.

On a more sombre note the County Crematorium is situated on the outskirts of Croesyceiliog overlooking the peaceful pastoral that is the heartland of Gwent and the bustling town in the valley below. Opened on 8th April 1960, it was dedicated by the Archbishop of Wales, the Most Reverend A.E. Morris, D.D. Within its well-tended garden of remembrance the silent whispers of the dead echo the past. Or so we wish to believe...

Llantarnam

Llantarnam, or more correctly Llanfihangel Llantarnam, used to be a sleepy village set in verdant countryside with the Afon Llwyd meandering by to the north and a feeder stream of the Monmouthshire Canal to the south. But much has changed over the years and the area is now engulfed by housing developments and flourishing commercial enterprises.

Today's Welsh name ***Llantarnam*** has many possible origins and derivations, all somewhat uncertain and problematical. ***Emsanternon*** was recorded in ca. 1179 and is derived from ***Ynys Nant Teyrnon***, meaning ***'Stream in the valley of Teyrnon'*** (an early ruler of Gwent Iscoed who actually features in the ancient and perhaps mythical tales of the ***Mabinogion*** in which he is described as ***'the best man in the world'***). Down the ages the naming of the hamlet has been gradually corrupted to the now recognisable 16th-century form ***Llanternham***.

LLANTARNAM CHURCH

The Parish Church of St. Michael & All Angels ***'on Teyrnon's brook'*** is set just back off the old main road from Newport to Pontypool next to the historic Greenhouse inn.

Described in 1535 as ***'The Chapel of St. Michael near the monastery'***, the building is mostly 15th-century, but between the north chapel and the chancel are two curious arches of very much earlier origin, possibly of some 500 years or more: the central pillar which supports these arches is remarkable for its cable ornamentation. The church belonged to the richly endowed Cistercian monastery nearby. During restoration work in 1921 evidence was found of an early Celtic church or 'cell' on the site, possibly dating from around the 6th-century.

The church building underwent extensive restoration in 1869 in the much admired Gothic style: it now consists of a embattled tower, chancel and the former Lady Chapel, the latter better known as the Morgan or Blewitt Chapel. This was probably built by William Morgan who purchased Llantarnam Abbey in 1554. Moreover, it is likely that the pair of depressed arches through which the church is entered were brought here from the Abbey close by.

The Morgan Chapel has stone memorials to both the Blewitt and Dowling families, the most prominent being the massive tomb of the 16th-century Morgan family on the north side which effectively now serves as a communion table. A tablet commemorating the death of a Martin Kuych Van Mierop, Esq., a London merchant who died from a fall (off a horse he was riding?) at ***'Mynydd Mane'*** in August 1775 seems strangely out of place. What was his connection with the locality?

Another tablet on the north wall recalls Martha Absalam who died in 1770 at the 'goodly' age of 82 years. The grammar may be weak, but a heart-warming sentiment from a lady who obviously suffered severely for many a year:

'Death in a very good old age
Did end my wery Pilgrimage
A sweet deliverance from my Pain
That I may Enter life Again
An happy Change and ever blest
When grief and Pain
Is turn'd to Rest.'

The stone font is believed to be pre-Norman and has fish decorations which may be associated with an early Christian symbol based on the Greek word for fish, ***'ikhthus'***. The church registers date from 1727.

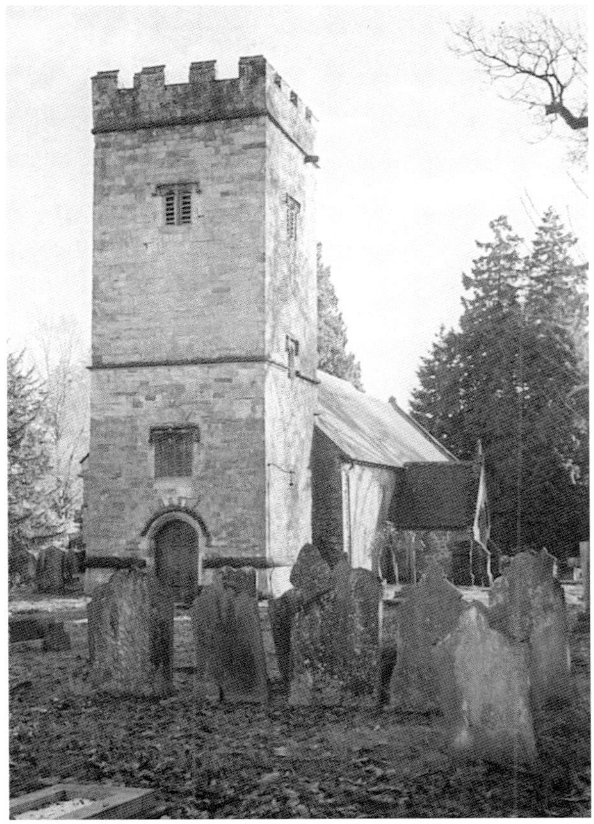

The Church of St. Michael's.

In 1919, and purely by accident, several beautiful murals were discovered in the nave. These were almost certainly of medieval origin and executed by Cistercian monks, but had been covered with a lime wash at the time of the Reformation and hidden from the view of thousands of worshippers down the centuries. (Similar murals were found at St. Peter's Church, Henllys.) When the flaking plaster was removed and upon exposure to the humidity of the air, all deteriorated and crumbled to dust within several weeks. More incredibly, neither drawings nor photographs recorded the wondrous spectacle. All that was reported was the scenes were painted in ***'gorgeous blue, gold and red'*** with curiously long brush strokes depicting:

(i) Mary enthroned with a boy server
(ii) A priest dressed in medieval clothing
(iii) Elijah in the wilderness
(iv) John the Baptist.

The chancel arch displayed large figures of floating angels. The murals represented the story of the New Testament and was the bible of the illiterate people of the parish. Sadly, these potent reminders from a distant past are irrevocably lost to historians and future generations.

Centuries of worship within such hallowed walls by both wealthy and humble stock alike is eloquently expressed by the contemporary poet Glynfab John who visited St. Michael's Church at Eastertide.

Worship

A choir of praise
In the bird-black trees,
And a sky of praying-blue,
A time of calm and quietude,
When Peace moves down
The green-aisled lanes,
And Hope strolls close behind.
Like white-robed hosts,
The surpliced clouds sing
Mist-scored anthems sweet,
And pious hills exalt the sun
With psalms of budded life.
May-incense fills the holy air,
And, in the silver-plated pools,
Coined hymns ring bible-true.

The churchyard contains the base and shaft of an ancient preaching cross. The stump of an ancient yew has a staggering girth measuring some 18 feet. If only it could tell of those who have passed this way or sheltered beneath its majestic canopy!

Of particular interest is the grave of Private John Williams/Fielding V.C. of the South Wales Borderers. A local hero who fought at the battle of Rorke's Drift, Natal, during the Anglo-Zulu War of 1879, his resting place is close to the highway at The Greenhouse inn side of the churchyard. Nearby, and until recently all but forgotten, is the grave of Private Penry Morgan who fought and was wounded in France during the Great War.

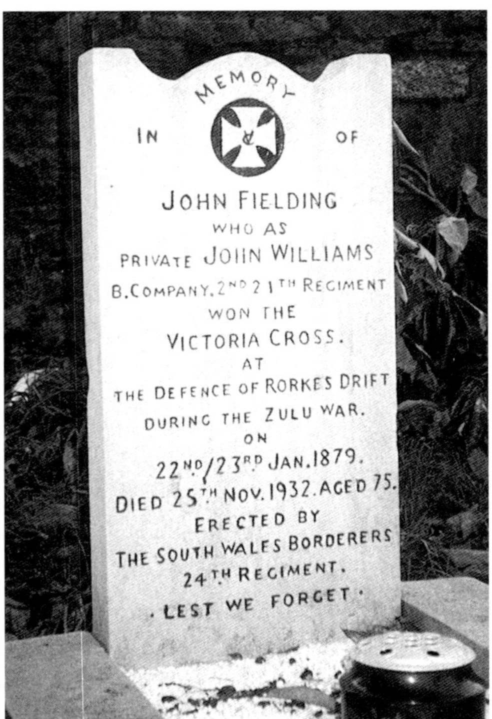

The headstone of John Williams, V.C.

The Church has always proved popular for the solemnization of marriage vows and continues to play an important role in the social fabric of the area. A rare archive photograph (seen opposite) taken at nearby Court Farm presents a fascinating insight into a late Victorian wedding between Rees William Spencer of Llangeview and Lily Maria Lawrence of Llantarnam on 8th September, 1896; it shows the fashions and culture of the day. The young lad in the front row is Albert Ernest Lawrence, father of co-author Graham Lawrence; the latter's grand-parents, Henry and Priscilla Lawrence appear seated in the same row.

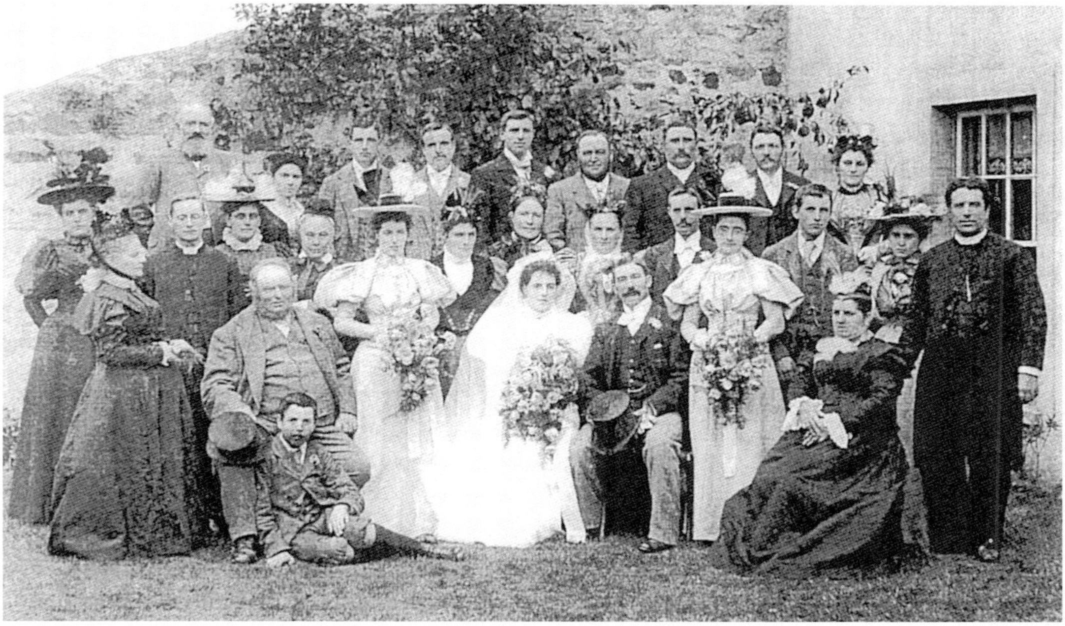

A Victorian wedding scene: the marriage of Rees William Spencer and Lily Maria Lawrence on 8th September, 1896, taken at Court Farm.

Well-known and highly respected was Vicar John Donne B.A. who officiated at the church from 1917 until his retirement in 1962. And how active he remained throughout those years. Daily he rode his bicycle wearing his black cassock and hat greeting all he passed-by with a cheery ***'Good Day'***. He visited the poor and sick regardless of their religious denomination and gave them his blessing. Clearly, a true Christian and a man of God.

The old blacksmith's shop opposite the church is long gone. The illustrations here and overleaf are evocative of days that have been. The first was taken in the 1880s when George Pritchard and his family lived there. The building was demolished to make way for a new smithy and Post Office in around 1910. The gentleman on the horse was Mr. Samuel Purkiss, coachman and gardener at the home of the Mitchell family at Llanfrechfa Grange. The wheel-wright's shop and smithy are no more, although until fairly recently an iron circle

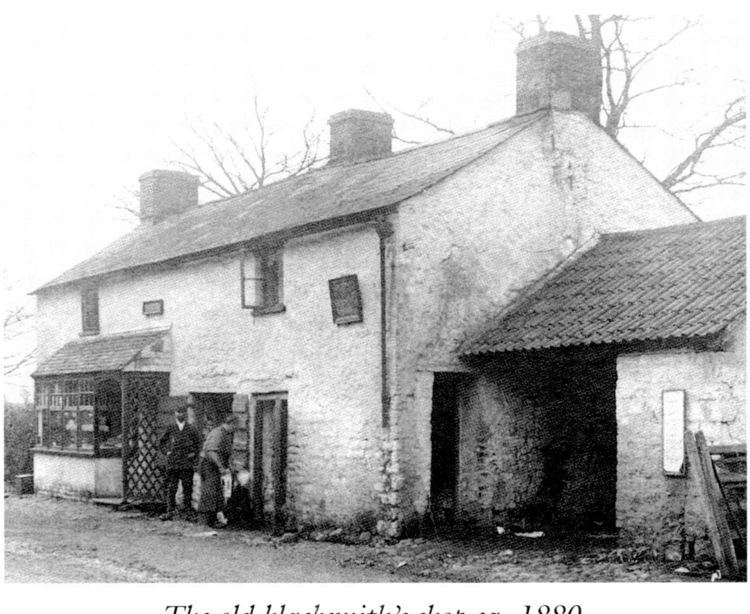

The old blacksmith's shop ca. 1880.

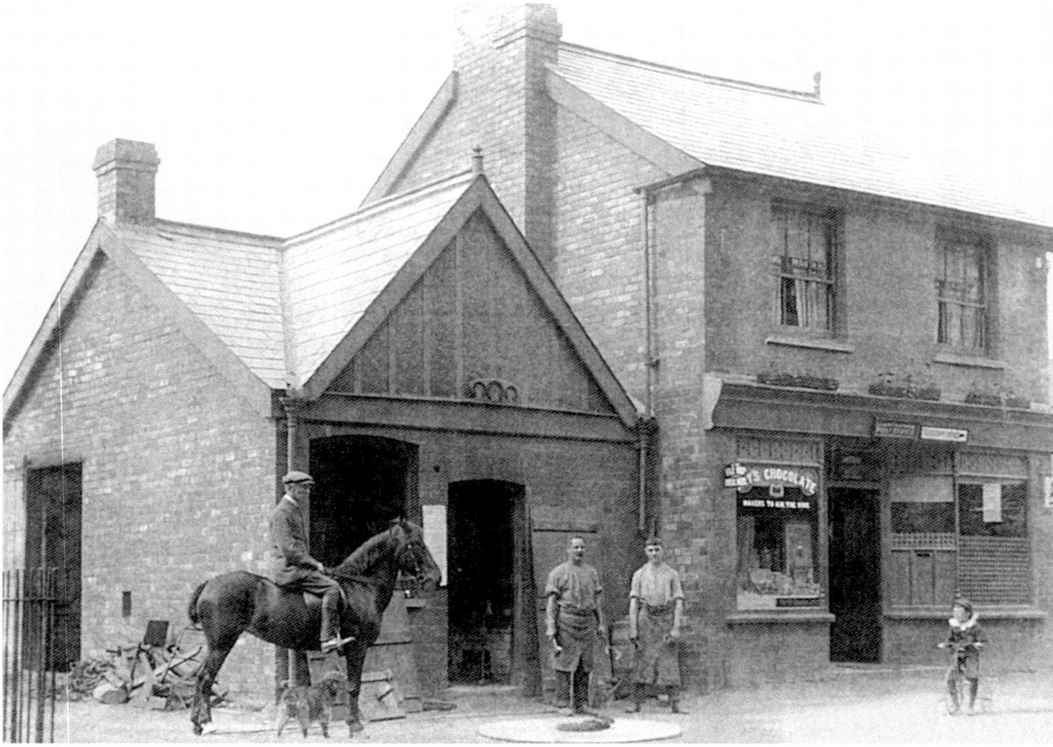

The new smithy and Post Office ca. 1910. Samuel Purkiss, coachman and gardener at Llanfrechfa Grange sits astride the horse.

just off the pavement marked the spot where the forge once stood, the tyring platform used to fit tyre rims on to wooden cartwheels. The red-brick Church Hall was built in 1922 and while in need of modernisation remains a popular venue for social and community activities.

THE GREENHOUSE INN

Next to the church can be found an emphatic reminder that Welsh was the spoken language in the area during the early 18th-century. The Greenhouse inn is an attractive hostelry with picturesque mullioned windows and green-painted exterior. Together, inn and church have for centuries satisfied the needs of both the flesh and the spirit. And continues to do so.

Yet it is the curiously unique inn sign that immediately attracts attention, remarkable both for its originality and artistry. The skilfully carved and brightly-coloured wooden sign set high in the rounded gable of the porch invites passers-by to step inside and sample good ale and cider. Its quaintness derives from the two jovial little men seated on opposite sides of a table upon which stands an outsize goblet, a candle in the middle and a tankard almost as large as the men themselves. Immaculately dressed, the tails of their frock coats are neatly draped over the backs of their chairs. One fellow is contentedly smoking a long-stemmed clay pipe, the other reaching for his tipple. A most engaging scene.

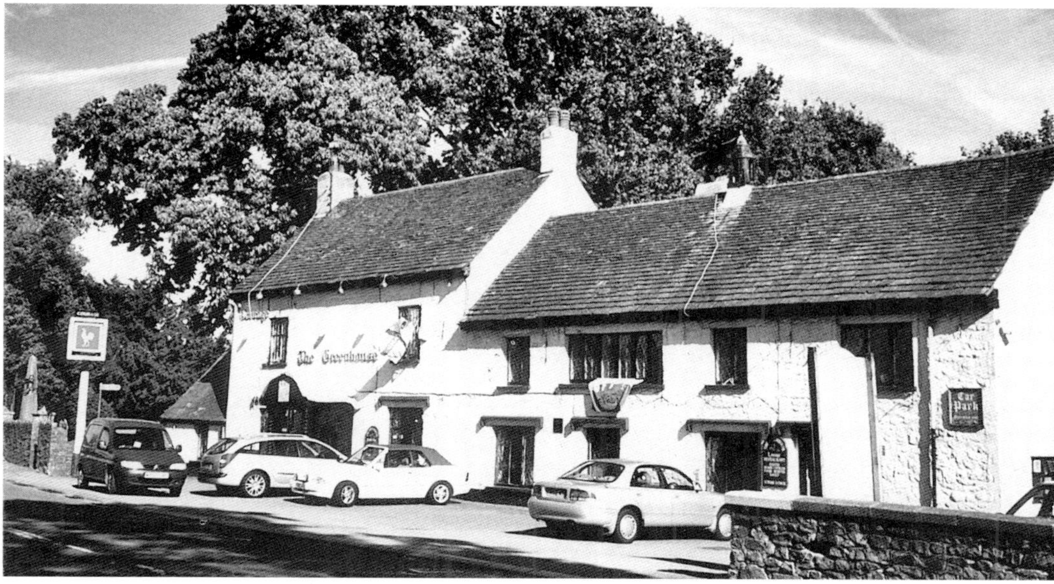

The Greenhouse inn, little changed over centuries.

Beneath this appears the Welsh inscription:

Y Ty Gwyrdd
1719
Cwrw da
A Seidir i chwi,
Dewch y mewn
Chwi gewch y brofi.

Translated, this means:

The Green House
1719
Good ale
and cider for you
Come in
You shall taste it.

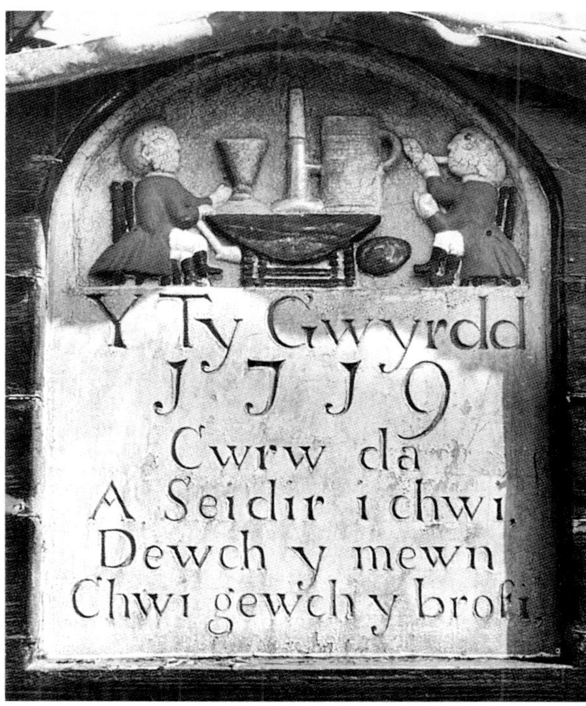

The quaint sign in Welsh.

The celebrated antiquary, Archdeacon William Coxe, accepted this invitation in 1799 while visiting the County and staying with the wealthy Hanbury family at Pontypool. He was less than impressed with his tankard of peculiarly Welsh Ale, for he wrote in his ***'Historical Tour Through Monmouthshire' (1801): 'Cwrw is new ale in a turbid state before it is clarified by*** *fermentation...this beverage is extremely forbidding to the sight, and nauseous to the taste.'* A description hardly likely to tempt the more discerning of taste buds. Today, The Greenhouse inn (now a listed building) remains a popular venue to relax, imbibe fine ales and to enjoy convivial conversation and fine fayre.

THE THREE BLACKBIRDS

A short distance away on the brow of the hill The Three Blackbirds public house looks out over the Vale of Henllys and Llantarnam village below. In the early 20th-century that famous son of Newport, the tramp-poet W.H. Davies, paused here for refreshment. He related in ***'A Poet's Pilgrimage' (1918): 'When I reached the Three Blackbirds at Llantarnam I had my first glass of beer of the day and enjoyed it very much. It was a good brew, mild and yet satisfying, frothy and yet without gas. I would most certainly have had a second glass if any company had been present. But as I was the only customer it was not long before I left.'*** Known to quaff ale, the above extract suggests he visited the pub somewhat early in the day before continuing his pilgrimage throughout the area. Was The Greenhouse next on his itinerary? Possibly.

Renowned and revered as a Nature poet, his copious verses extol the virtues of the countryside which were obviously coloured by his love for the county of his birth. Ironically, though, his upbringing was in the rough and tumble of late 19th-century dockland Pillgwenlly. No matter, for he wrote with a warmth and sincerity few since have matched. The following lines from his nostalgic poem ***'Days That Have Been'*** immortalise ***'Llantarnam's green'***:

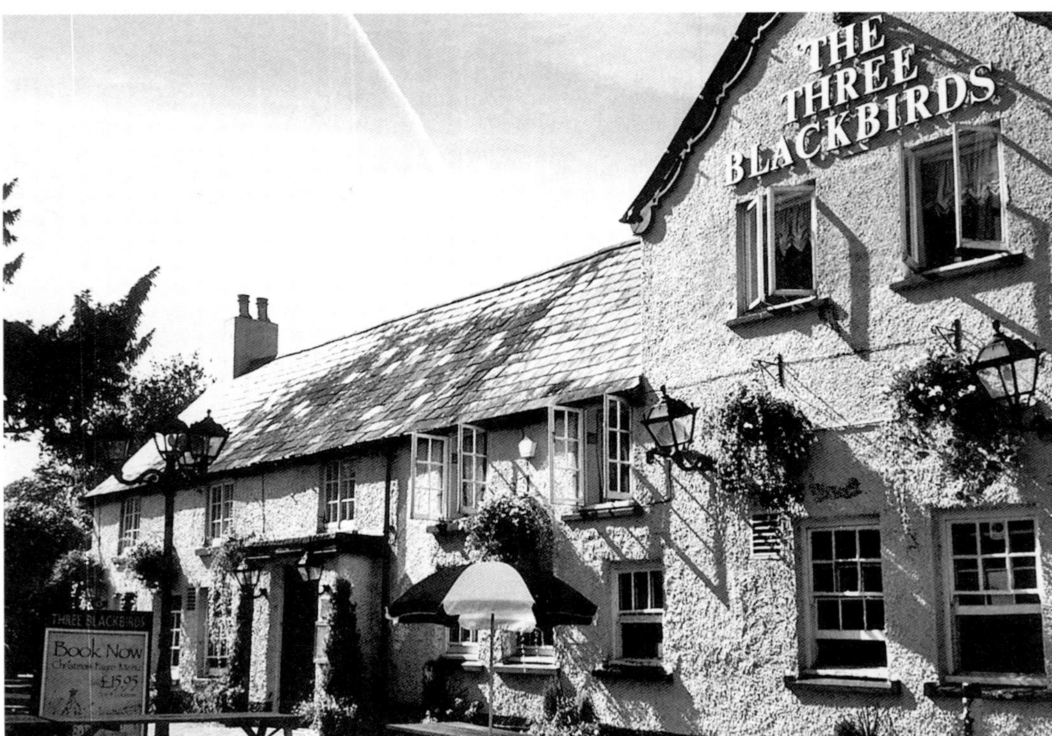

Another ancient hostelry, The Three Blackbirds.

Ah, when I see a leafy village now,
I sigh and ask it for Llantarnam's green;
I ask each river where is Ebbw's voice -
In memory of the sweet days that have been.

Since his historic visit to the inn, the landscape has changed greatly. Where once there were fields in all directions, these have been swallowed up by housing, light industrial units and what is euphemistically referred to as 'call centres'. What would the great man have thought?

ABBEY COTTAGES

An interesting part of Llantarnam's heritage is centred in the area known as Abbey Cottages, a small cluster of stone-built dwellings believed to be of 18th-century origin, if not earlier. Referred to by various names, such as ***'the monastery'***, the census of 1891 lists the cottages in ***'Old Police Station Row'***. The census further records the ***'Coopers Arms and cottages'***, the former being an inn until it closed in 1916.

THE OLD POLICE STATION

It is hard to imagine a police station hereabouts. Yet that is precisely what existed during the 19th-century when one of the cottages became a focus for the judiciary attempting to bring law and order to the village. Though long redundant for this purpose the front of the building retains its ornate heraldic plaque which, while painted over, is recognisable. Inside there were two cells. The bars of one cell can still be seen recessed in a small window which now forms part of the kitchen. One original heavy wooden cell door reinforced by iron struts

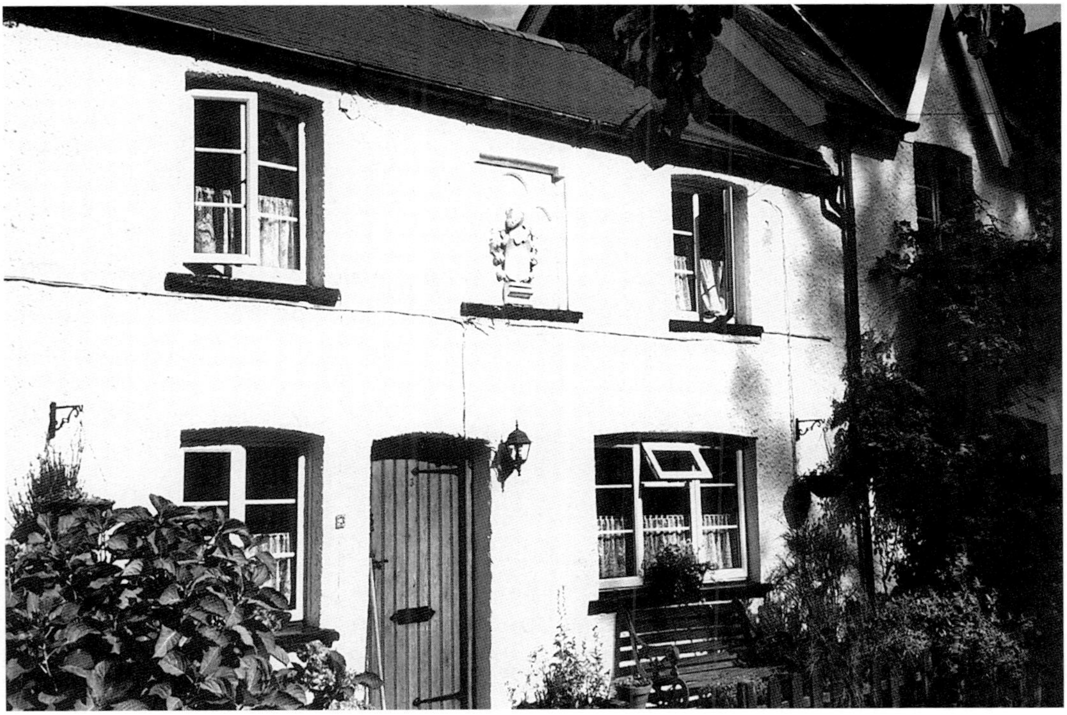

The Old Police Station at Abbey Cottages still displays its heraldic plaque.

remains in place. The magistrate's court was held upstairs and it is easy to imagine Member of Parliament and local Justice of the Peace, Mr. R.J. Blewitt, dispensing justice there to those who flouted the law.

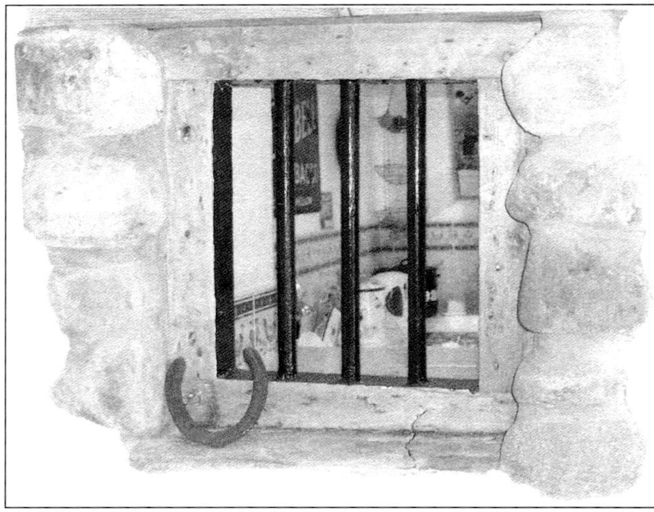

Cell bars recessed in a small window looking into a modern kitchen.

Interestingly, the first salaried constables were authorised by an Act of Parliament in 1792. A later Act in 1842 empowered Justices in Quarter Sessions to provide a ***'Lock-up'*** in the Petty Sessions Division under the control of local Justices. When the Monmouthshire Constabulary was formed in 1857 a parish constable was appointed at the not inconsiderable salary of £1 per week together with free use of a cottage. The old police station in Abbey Lane was most certainly such a ***'Lock-up'***. The cottage has long been a private dwelling.

THE OLD DAME SCHOOL

A Dame School was usually run by an elderly woman in her own home and offered a rudimentary education to local children. In the early 19th-century the Old Llantarnam School, also known as ***'Mary Ann Jones' Cottage'***, began but only a handful of pupils could be taught there at any one time. Earlier attempts to establish some form of organised education for the small rural community of Llantarnam (and that of neighbouring Henllys) through a ***'circulating school'*** based on strong religious values and set up in cottages and barns not surprisingly floundered after only a few months.

A report to the Lords Committee Council on education in 1847 emphasised the generally poor quality of instruction by teachers in the Cwmbrân area during the first half of the 19th-century. Particular reference was made to a schoolmaster at Llantarnam School who held classes in his cottage and who was described as ***'advanced in years and very unfit for the office'***. This surely refers to the ***'Old School House'*** at Abbey Cottages.

However, with the opening of the Lower National Church School at nearby Llanfrechfa in September 1864, children from the vicinity trudged daily across the fields to gain a fitting education. This saw the demise of the old Dame School. The photograph opposite shows the building abandoned and in ruins. During the 1970s it was rescued from oblivion and transformed into a comfortable dwelling.

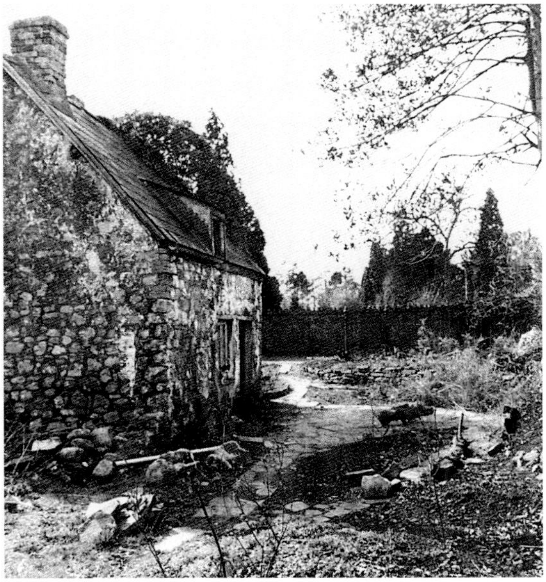

The early 19th-century Dame School known as 'Mary Ann Jones' Cottage'.

The census of 1891 provides a fascinating insight into the trades, professions and ***'Where Born'*** of residents of this ***'hamlet within a village'***: Brook House, secretary to Gas Company, from Cambridge; Coopers Arms Cottage, bricklayer, wife dressmaker, from Longstow; Coopers Arms Inn, publican and dairyman, wife dairymaid, from Bridgwater, Somerset; Number 1 Old Police Station Row, head of household, a widow, living on our means, and two sons both labourers, from Devon. This shows unequivocally that in days gone by people moved to seek work and population migration is no new phenomenon.

LLANTARNAM ABBEY

Llantarnam Abbey has a history to rival that of the world-famous Abbey of Tintern, yet it has all-to-often shunned the limelight in order to retain its privacy: little is known about it by present-day folk. Why ever not? Probably because it is hidden from view surrounded by parkland. It is approached from the highway through the Magna Porta and along a winding lane. Yet the Abbey offers a fascinating story on the very doorstep of local history.

Around the year 1179, in the reign of Henry II, a colony of Cistercian monks from Strata Florida established a daughter ***'house'*** at Nant Teyrnon supported by Sir Hywel ap Iorwerth, Lord of Caerleon and a Prince of Gwent, who was generous in his grants of land for all its upkeep. History abounds with uncertainties regarding the original siting for there are many references to the Abbey of Caerleon. However, there exists much evidence to suggest a change of site. For what reason? At the time Caerleon was a bustling port (hard to envisage

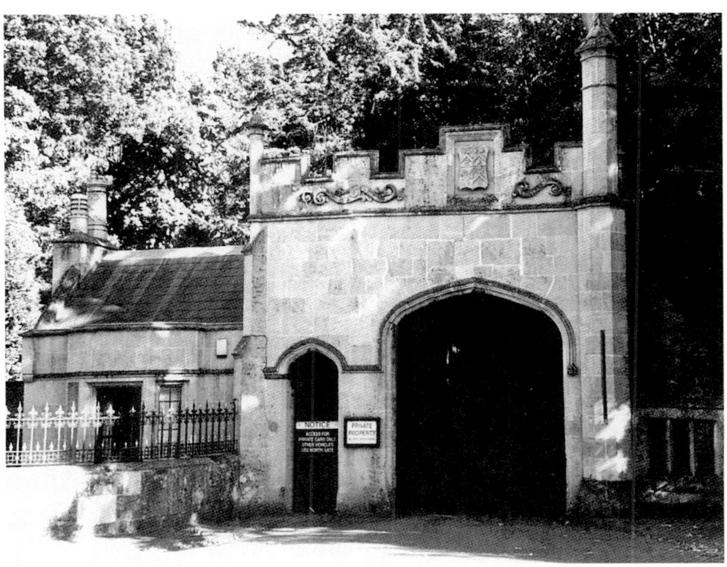

'Magna Porta' - the main entrance to Llantarnam Abbey.

nowadays) and probably far too noisy and boisterous for the monks seeking quietude for silent prayer. No matter, for what is certain is that the Abbey dedicated to Saints Mary and Deuma of Caerleon was built in secluded woodland between the Dowlais Brook and the Afon Llwyd i.e. at Llanfihangel Llantarnam. This cannot be doubted. Several stories claim that the Abbot of Llantarnam kept a well-furnished town house in Caerleon to provide hospitality to weary travellers and pilgrims. This might well be true.

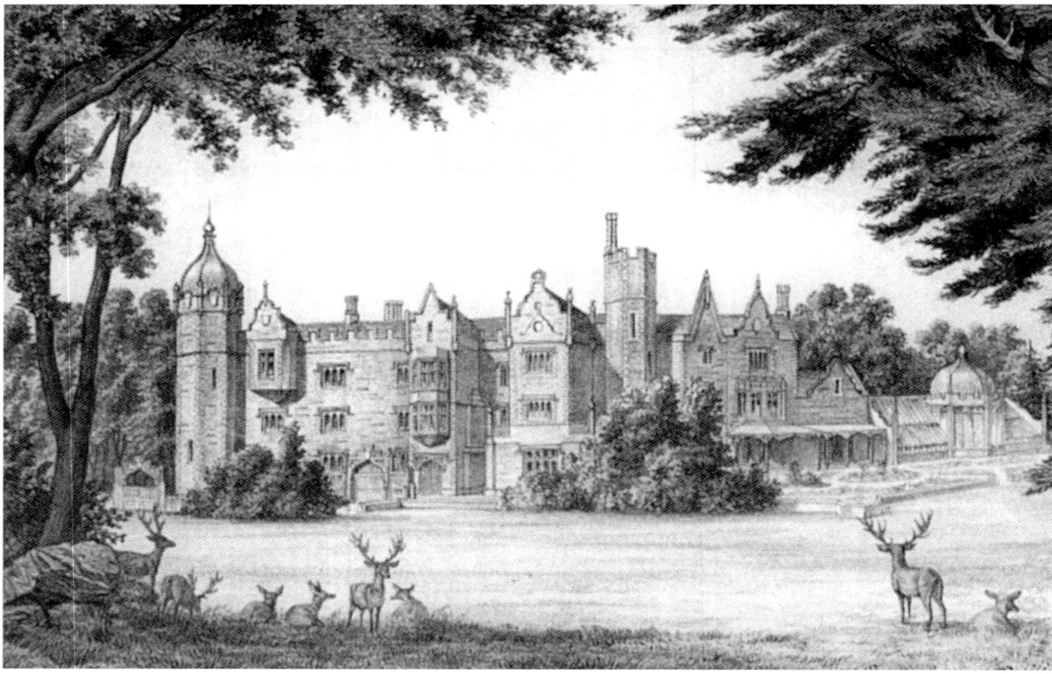

The splendour of the Abbey aspiring to Heaven.

The monks were predominantly agriculturalists and sheep rearers, and their influence profoundly affected life in the community hereabouts for nigh on three and a half centuries. Though their lives were austere and devoted to the sanctity of prayer and seclusion, they still needed wood for fuel and building shelter from the elements, a regular supply of clean water to drink and a river to fish in for they ate neither meat nor partook of wine. Llantarnam was a natural place to settle, nestling serenely in Nature's bosom.

In such times it was not uncommon for wealthy members of the nobility to bequeath a substantial sum of money to their local monastery in return for the favour of daily prayers from the monks. Whether such patronage was prudent can only be attested to in the after-life. Hywel ap Iorwerth was such a man and was described as ***'a man of war from his youth up'***. It is known that in 1175 he had his uncle, Owain ap Owain Wan, a rival claimant to his title, imprisoned, took out his eyes and castrated him. Times were indeed barbarous with sentiment lacking. Perhaps Iorwerth possessed a conscience after all and helping the White Monks was a way of atonement for his former vile cruelty lest his soul rotted forever in the pit of unimaginable darkness.

'Be it known to all the faithful
of the Church of God that I,
Hywel ap Iorwerth, son of Owen,
for the salvation of my soul
and that of my parents and
predecessors, I have settled
the White Monks at Llantarnam
and have given the lands to
the White Monks.'

A fire in 1398 all but destroyed the Abbey. Yet with an unshakable belief and considerable fortitude the monks undertook the task of rebuilding their place of silent worship, a shrine to the glorification of the Almighty. A few years afterwards the region was under siege by the rampaging army of the Welsh chieftain Owain Glyndŵr. One of the Abbey's Priors, the seemingly stalwart and militant John ap Hywel, exhorted those defending their territory to remain defiant before God and that all who fell that day would sup in Heaven. Sounded plausible enough, but he was taunted as he quietly tried to slip away from the field of battle when he realised the cause was lost, maintaining that since it was a period of fasting he must deny himself the prospect of a meal! He became yet one more casualty at the Battle of Usk of 1405. Which, as some might argue, is precisely what the sanctimonious cleric richly deserved.

The Act of Supremacy in 1534 and the subsequent Dissolution of the Monasteries in 1536 inevitably took their toll on Llantarnam. According to the ***'Valor Ecclesiasticus'***, the possessions of the Abbey in that year amounted to £71-3s-2d. These were confiscated and surrendered to the Crown and the 60 Cistercian monks dispersed and reduced to six. Where did the brothers go? The Abbey was suppressed and closed after just over 357 years. Together with the later ravages of the Reformation, the monastery lay in a ruinous state. It is well worth recalling the original directive at the time of the Dissolution that the Commissioners:

'Should pull to the ground
all the walls of the
churches, steeples, cloisters,
fraters, dorters, chaper houses ect.'

In 1539 a certain John Parker acquired the Abbey buildings but having no heirs the property reverted to the Crown in 1552. Queen Mary later bestowed the property to William Carpenter and William Savage. But this acquisition was short-lived. In 1554 it fell into the grasping hands of the extremely wealthy local squire William Morgan, a grandson of Sir Thomas Morgan of Pencoed Castle, and the eldest son of John Morgan of Caerleon, who also acquired neighbouring Pentre Bach.

There were Morgans at Llantarnam for some 200 years, almost all loyal to the Roman Catholic faith, several being regularly fined for harbouring recusants on their land (i.e. one who refused to conform to the Established Anglican Church). By his death in 1633, Edward Morgan had paid fines in excess of £6,900.

His faith was strong! There again, he could well afford such monies for the *'inconvenience to his beliefs'*.

On 17th November, 1678, Father David Lewis, possibly a nephew of Lady Frances Morgan, was arrested by six dragoons when found *'under a clay floor cunningly contrived'* next to the blacksmith's workshop opposite St. Michael's Church for preaching mass to his parishioners. His outspoken views did the Jesuit priest no favours for despite a lengthy trial in which he defended his actions he was found guilty as charged. The judge Atkins epitomised the situation by stating: *'He that uses to read Mass commits treason.'* Harsh times, indeed. Subsequently, the priest was hanged, drawn and quartered at Usk on 27th August, 1679. His last words when brought to the scaffold are perhaps pertinent to modern-day beliefs, for all extremes of religious faith invariably create a social if not a moral vacuum:

'I was condemned for reading the Mass;
Hearing Confessions; Administering the Sacraments;
Anointing the Sick; Christening; Marrying; Preaching.
As for reading the Mass it was the old and still is
the accustomed and laudable Liturgy of the Holy Church
and all other Acts of Religion today, tending to the
worship of God, and for this dying, I die for Religion.'

David Lewis preached the noble word and blessing of God. Enough said. His remains were interred near the porch of St. Mary's Priory Church, Usk. In 1970 he was canonised in Rome by Pope Paul for being a Welsh Roman Catholic martyr. Surely, somewhat late?

The last member of the family was Edward Morgan who lived until his 84th year. Having no male heir the estate passed to the female line through the law of equal inheritance, his eldest granddaughter who had married Edward Bray. Upon marriage his two daughters became Ladies, Mrs. Blewitt and Mrs. Fettiplace, both of whom inherited the Abbey on the death of their father. But the two women could never agree about anything, quarrelling endlessly, and the estate slipped into inexorable decline.

During the late 18th-century, William Coxe visited the estate and recorded what he saw. Strangely, it was the venerable Archdeacon's niece, the Lady *'Miss Coxe'*, who in 1802 penned an abridgement entitled *'Picture Of Monmouthshire'* which began thus:

'Llantarnam House, an ancient seat of the Morgan family...was built
on the site of an abbey...the stone cells, and a beautiful gothic
gate-way to the ancient structure, still remain...The house, which
is large, dark, damp, and dreary, contains nothing remarkable,
except several portraits of the kings and queens of England, and
many family pictures; but the park is extensive and diversified,
swelling into gentle undulations, and interspersed with thick
plantations and dark avenues, which make a conspicuous figure
in the adjoining landscape.'

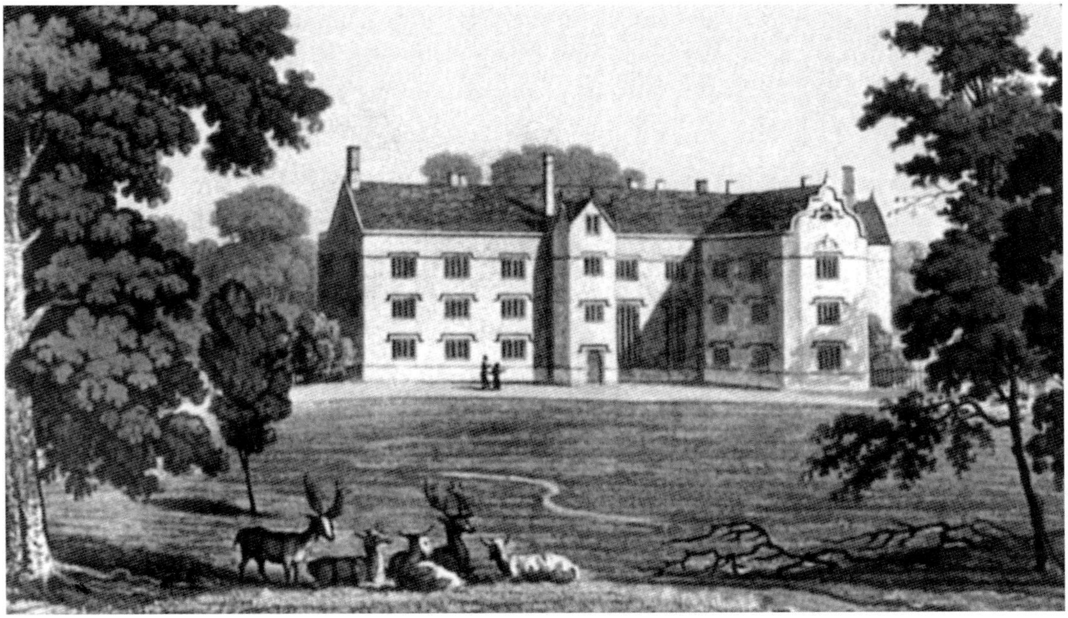

The west front, ca. 1826, in the Elizabethan style.

The accompanying engraving shows the west front of the Abbey in 1826 when it was tenanted by Sir Henry Protheroe, a Bristol merchant. Though appointed High Sheriff of the County in 1816, he quickly fell from grace as on 23rd January of the following year an order was issued for the Coroner to arrest him at the Abbey ***'to answer to Edward Blewitt in respect of debts of £700 owing to the said Edward Blewitt'***. It was later asserted that Sir Henry had disposed of many fine treasures and caused damage to the roof.

In 1834 Reginald James Blewitt, a grandson of one of the ladies (and already established as a successful industrialist in the area, Editor and Proprietor of ***The Monmouthshire Merlin***), claimed the property as rightfully his. Straightaway, he set about demolishing the ruinous parts and using the stone to rebuild the oldest part of the house itself: this ultimately cost him the quite staggering sum of £60,000. What he created was a typically ornate Georgian mansion complete with - yes - a minstrel gallery. The front of the house has remained largely unchanged since then. Such an expense probably contributed in no small measure to the collapse in 1851 of the Monmouth & Glamorgan Bank in which Blewitt was a foremost figure: he was forced to resign his seat in Parliament as a member for the Monmouth Boroughs. Notwithstanding, he was afforded the luxury of residing abroad for the next 15 years. How the influential and wealthy suffer for their fraudulent actions!

An honourable gentleman not without compassion, he annually made a gesture of goodwill towards those within the community. ***The Monmouthshire Merlin*** of Saturday, 26th December, 1840, duly reported:
'On Christmas Day the poor inhabitants of the parish of Llantarnam were supplied by Mr. Blewitt, M.P., with an ample and substantial Christmas dinner, consisting of a pound of meat and a pound of bread for each individual in each family. This custom, so honoured in its observance, Mr. Blewitt commenced in the

first year of his residence at the Abbey, and he has continued it ever since. Mr. Blewitt has also directed that the poor of the same parish shall be supplied with coals during the present inclement season; and we hear that he has ordered fifty tons of coal to be distributed amongst the poor inhabitants of the town of Newport.'

The coal magnate Sir Clifford Cory bought Llantarnam Abbey in 1895 and upgraded the house, installing central heating, marble-lined bathrooms and a monks' cell. Some innovation! He entertained lavishly and his lifestyle became the talk of the neighbourhood. His polo matches were occasions of extreme exuberance. The story concerning the monks' cell was greatly exaggerated yet revolved around his housekeeper who vehemently objected to the mess the polo players brought into the house. To diffuse the situation, Sir Clifford Cory had a monks' cell built together with a Swan Lake in the park where polo players could change their dress. The monks' cell is now a residence used by a gardener, the stagnant lake filled in. Like so many successful businessmen today, the ruthless industrialist lived off the ***'sweat and toil'*** of those desperate for a pittance to feed their families. What's new? The 'masters' still continue to exploit the pauper - which remains acceptable to present-day society by and large.

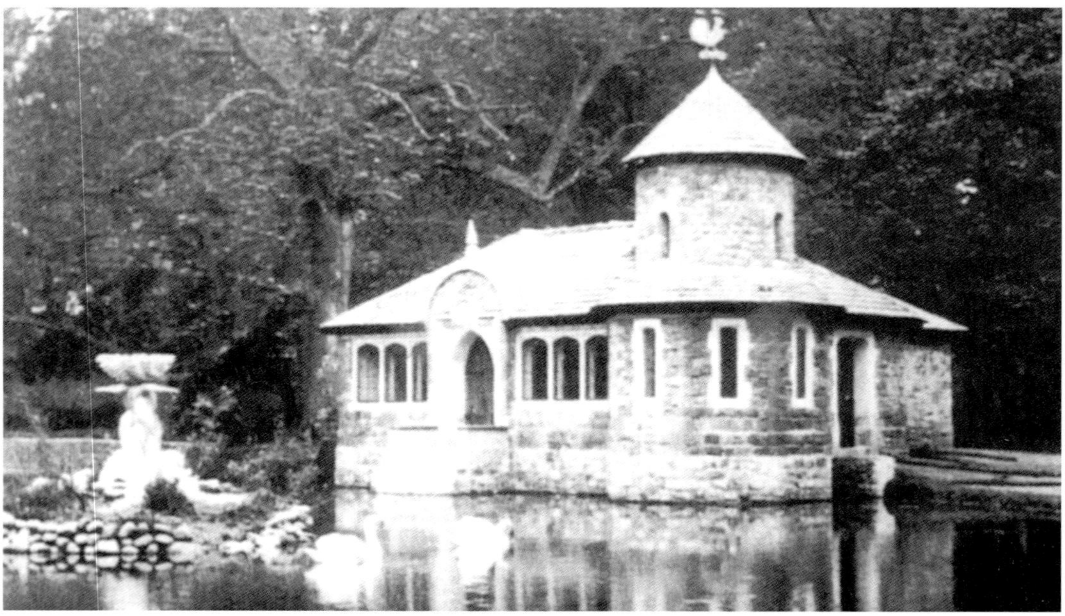

The Monks' cell and Swan Lake.

Though a man of supposedly high principle, he often found himself at odds with the local council over ***'rights of way'*** on his lands. Unsuccessfully, he tried to compromise land in exchange for footpath closures.

Following Sir Clifford's death in 1940 Llantarnam Abbey was sold to the government and appropriated by the Ministry of War for use as a Red Cross storage depot and later by the Americans for ***'ordnance purposes'***. What that precisely means is an enigma. Nonetheless, there was a large GI camp in the grounds of the Abbey, all awaiting the D-day landings of 1944. Llantarnam, like so many other places throughout the County became the temporary home to

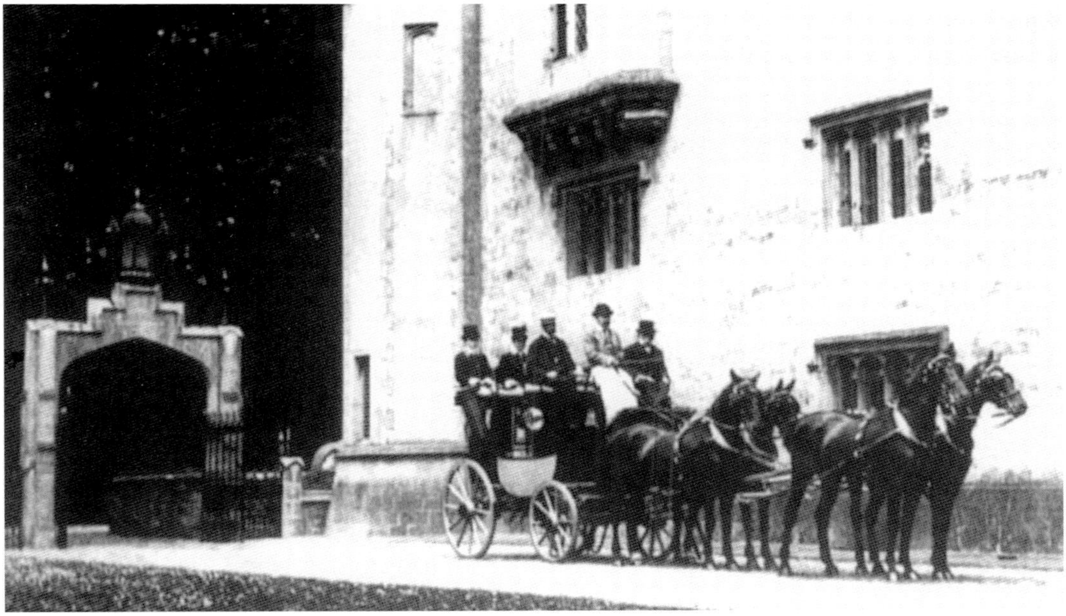

Sir Clifford Cory and his magnificent coach and four-in-hand ca. early 1900s.

American servicemen. Their easy charm, ready money, ***'gum'*** and ***'nylons'*** seduced many a vulnerable female. Sadly, many of these brave fighters became casualties on the beach at Omaha never to return to their loved ones nor to their homeland. After the departure of the Americans, the camp was made ready to accommodate prisoners of war.

During 1946 Llantarnam Abbey was again put up for sale. Few purchasers were forthcoming due to the dilapidated state of the place, the result of years of neglect. Surprisingly perhaps, the Order of the Sisters of St. Joseph of Annecy within the Church of Rome were looking for a retreat to replace their convent in Newport. Llantarnam Abbey and surrounding grounds fitted the bill. Following much upgrading of the site whilst retaining, as far as possible, the former character of the Abbey it is now a delightful place to visit which offers an ongoing

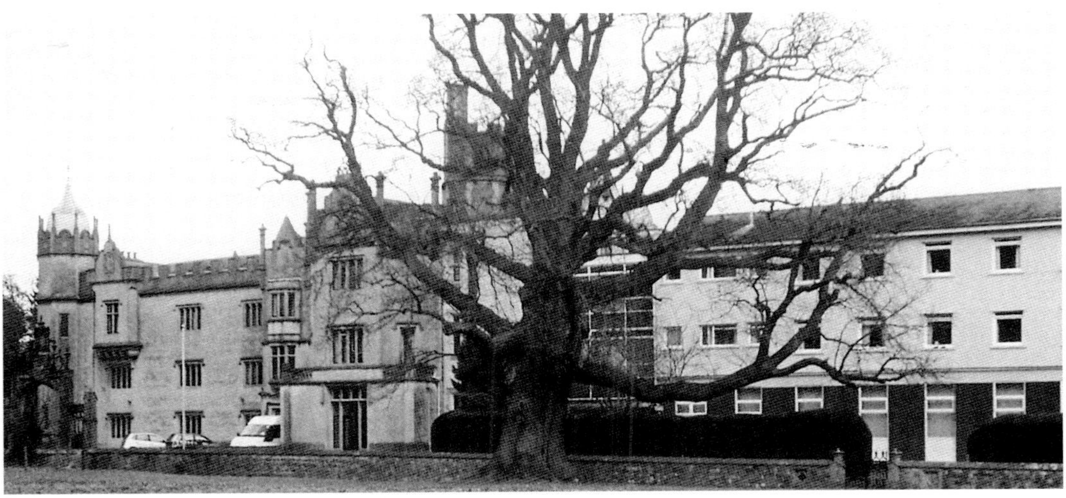

The Abbey with its modern extension.

opportunity to bear witness in prayer, peace and humility before the compassion of the Lord most supreme.

Of particular interest were a number of stone statues which adorned the boundary wall of a formal garden. Yet in the wild part of the park, obscured by overgrown trees and bracken, was an old stone figure of a man with a dog at his feet. Known as Robin Hood, had this any connection with his Merry Men and the monks' cell? Who can say...and what happened to the statue?

The ruins of an ancient Tithe Barn exist in the grounds and was probably built with stones pilfered from the original simple monastery.

Evidence of the antiquity of the Abbey is also provided by a rare manuscript and two seals. The manuscript details the Homilies of St. Gregory and is of late 12th or early 13th-century origin. The one seal, found in the grounds in 1987, shows a squirrel with the words in Old English ***'I crack nuts'***. Curious. The second seal, surely the seal of St. Magdalene, depicts a monk, presumed to be Bernard, an early Cistercian founder, blessing three people and dates back to the 14th-century. This seal is displayed in the National Museum of Wales. Because of their historical importance the other two artefacts are displayed in the British Library, though a photograph of the second seal is held in the Abbey's archives.

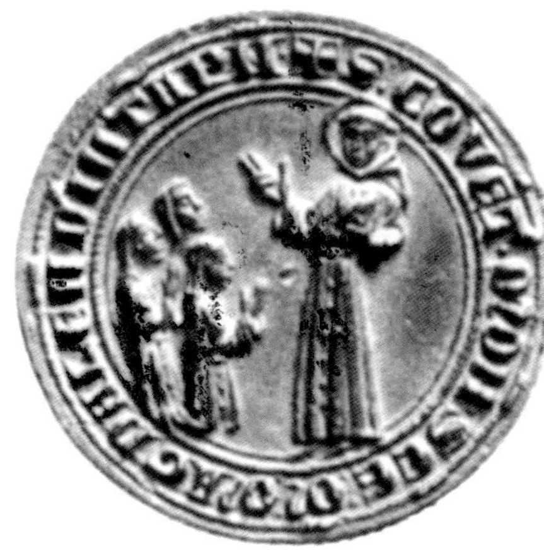

The 14th-century seal of Mary Magdalene.

Many legends surround Llantarnam Abbey. One is of the ghost of a lady in white - more likely that of a White Monk - which to this day roams the Abbey and lands, and along tunnels that run to the grange of Pentre Bach. And that, in fact, is all that is known. The latter may seem improbable, for many such stories concern fine buildings of antiquity elsewhere. Yet during a turbulent age of dissension and with the persecution of Catholics all too prevalent, underground hiding places were very much a reality.

A DAY AT THE RACES

Surely the title from a well-known Marx Brothers farce. But racing at Llantarnam? Apparently so. An old document purporting to be a race card was unearthed during the 1950s among the records of the former Llantarnam Urban District Council. Headed ***'THE LLANTARNAM GRAND NATIONAL, Monday April 4th, 1910'***, it lists the horses running together with all the information necessary to judge the likely winner of the race. A copy of the original is shown opposite.

At first glance the race card appears genuine and certainly conveys the impression that a great Steeplechase had taken place in the vicinity. Yet there is no record of a racecourse anywhere close by, although Point-to-Point meetings no doubt took place on surrounding farmland. By coincidence, an elderly Cwmbrân resident was able to reveal the document's true identity.

The write-up on the card does not refer to horses nor to an actual race, rather to candidates standing for the local council election. The ***'horses'*** listed are merely the nicknames and pseudonyms of real people. The person who wrote the card obviously had a good working knowledge of the sport for the comments are both witty and authoritative. Remember, the Representation of the Peoples Act of the time prevented real names being used in case of ***'undue influence'*** on the outcome of the election.

The author of this ingenious resumé concludes his description of the race thus:

> ***'To the victors, all enjoyment – may they increase their zeal***
> ***To benefit their neighbours and work for public weal:***
> ***We extend our sympathy to those among the slain,***
> ***May they enjoy the best of health and live to fight again.'***

As nowadays, local elections were hotly contested with each candidate striving to persuade the electorate to vote him into office rather than any of his rivals.

THE LLANTARNAM GRAND NATIONAL, Monday, April 4th, 1910.

Who's Who in the Race.

HORSE.	SIRE.	DAM.	REMARKS.
I.L.P.	Socialist	Merrie England	Green colt out of an entirely new stable: can hardly reach home at the first attempt.
Fire Engine	Hose Cart	Hose Pipe	Third exhibition: close up last time: will join in the scramble for twelfth position.
Welsh Mutton	Brisket	Rump Steak	Rather weedy: obtained a place three years ago: likely to repeat this performance.
Whiskers	Spring Poet	Cabbage Plant	Completely outclassed each time: likely to benefit by change of stable.
Whippett	Star Seconds	Border Tile	A young colt that is inclined to be rather fretful: the stable lads appear rather confident.
Local Veto	Hop Bitters	Stone Ginger	Ran a dead heat for first place six year ago: not so fast as of yore.
Tim	Patsy	Bridget	Best of the heavy-weights: belongs to a clever stable; good business for 1—2—3.
Nil Desperandum	Pluck	Ability	Disappointed his backers a few weeks back: the shorter course may suit him better.
Critic	Co-op.	Federation	Unsuccessful three years ago: not likely to improve his position this time.
Smart Boy	"How are you to-day?"	"How's Johnny?"	Won in a canter last time: favourite on this occasion: almost certain to repeat his performance.
Irish Smile	K.E.	L.L.Y.	Just managed to scrape in last time: greatly improved since: undergone a thorough preparation.
Councillor	Good Attendance	"Remember my brother"	Won [illegible] sure to be in the first flight: expected to be a great success at the stud.
Lamp Oil	Scrubbing Brush	Emery Cloth	Knows every inch of the course well: honest horse: expected to get a place.
Old Tom	Johnnie Walker	Uam Var	Brought off a great surprise last time: stable connections still confident.
Club Swinger	Dumb-bell	Parallel Bar	If physical culture could win there would be no one else in the race.
Dressmaker	Science	Mathematics	Another of the weedy kind, who will find the distance too far.
Collier	Pick	Shovel	Made an attempt 15 years ago: lack of training will prove detrimental.
Sunny Jim	Pippin	Mangold Wurzel	Great favourite with the crowd, who are not likely to repeat their mistake of three years ago.
[illegible]	Independence	Integrity	Thoroughly honest horse: may get a place if the pace is not too fast.
Straight Jacket	Screws	Timber	An old and useful performer, who will take a lot of beating.
Mealk	Dairyman	Milk-tin	Very erratic colt: wild as a March hare: cannot stay the distance.
Galloping Major	Bombardier	Fusilier	Too much of the military prance to meet with success on Grand National Course.
Jupiter	Saturn	Mars	Clumsy colt that cannot jump: has only negotiated one fence in his life.
Engineer	Cog-wheel	Cylinder	One of the most useful horses in the race: ought to secure a shop.
Weary Willie	Tired Tim	Benjamina	Would make a useful cab-horse: too slow for steeplechasing.
Post-boy	Fruiterer	Greengrocer	Thoroughly used to the course, and having a thorough preparation will make a good show.

Description of the Race.

An April morn, a cloudless sky, the birds are mating in the trees,
When lo, the sound of horses' hoofs is early wafted on the breeze;
Clearer and clearer the noise is heard, and as the steeds bound into sight,
Spectators throng from every part to hear Friend Haden shout "All's Right."
A false alarm! Another start, for Whiskers, Mealk and Jupiter
Have bolted right across the course, creating quite a little stir.

Away they go, right up the hill, with Galloping Major leading on,
Followed by Stedfast and Engineer, Local Veto and Old Tom;
Across the fields to Maesyrhiw, Councillor begins to cock his ears,
John sees his favourite fresh and strong, the sight alleviates his fears.
Smart Boy now makes the pace with Whiskers, I.L.P. and Tim,
Closely followed by Irish Smile, Weary Willie and Sunny Jim:
Down the slope to Glanynant, Nil Desperandum takes the button,
Neck and neck with Dressmaker, Club Swinger, Critic and Welsh Mutton.
Along Tyooch they're startled—the visage of a "County Copper"
Frightens poor Mealk, his legs give way and down he goes a regular cropper.
Through Pentrebasket and Pantglass then make their way to Cider Mill,
But sad to say that on the way poor Weary Willie had a spill.
'Tis now the fun commences, excitement starts just here,
This is the place folks congregate to give a little cheer
To those who jump the water, to laugh at those who fail—
When near the locks, some of the jocks turned red, then deadly pale;
Over they go, three parts of 'em, but Jupiter and Whippett,
Galloping Major, Dressmaker, Collier and Critic,
Are sorry spectacles indeed, and [illegible] to relate.
We must follow up the others and leave them to their fate.
Fire Engine and Post-boy now bound along the soil,
Their near attendants being Straight Jacket and Lamp Oil.
Just hear Ted Thomas shouting—"Now then my lads come on,
If you don't jump the Greenhouse Brook, your chance of victory's gone."
Where's Whippett? shouts the crowd—Oh, dear! exclaimed his sisters,
When straight into the brook goes I.L.P. and Whiskers.
Now the heavy-weights start travelling, nostrils to the full expand,
Veins stand like whip-cord on their frames—Was ever sight so grand?
Up past the Star, along Grange Road, they keep together in a cluster,
Where a little spill to Club Swinger createth just a little fluster.
O'er to Forge Hammer at top speed, the pace begins to tell a tale,
Fifteen have now a chance to win, but three of them must fail.
On entering Coronation Road excitement reaches fever heat,
Smart Boy commenceth leading, his jock can hardly keep his seat.
Up o'er the bridge they scramble, the winning post is near,
And as they come along the dip, up goes a hearty cheer
From those who've backed the favourite to land in front of Tim,
Councillor and Irish Smile, Old Tom and Sunny Jim;
Next comes Lamp Oil and Engineer, Nil Desperandum sore distressed,
Welsh Mutton taking tenth place, but what about the rest?
Now for the last two shops the struggle is severe
[illegible] Local Veto and Post-boy, Straight [illegible] being near,
With Fire Engine and Stedfast a fighting might and main
To secure the last positions in this steeplechase of fame.

To the victors, all enjoyment—may they increase their zeal
To benefit their neighbours and work for public weal:
We all extend our sympathy to those among the slain,
May they enjoy the best of health and live to fight again.

Printed and Published by Joyce and Sons, 32 High Street, Newport, Mon.

The race card for The Llantarnam Grand National, 1910.

Extensive coverage was given to the 1910 election by ***The Free Press of Monmouthshire***. Through its columns on Friday, 1st April, a letter signed by nine of the candidates stressed that the most urgent matter to be addressed by the newly elected Council would be that of a proposed sewerage scheme ***'rendered absolutely necessary by the varied nuisances existing in our midst'***. Public health was a major issue of the time: the intent was a wholesome water supply together with a proper sewerage system to avoid the dreadful diseases associated with a lack of these basic amenities. The subject continues to be a matter for concern and a powerful political bullet. The letter concludes: ***'If favoured with election, we shall endeavour to give this and other matters affecting the welfare of the inhabitants our very best consideration.'*** Sounds all too familiar, doesn't it?

In common with other parts of the County, polling took place on Monday, 4th April, at St. Dials School, Cwmbrân The twelve seats were contested by twenty-six candidates. Voting was quiet throughout the day, but became ***'very brisk'*** during the early evening. The count was carried out in the Temperance Hall under the presidency of Mr. H. Haden, Returning Officer. A large gathering ***'waited patiently in the biting wind and squalls of rain for the declaration...a party of young men passed away the time by singing snatches of popular songs and patriotic airs'***. The results were finally declared well after 11.30 p.m. and ***'were cheered, counter-cheered, and laughed according to how their feelings were 'tickled' by the run of events'.***

The number of electors eligible to vote was 1,400 and 1,104 actually voted giving a 79% turnout, a remarkably high figure compared to contemporary voting patterns. But why was the electorate so small in number? At the time only males over the age of 21 were entitled to vote. Though the Suffragette movement was starting to find its voice in a male-dominated society, it was not until the Representation of the People Act of 1918 that women over 30 years of age were given the right to vote (and then with certain property qualifications); all women over 21 years, irrespective of personal circumstances, were eventually given the right to vote in 1928.

The same newspaper reported the annual meeting on 1st May of the newly-elected council: this contained much that was predictably bureaucratic and downright mundane, of issues dealing with everyday matters viz. the state of Grange Road, Llantarnam, a breach of bye-laws relating to alteration of property without proper planning consent and - wait for it - the deplorable state of the Fire Brigade's uniforms! True. Little mention of election pledges regarding sewerage...

Notwithstanding, one item is pertinent to the modern lifestyle - that of Sunday trading: ***'...a shop owned by Mr. Capper, which was opened every day in the week, including Sunday. Councillor Kelly said that it was the cause of a great deal of comment in the district, and children spent their pennies in the shop on Sunday, instead of putting them in the plate at church.'*** The latter remark shows where the Councillor's affinities lay. It was pointed out that the shopkeeper held a seven days' refreshment licence granted by the County Council and this could not easily be revoked. The Clerk was duly instructed to look into the matter.

The race card of Llantarnam's **GRAND NATIONAL** in 1910 is an extraordinary document for it takes the reader on an enthralling tour through the length and breadth of the urban district, meeting characters familiar to everyday early 20th-century society. In short, card and press reports offer a nostalgic insight into the way things were, long before the advent of Cwmbrân New Town. Moreover, they provide a poignant reminder that our forebears took politics very seriously. Even so, they possessed a canny ability to communicate and to generate enthusiasm and commitment among the electorate. Politicians today of all persuasions should take note and learn from the lessons of the past. For it is apparent that in the current climate of political mediocrity at both local and national level, apathy creates a bureaucratic state bordering on the inept and dictatorial.

Yes. The race card of 1910 is a valuable and important part of Cwmbrân's social and cultural history. Which, after all, is as it should be.

CURSED THE MAGISTRATE

In this country the right to a fair and unbiased trial is paramount to the Justice System, for this is an essential cornerstone of Democracy. Herein follows an account taken from the ***Magistrates Journal*** and which appeared in the ***The Pontypool Free Press*** dated 1st December, 1922. This surely is an unusual case for the defendant was only too well-known to one of the ***five*** magistrates sitting at Cwmbrân Police Court in judgement of his continual anti-social behaviour.

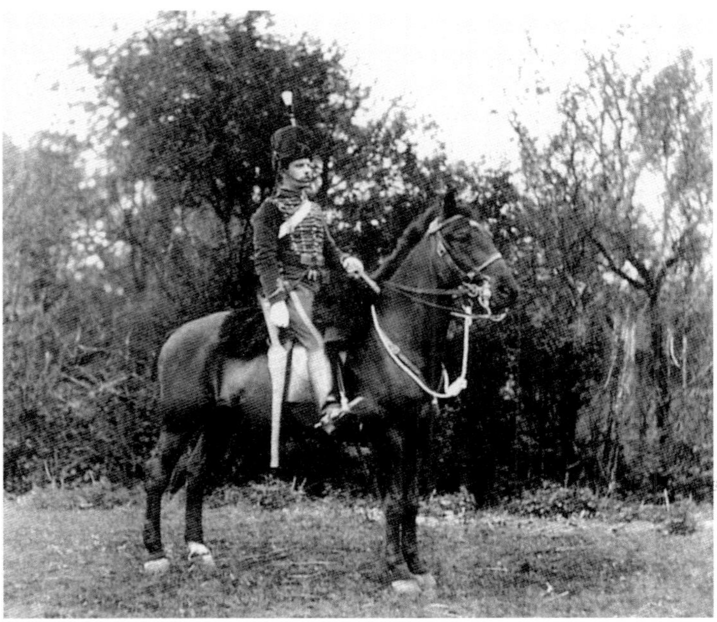

Lewis Lawrence of Gloucestershire Yeomanry & Monmouth Troop in regimental uniform ca. 1894.

The magistrate in question was Lewis Lawrence of Court Farm who in 1901 married Eleanor Powell of Tan House, Caerleon: their union produced ***eleven*** children - a very 'busy' man! Plas Newydd farm was built on Court Farm land and the happy couple took up residence there in 1905. Lewis was a much respected local councillor and a J.P. He and his wife were invited guests at the Investiture of Edward, Prince of Wales, on the 13th July, 1911, at Caernarfon Castle - a most prestigious honour. By sheer chance, Lewis found himself in the dual roles of magistrate and plaintiff. Read on.

'Formerly a motor driver in the employ of the Union Construction Co., Newport, Eugene Lyons appeared in custody on a charge of using profane Language on the highway at Llantarnam on October 10th. Evidence was given by Mr. Lewis Lawrence, one of the sitting magistrates, to the effect that he had occasion to speak to Lyons with regard to his conduct in getting over the railings at his premises to take water for the steam engine. Lyons became most abusive, and used filthy expressions. Mr. Lawrence added that he had no objection to defendant getting the water, but protested against his conduct in tearing the fence...(the defendant denied all allegations made against him). The Chairman: So all Mr. Lawrence says is untrue, is it? - Yes. Can you suggest why he should say anything untrue about you? - Only because I was on his ground. Mr. Russell H.P. Lawrence, son of the magistrate, gave corroborative evidence.'

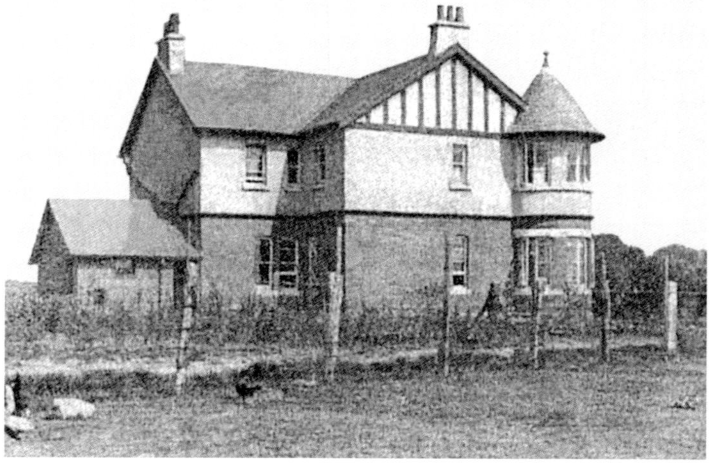

Plas Newydd Farm 1905.

Needless to say, the scoundrel Lyons who had a string of previous convictions, principally for theft, was found guilty of said verbal abuse and trespass. A fine of 20 shillings (or 14 days) was imposed and time to pay refused. Justice, at least, was seen to be done.

PENTRE BACH

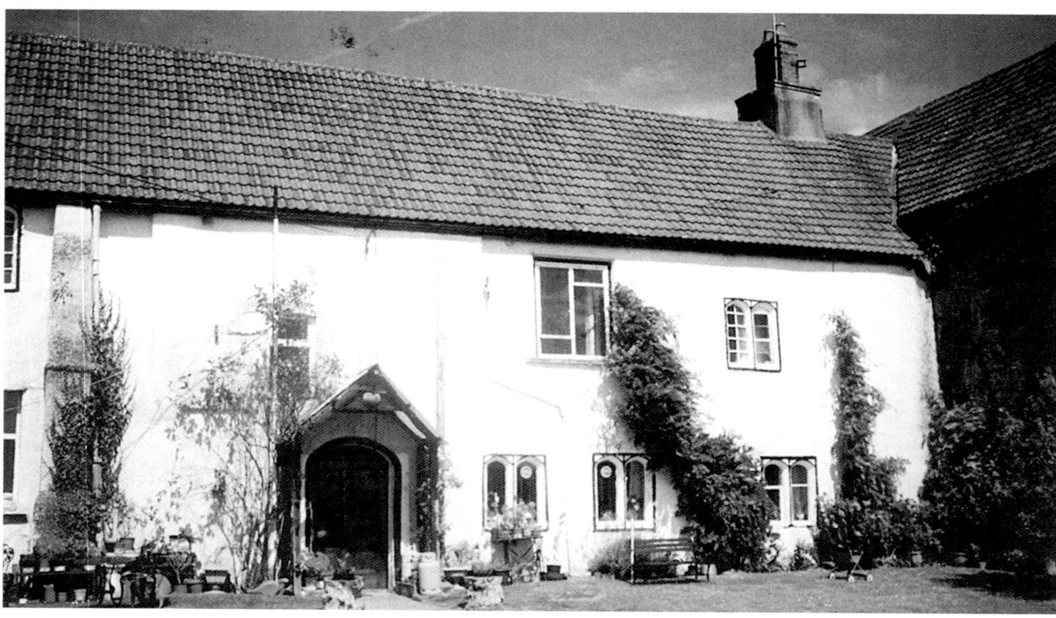

16th-century Pentre Bach.

Gunpowder, Treason & Plot. Pentre Bach has it all. Pentre Bach lies about a mile from the crossroads near the Three Blackbirds Inn leading to Henllys Vale and Castell-y-Bŵch. The former manor house dates from the end of the 13th-century and was, initially, a grange (i.e. a place for storing grain) which belonged to the Cistercian order of ***'White Monks'*** at Llantarnam Abbey; it is set a little way off the monastic trackway to Twm Barlwm.

Very early documents (ca. 1291) refer to it as ***'Mynachty-tir-Waun'*** i.e. ***'the Monks' Meadowland'***. This did not last long for even before the closure of the Abbey by Henry VIII in 1536 the building was actually leased as a private residence to a minor branch of the Morgans of Tredegar.

Following the closure of the Abbey, the Grange was purchased together with Llantarnam Abbey in 1554 by William Morgan, M.P., and High Sheriff of the County. Contemporary sources then mention the house by the name of ***Cefn Vynoche*** (properly ***Cefn Mynach***), the monks' ridge, which seems rather appropriate since it stands directly under the lee of Castell-y-Bŵch.

Mystery surrounds this former grange. For herein lies the original story of the plot to blow up the Houses of Parliament in London with gunpowder - long before Guy Fawkes' ill-fated attempt. The Popish Plot is well known to every school child and has for long become part of political history and folklore; the event is celebrated annually upon 5th November in the traditional manner. Yet Thomas Morgan was the first person credited with such a daring scheme.

Thomas Morgan was born in 1543 into a devoutly Roman Catholic family at the former manor house of Pentre Bach. Though his early years remain somewhat obscure, in later life Thomas became an arch-conspirator in an age of conspiracy, treachery and intrigue. Like many others around him, Thomas was fanatically

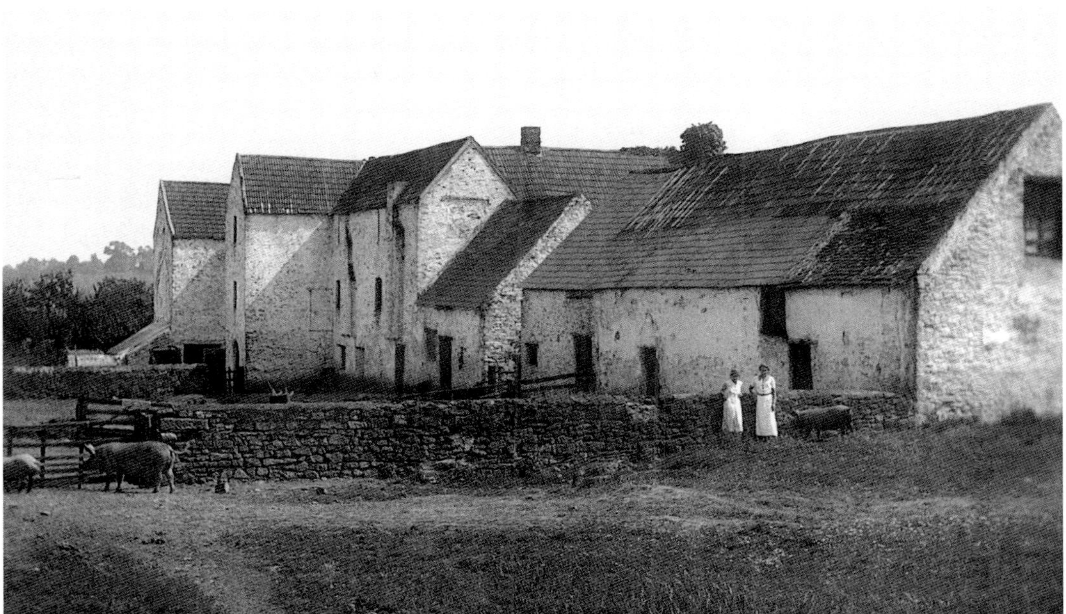

The scene taken from a postcard ca. early 1900s with its 'Haunted Hall'

loyal to the cause of Mary, Queen of Scots, who held a natural birthright to the throne of England, but whose destiny ultimately lay on the executioner's block.

As a trusted Secretary to Lord Shrewsbury, he usurped his position and smuggled messages to the imprisoned Mary at Tutbury. But he was caught out, his treachery to the English Establishment exposed, and he was taken to the Tower of London to languish, uncertain of his fate, for some 10 months. His considerable influence in higher circles prevailed and secured his survival. Upon release, the fortunate Thomas was banished to foreign shores and compelled to find refuge in exile in Paris. Yet even in exile he repeatedly and unsuccessfully plotted the assassination of Elizabeth, the bastard Queen of England - and blow up Parliament. A tricky task! Clearly, Thomas Morgan possessed both the cunning and necessary wit to ensure his skin remained intact. Thus, he survived unscathed to enjoy life abroad for many years and apparently died of natural causes sometime during 1606 aged 63 years.

Pentre Bach is a curious building, rambling and of two distinct parts, of both Tudor and Jacobean origin. Like other middle 16th-century stone houses, the older part has a passage running directly from front to back porch and garden, thus separating the hall from the kitchen with an oak screen. The hall was subsequently divided into several smaller rooms. During the 17th-century the estate was enlarged, a sizeable new wing constructed of very small bricks covered in places with rough plaster and joined on at right angles to the earlier section. Following this enlargement, the ***'house'*** acquired its present Welsh name of ***'The Little Village'***. Thereafter, Pentre Bach became the dower-house or supplementary dwelling for the Morgans of Llantarnam.

The older section of the building with its quaint windows, each with its dripstone above, remains little altered down the ages. The later wing contains the famed ***'Haunted Hall of Pentre Bach'***, some 50 feet long and once renowned throughout the parish as a venue for sumptuous banquets and brilliant old-time balls - and reputedly the venue of mysterious poltergeist activity and other strange phenomena.

At the time the great hall possessed a fine ceiling and the walls were hung with fine paintings. On one particular occasion the guests were enjoying themselves when, quite suddenly and without warning, the walls trembled and the pictures fell to the ground. All present fled from the hall 'in dismay'. No date has ever been found relating to this terrifying event. Was it simply an earthquake? Minor earthquakes have been observed in the Cwmbrân area in the past 20 years. Whatever, though, such tales continue to delight the folklorist.

With the glory days as a grand mansion long gone, its splendour dulled, Pentre Bach passed into various hands, including the influential Blewitts who, by a stroke of good fortune, had eventually inherited much of the Abbey's lands. Nowadays, the former grange survives as an impressive farmhouse; its spacious hall now serves as a dimly-lit and dank barn, the home to domestic fowl and agricultural machinery. Notwithstanding this, Pentre Bach remains the birthplace of Thomas Morgan, a man of deep religious conviction and astute political ambition. What would have happened if he and his arch conspirators succeeded in placing the Catholic Mary upon the throne of England? Now there's something to ponder…

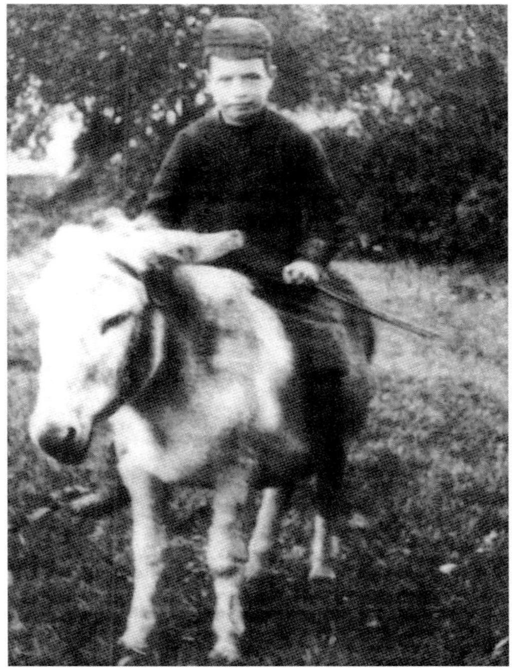

Albert Ernest Lawrence as a youngster riding a donkey at the farm in 1887.

Evidence still remains of extensive earthworks and a moat around the house which are probably of even older origin. At one time quite a considerable community dwelled in this enchanting rural idyll and daily worked the land.

By coincidence, the joint author's father, Albert Ernest Lawrence was born in 1880 and raised on the estate and in adulthood was an ironmonger before emigrating to America in 1904. The accompanying photograph shows him as a youngster astride a donkey at the farm in 1887. What a powerful image this is!

COURT FARM

The farm was probably of 13th-century origin, possibly much earlier. Records show that in 1291 Court Farm was one of the largest farms on the vast Llantarnam Abbey Estate. When the Abbey was 'Dissolved' in 1536, the farm was valued at £71-3s-2d. Thereafter, the original name of the farm reputed to be the Grange of Scybor Court was valued at £1-6s-8d. The sums may seem a pittance by today's monetary value but, remember, centuries ago these were considerable amounts of money.

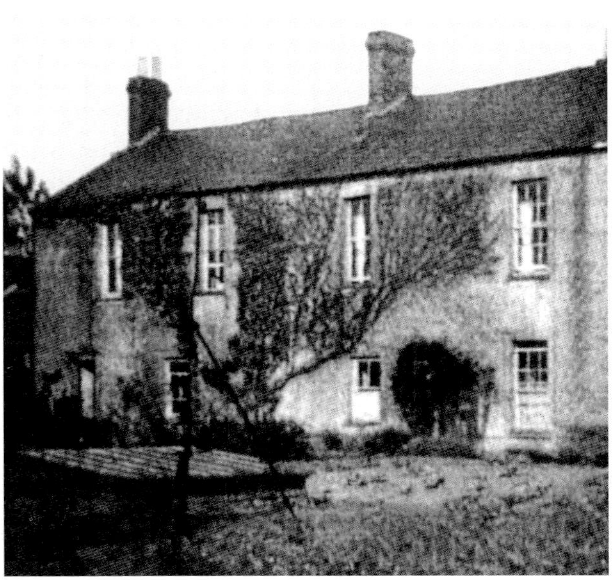

Court Farm ca. 1950.

The farm was occupied by a number of people, but members of the Lawrence family lived there. Most notably, a John Lawrence (one of many such Johns in the family down the years) was born here on the 26th November, 1807. He lived to nearly 94 years of age and was widely known as the ***'Grand Old Man of Monmouthshire'*** and described as ***'the beau ideal of the old world squire'***. A famous raconteur, sporting gent and compassionate industrialist, he was much-admired and greatly respected.

John's father had sold land at Abersychan to three London capitalists and directors of the Bank of England, resulting in the formation of The British Iron Company. Years later he purchased the iron works in Cwmbrân formerly owned by Messrs Blewitt & Co. He went on to become a director of the Monmouthshire Railway & Canal Co, but kept his associations with the iron and steel trades.

John Lawrence was well-known in sporting circles and was Master of Hounds for an amazing 77 years, latterly with the Llangibby pack. He began by founding the Cwmbrân Harriers and regularly hunted both fox and hare on Mynydd Maen and in Henllys Vale.

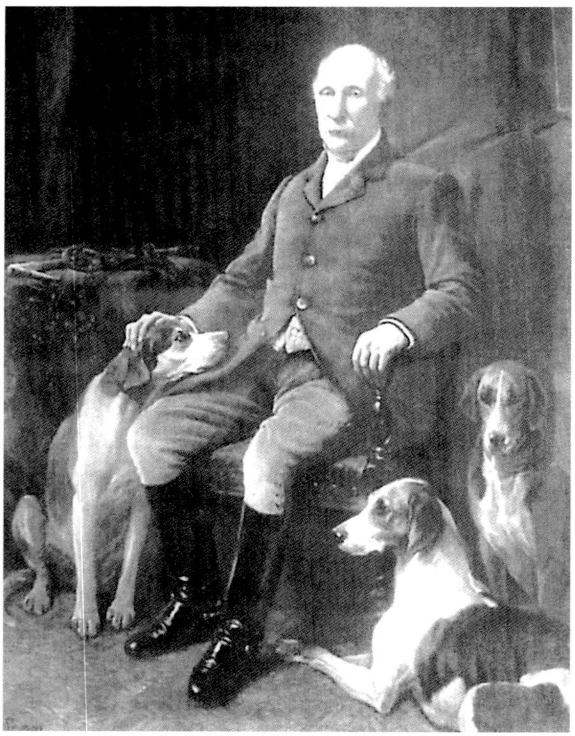

John Lawrence, Master of Hounds.

The crowning honour of his career came on his 91st birthday when he was presented with a magnificent life size portrait in oils of himself painted by Mr. John Charlton. Among those present were Lord Tredegar, His Grace the Duke of Beaufort and other illustrious names. The portrait shows John seated with his three favourite hounds, his hand affectionately laid upon Bluebell's head.

John married Adelaide Lucy and the couple had six children. When he died in November 1901 he was laid to rest in Caldicot Churchyard; the funeral cortège was accompanied by neighbouring Hunts. Truly, John Lawrence typified a social class long gone.

The late Lord Raglan, himself erudite and knowledgeable in architectural grandeur, lamented that so many features of the original house were irrevocably lost. For example, the old stone porch, one of the glories of the ancient building, was removed around 1890 and a smaller nondescript one put in its place. For what reason is unclear. When other alterations were later carried out, a concealed opening was discovered leading to a secret compartment in which Catholic priests and parishioners hid and prayed to the Almighty during the former bloody times of Catholic persecution.

In 1930 Court Farm was purchased by Frederick Lawrence for the princely sum of £5,600, but he died shortly afterwards. It was advertised as a commodious and comfortable dwelling with well-appointed farm buildings and fertile lands of good arable pasture. Subsequently, the farming activities were taken over by the Williams family who lived there until forced out during the 1950s.

Notwithstanding, the grounds of the farm were swallowed up for housing with the development of the emerging Cwmbrân Town Centre, together with the need for a new large school to cater for the fast growing population. The school opened in 1954 and was the first school to be built in the County since World War II: in 1971 it became a Comprehensive. Despite efforts by the local community to preserve the farm as a historic monument, in 1955 faceless bureaucrats decided that the farm and its out-buildings should be demolished to make way for a road-widening scheme. Centuries of history destroyed. Yet another damning indictment of urban vandalism!

THE TRAINS DON'T STOP HERE ANYMORE

The railway ran through the heart of the village and was mainly a line to convey heavy mineral traffic such as coal, iron and steel from the plundered Eastern Valley to the burgeoning port of Newport and beyond. The line also connected with the Midlands. Llantarnam station itself was built in the 1860s. During the early years passenger traffic was minimal and considered of little importance.

Incidentally, before the age of refrigeration large quantities of ice were brought by rail to the station to be delivered to the coal magnate Sir Clifford Cory on his nearby estate at Llantarnam Abbey. Presumably, he had a below-ground ice-house for chilling his vast vintage wine stock and champagne.

During the infamous Dr. Beeching era of the late 1950s and early '60s, most of the minor branch lines in Wales saw their demise - for whose services a grateful government awarded the honourable gentleman a peerage! Anyway, on 30th April, 1962, the last passenger train ran from Newport to Blaenafon via

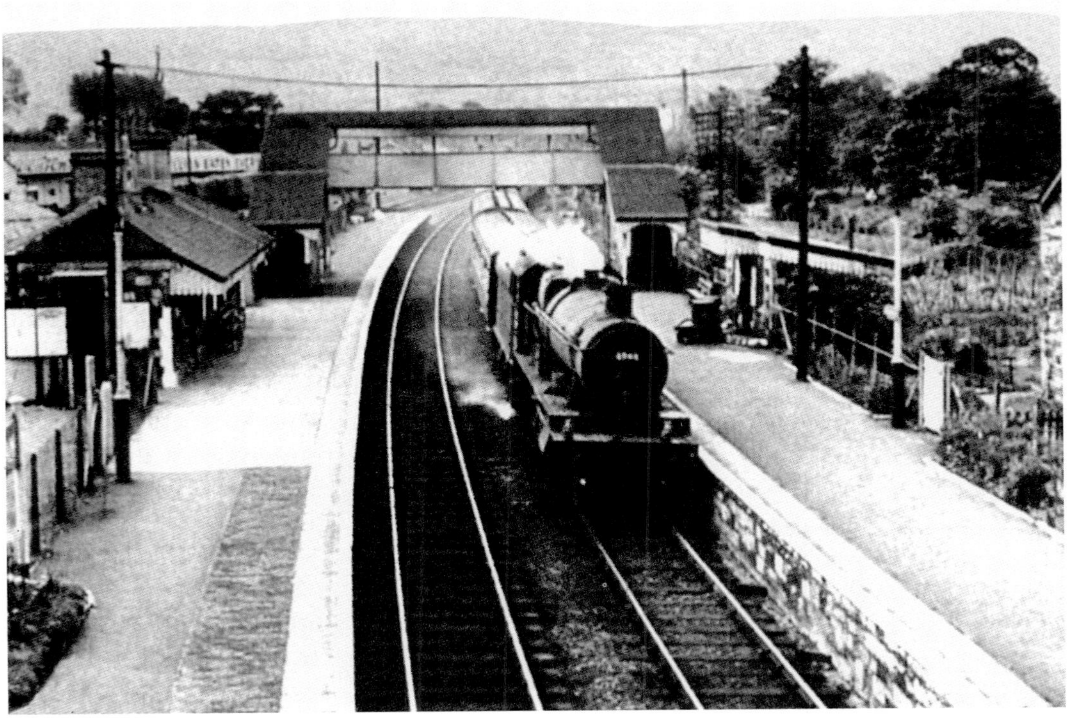

Llantarnam Station typifies the bygone 'age of steam'.

Cwmbrân and Pontypool. A hundred years of railway history had come to an end. Llantarnam Station was closed as a passenger station, although the main line going north still passes through the village. Station House has been renovated and is currently two dwellings.

BURTON'S FOODS

The story of Burton's starts way back in the late 19th-century - in Canada! George Weston was an ambitious 18-year-old baker's apprentice who managed to scrape together enough money to buy his first bread round. Through sheer hard work and commitment to both quality and customer care his business quickly took off. George's company went on to become the largest biscuit manufacturer in Canada. His son, Garfield followed in his father's footsteps and was equally enthusiastic to promote the business with a vision to conquer the British market; this came to fruition with the opening on 1st November, 1938, of the Weston Biscuit Factory - at Llantarnam of all places. This produced biscuits not only for Britain, but for a highly lucrative export market. The new factory was a Nuffield National Trust-assisted project to stimulate the severely depressed economy of the area and ease the high level of unemployment.

The factory was sited discreetly in a hollow a mere 200 hundred yards from Llantarnam Railway Station, an ideal spot for transporting its products. During the war years a huge sign fronted the main entrance stating: **WORK HARDER FOR BRITAIN**. Garfield was supportive of the British war effort and generously provided the finance for four 'Spitfires' which made him a hugely popular figure amongst his largely female workforce, many of whom arrived by train at the station.

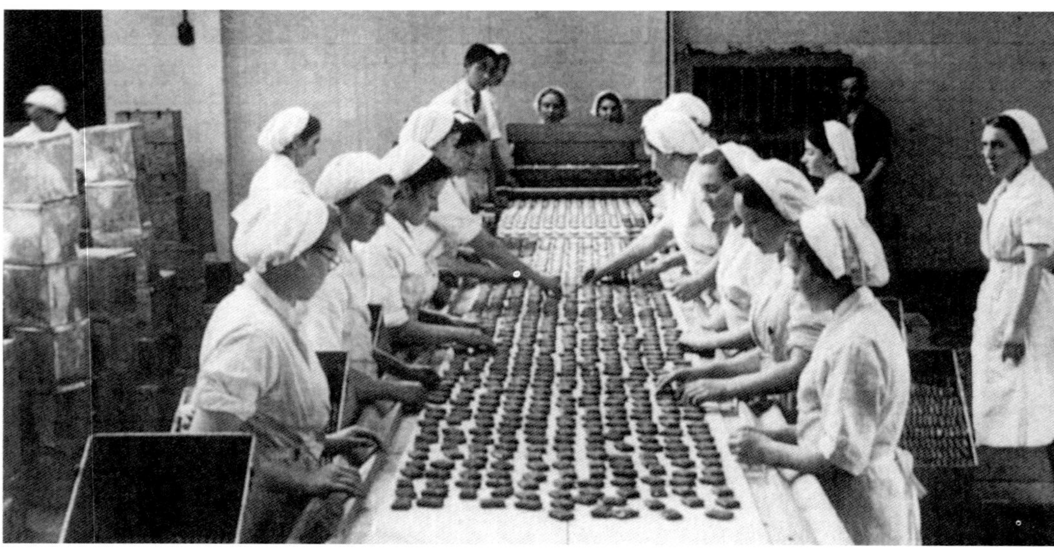

Workers at Weston Biscuit Factory in 1938. A happy bunch of ladies.

Predictably, like all successful businesses, Weston's merged with another company to become 'Burton's Gold Medal Biscuits': further takeovers led to the present-day 'Burton's Foods', a massive conglomerate of business power. And the name 'Weston' has been lost. What's new in the cut-throat world of commercialism?

Today, the factory is a key biscuit manufacturer in the United Kingdom, producing such favourites as the traditional 'Wagon Wheels', the only place in the entire world to produce them. What sort of tribute is that to the company? Other famous products include 'Jaffa Cakes' and 'Jammie Dodgers'.

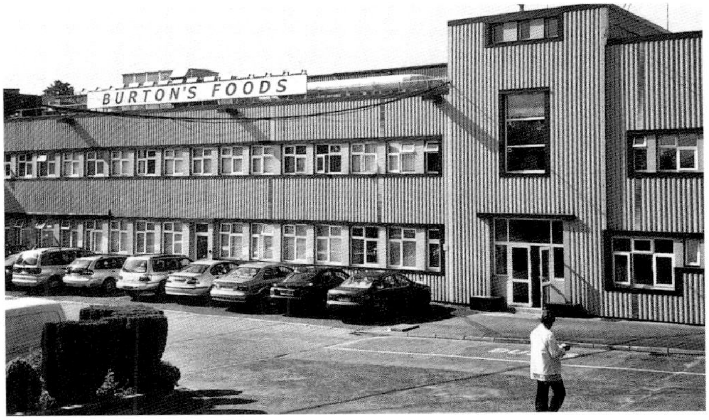

Burton's Foods today.

THE SPORTING SCENE

Sporting activities were an integral feature of the social life in a predominantly rural environment. The cricket club established in the early 20th-century was well known throughout Monmouthshire and South Wales. Many photographs exist of the teams, but that taken of the 1913 side outside The Greenhouse inn is remarkable in that all the players are named.

For many years, the most important cross country events in Wales were held at Court Farm. The Midland Championships, junior and senior, and the various

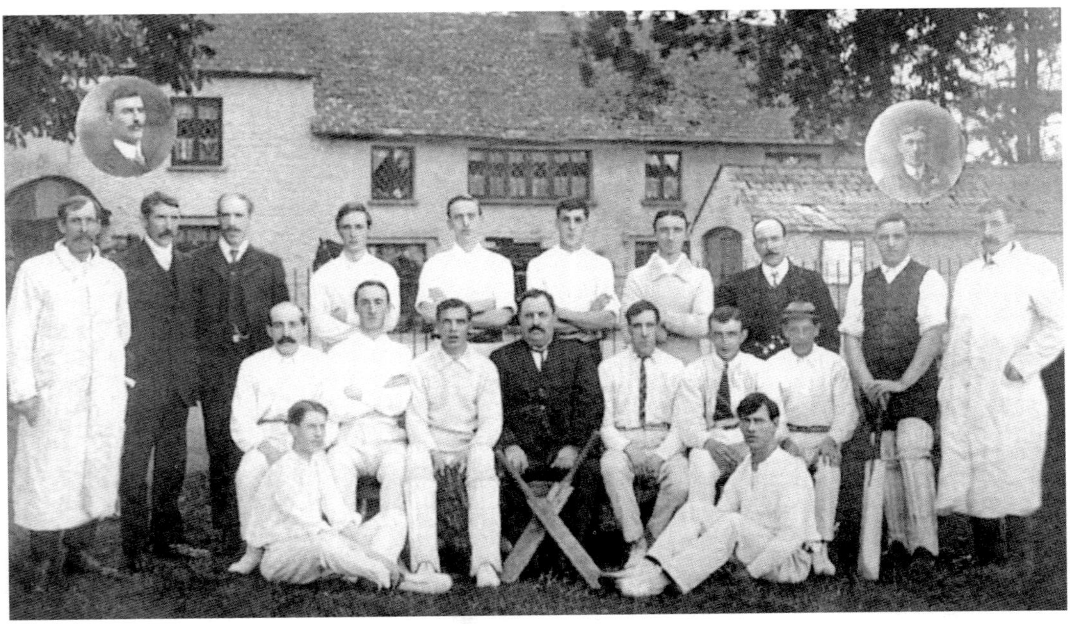

Llantarnam Cricket Club 1913.
Inset left: J.T. Evans. Inset right: A. Edwards (Hon. Treasurer)
Back row: T. Hewlings (Umpire), R. Travers (committee), W. Mapps, J. Bevan, C. Crocker, F.H. Johnston, A.H. Pryer, W. Pritchard (committee), C. Tucker, C. Johnston.
Middle row: J. Falle, F.C. Evans, H. Holmes (Captain), Councillor L. Lawrence, J.P. (President), W.W. Johnston, T. Male (Vice-captain), A.G. Thomas.
Front row: J.T. Thomas (Hon. Sec.), B. Williams.

Welsh Championships were run there. Famous Welsh internationals such as D. Phillips, E. Thomas, J. Prosser, S. Driscoll, E. Leyshon, F. Denmead, Gwyn Morgan, J. Hughes, all of Cwmbrân Harriers, would have been familiar with the Court Farm venue at which they regularly participated.

The photograph of Cwmbrân Harriers and officials was taken outside the Drill Hall, Cwmbrân, circa 1930. A fine bunch of athletic young men in their prime with their trophies. Several Welsh internationals in the front row are named.

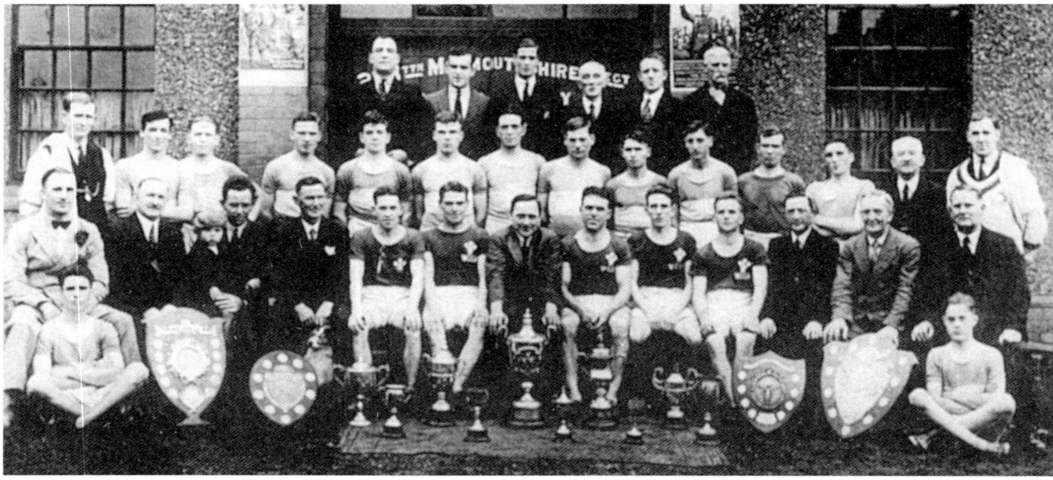

Cwmbrân Harriers and officials ca. 1930. Welsh internationals in the front row include: Harvey, Danny Phillips, Ernie Thomas, Jack Prosser, Harry Gallivan.

The best known athlete of his day (the 1930s) was Ernie 'Curly' Thomas. Among his many achievements he was Welsh cross country champion. A competitor of outstanding prowess, the accompanying photograph shows him standing alongside his vast collection of cups and trophies. In later years he coached youngsters at various youth clubs throughout the Cwmbrân area. How many sportsmen of today 'plough' anything back into their sport upon retirement?

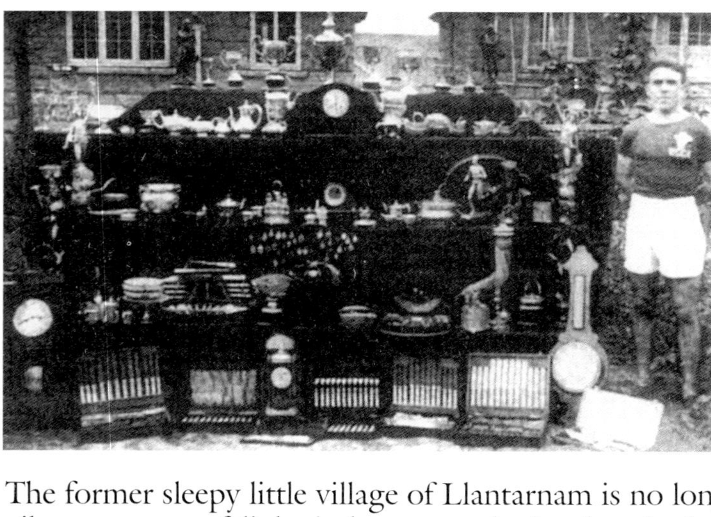

Ernie Thomas, supreme athlete of the 1930s, with his spectacular collection of trophies.

The former sleepy little village of Llantarnam is no longer sleepy. It has become a vibrant centre of light industry employing hundreds of workers. For better or for worse? That's hard to say for surely jobs are more important than acres of beautiful pastoral scenery.

Cwmbrân Town Centre

Cwmbrân currently boasts well over 55,000 residents and has grown to become the sixth largest town in Wales. It has seen many changes since August 1949 when it was designated the first Welsh town under the New Towns Act of 1946 to meet the desperate need for proper housing and employment following the devastation of World War II and to provide a ravaged community with ***'a balanced social structure'***. An admirable phrase, but utterly lacking in meaning. The population has since increased steadily over the intervening years. The vicinity of Cwmbrân was chosen primarily because of its ***'pleasant situation with good existing facilities'***. Predictable political ideology.

The purpose-built town centre covers some 55 acres and was constructed in stages between 1958 and 1980. With the co-operation and advice of an eminent firm of town planners appointed by Cwmbrân Development Corporation a Master Plan was drawn up in 1951 with numerous suggestions regarding future housing developments within the outlying areas. (Hardly a precise or sacred text which later proved to be seriously flawed in its lack of perception for the needs of the very people it was intended to serve.) This 'Plan' - one of several - was intended primarily to transform 'Old Cwmbrân' from a well-established and thriving village community into ***'a proper town'*** on a flat site nearby which would eventually gain Borough Status with a ***'smiling face'*** befitting the modern era.

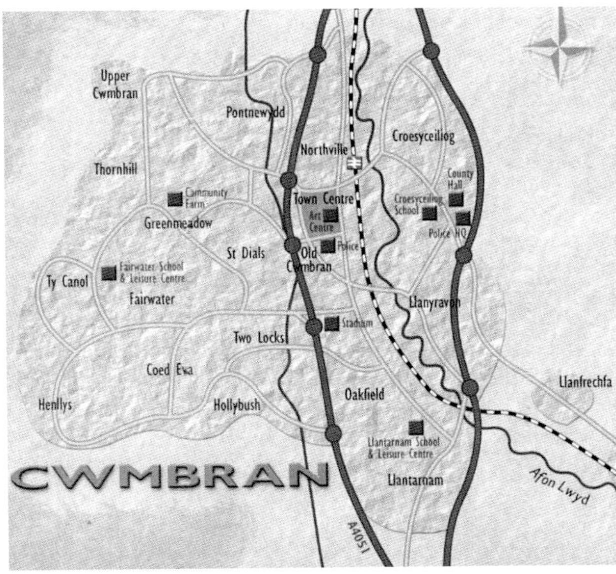

Cwmbrân and its environs.

The task of assimilating and grafting new on to old communities was a formidable social one and was entrusted solely to the Development Corporation. Gradually, over time, this was achieved surprisingly successfully. The early 1960s saw the new town centre slowly taking shape with much more to follow. Llantarnam Grange was restored to become an Arts Centre of considerable international repute; while the police station and magistrates court in Tudor Road were officially opened for the expected ***'regular business'*** of public disorder management - i.e. controlling the behaviour of unruly and often drunken miscreants. Little seems to have changed with the passage of time.

Yet the story could have been so different. For on 7th June, 1912, it was reported in ***The Free Press of Monmouthshire*** that Sir Clifford Cory, the wealthy owner of Llantarnam Abbey, was prepared ***'to buy a piece of land abutting***

on Coronation Road, Cwmbrân,' of over 7 acres and ***'to hand it over to the Council for the purposes of a public park and recreation ground'***. Curiously, such a magnanimous gesture of goodwill was rebuffed by members of Llantarnam Council as being too vague. Had the offer been accepted it is reasonable to assume that the later concept of a new town on such land would never have come to fruition. Strange old world...

Under a Welsh Office directive the transfer of housing stock to Torfaen Borough Council took place in June 1986. By 1987 the Development Corporation was deemed to have fulfilled its projected objectives and was finally wound up in March of the following year.

The town centre was subsequently purchased for a staggering £11 million by the City and County Land Co. Ltd., which was part of the giant leisure chain Ladbrokes. They invested heavily, modernising the centre and rebranding it as ***'Cwmbrân Shopping'*** with the added slogan ***'Where our valley comes to shop'***. With so many people from miles around visiting the centre by bus and car the slogan proved highly irrelevant and was quickly dropped. The town's new owners even financed the erection of a massive glazed canopy over Monmouth Walk at a cost of £1.5 million to become one of the largest unsupported span structures in Europe. Most impressive, though how many passing under its graceful arch appreciate its true beauty and worth?

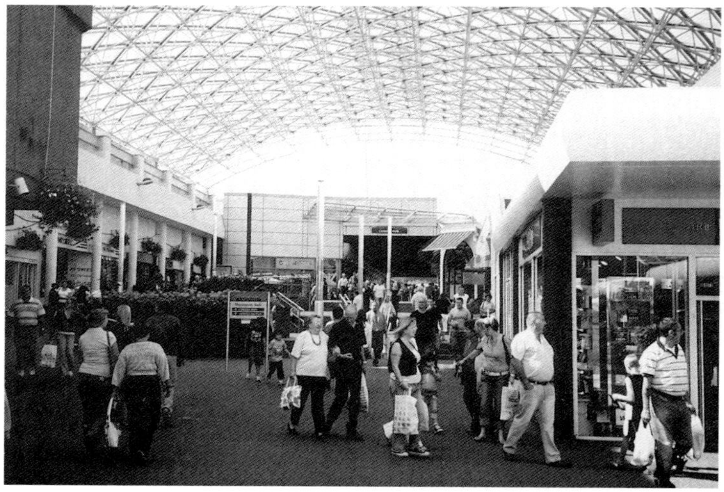

Monmouth Walk with its huge unsupported canopy.

During 1994 Prudential Holdings, a far more progressive and forward-looking company, gained outright ownership of the town centre for the princely sum of £73.5 million and reflected the ongoing success story of a hugely valuable commercial asset. Like their predecessor they, too, continue to invest heavily in improving the shopping area. 1999 saw Cwmbrân Shopping celebrate its 50th anniversary as a New Town in grand style.

In recent times the town centre has seen much to make it a more colourful and attractive place and to be ***'shopper-user-friendly'***. Numerous works of art including murals and sculptures were commissioned by Cwmbrân Arts Trust to mask what was formerly and most certainly a grey and sterile concrete jungle; these adorn the precinct areas, Gwent Square and the Water Gardens in Monmouth Square, and lend a vitality of interest to the hustle and bustle of shoppers scurrying by. And many more are planned.

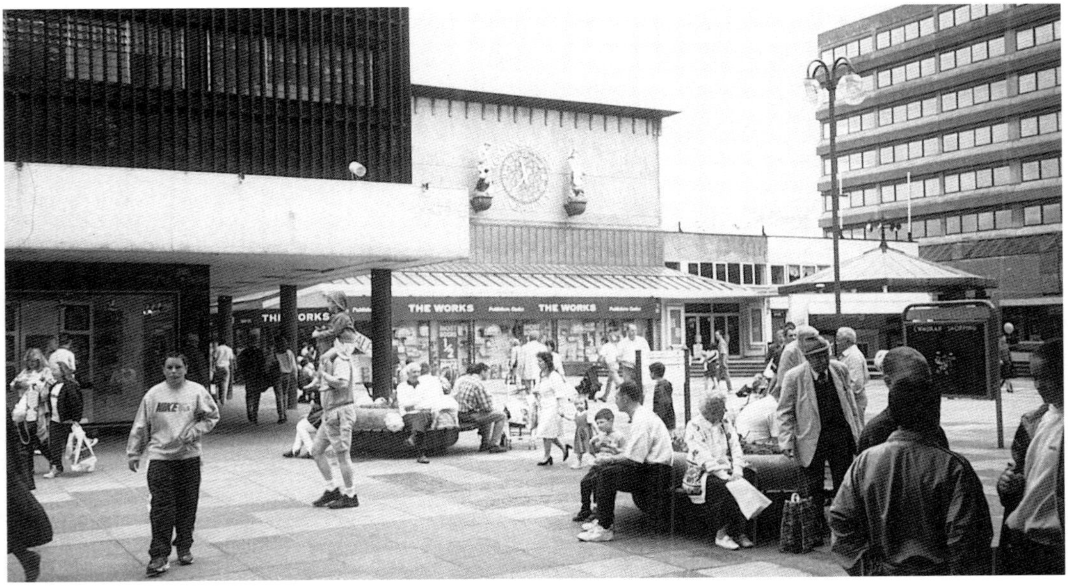

A bustling Gwent Square.

In summertime, the malls are ablaze with a riot of colour from close on 300 hanging baskets, each displaying a wide variety of blooms. This contrasts with many English towns which adhere to so-called 'political correctness' in the false belief of safety issues which deny those who appreciate the beauty Mother Nature annually offers. Certainly Cwmbrân's boast to be the ***'Garden City of Wales'*** is no exaggeration.

The town has become well-known throughout South East Wales for its large pedestrianised and under-cover shopping centre which is home to very many leading high street favourites stores. With well in excess of 3,000 free car-parking spaces in multi-storey blocks around the four corners of the centre, the town caters for all needs and deservedly has become a popular place to spend a day. And an unusually safe place too for all areas are covered by CCTV. Surely the envy of lesser towns where petty crime is often rampant. The centre also continues to prove attractive for retailers who enjoy the close and convenient links directly to the M4 motorway and to every major city in the country. Set against the stunning backcloth of Mynydd Maen, Cwmbrân seems to offer it all - by day at least.

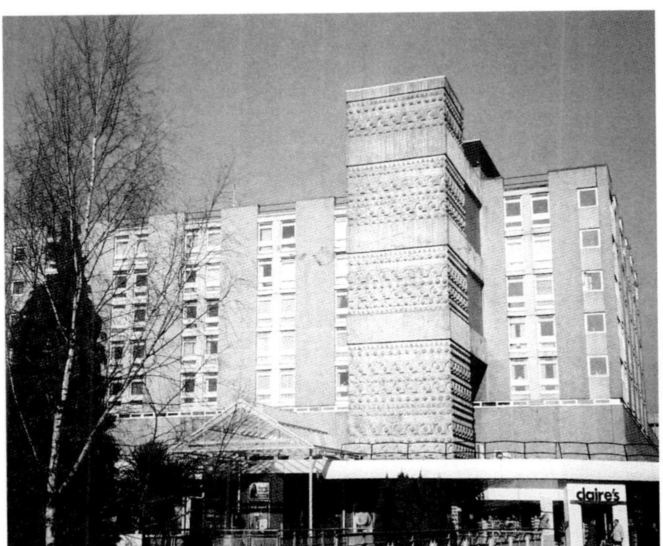

Residential Monmouth House overlooking the sunken Water Gardens.

Around the town centre are clusters of residential neighbourhoods. A supposedly successful blend of architectural styles and layouts has been achieved, thereby avoiding the drab monotony of outlook inflicted upon so many residential areas in towns and cities elsewhere. All open to question, of course.

To cope with the unprecedented influx during the 1950s of those seeking work in a fast expanding town, literally thousands of very basic quality homes were hurriedly constructed to cope with the demand for accommodation at affordable rents within proper acceptable standards of the day. This Master Plan was considered essential for the cultural well-being of a new town. Numerous housing estates were established around and on the outskirts of the town centre under the guise of ***'progress and modernisation'*** - often to the detriment of the old and well-established if somewhat rundown housing stock a great many of which were summarily demolished without question of modernisation.The Development Corporation's mandate was a simple one: ***'Out with the old and in with the new'***. After all ***'We must move with the times...'*** Which then seemed a reasonable philosophy.

The first new estate to be built was Northville in 1953 and planned meticulously. Free from busy roads and with open play areas for children it appeared to be ideal. Yet quickly proved a disaster largely due to the incredibly high density of housing crammed into too small an area. People complained openly of having no privacy in their homes. And by the 1960s a host of social and community problems were emerging. To a lesser extent Southville suffered similar problems in its early days, but with a far better feeling of spaciousness people bonded more readily and a true community spirit developed.

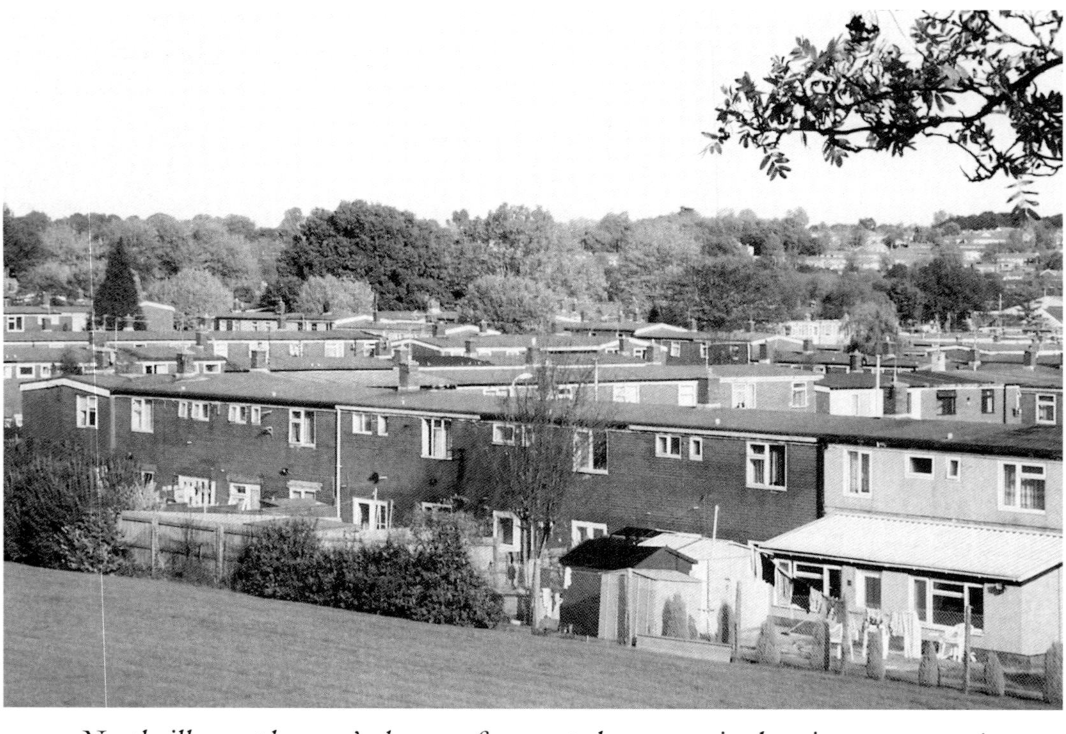

Northville - a planner's dream of congested community housing come true!

Nearest to the southern end on the fringe of the town centre in Southville is a massive 22-storey tower block of flats which was completed in 1967 and which happens to be the tallest residential building in the Principality. Built at a cost of over £385,000, it contains 81 flats and dominates the landscape from miles around. Despite its ***'brutal and unresolved'*** impact on the current valley community, at least it gives Cwmbrân a recognisable identity. But for the right reasons?

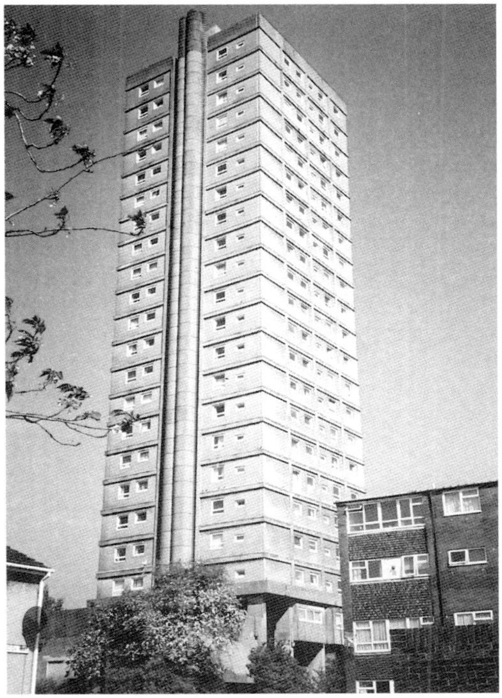

The distinctive 22-storey block of flats alongside the town centre.

But the CDC ran headlong into serious trouble in the 1970s when its decision to expand the housing stock northwards from Pontnewydd towards Griffithstown became unstuck. Public consensus was unanimous to preserve at least something of a ***'green belt'*** between town and country. All very well, but in 1974 Henllys unfortunately bore the brunt of a vast expansion of the housing stock to the detriment of its ancient village status.

To its credit, though, over the years Cwmbrân Development Corporation built well in excess of some 10,000 houses. Yet many were sold to sitting tenants under the ***'Right to Buy'*** legislation during the 1980s by a very right wing government.

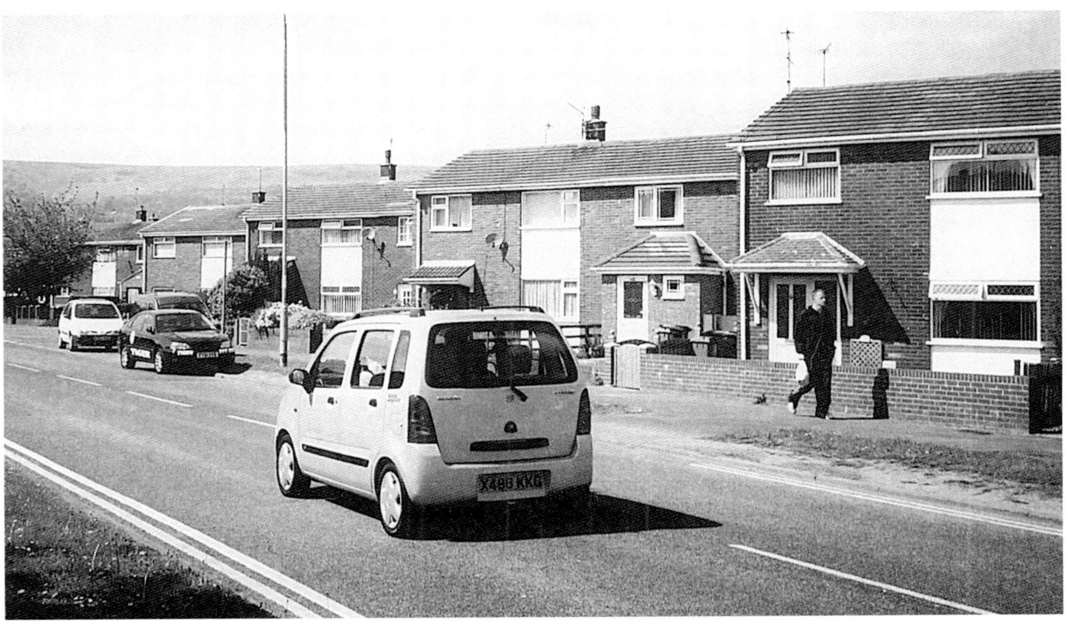

Southville with its spacious character.

THE TRAINS ONCE AGAIN STOP HERE!

Cwmbrân was effectively cut off from a passenger rail service on 30th April, 1962, when the last train ran from Newport to Blaenafon via Cwmbrân Village on the former Eastern Valley branch line. A result of the notorious Beeching 'axe', this deprived the burgeoning new town entirely of rail transport. This was a ludicrous situation when the Newport to Shrewsbury main line continued to pass through the very heart of the town. But few in a position of trust seemed to care one iota.

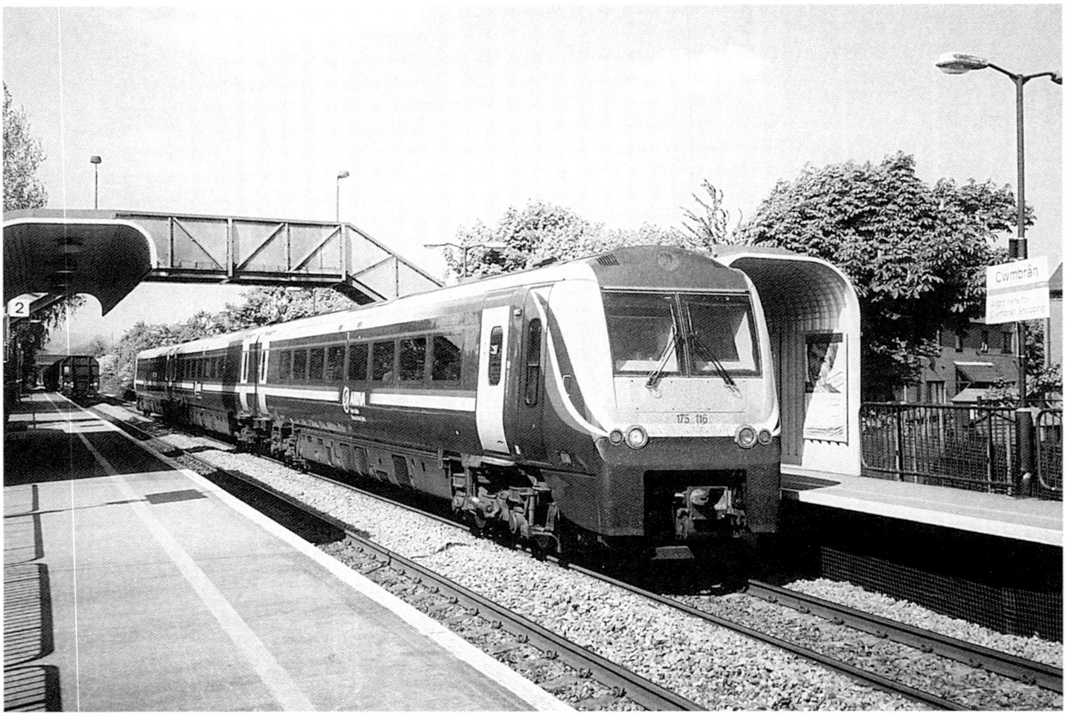

The trains once again stop in Cwmbrân.

The former Cwmbrân Urban District Council and the late Councillor Oliver Price in particular ran a determined campaign to re-establish a new station; British Rail were indifferent to such overtures. Not economically viable was their answer. During the 1970s supporters of the Master Plan (which one?) argued that a rail link to the outside world was the least of its priorities and that the future lay in the investment of infrastructure and road transport. Eventually, common sense prevailed and a new station was built slightly to the north of the Town Centre near Edlogan Way and opened on 11th May, 1986. Over 20 years lost in a major transport desert. Is the plaque at the station really a fitting tribute to the lack of vision of the former Cwmbrân Development Corporation and British Rail?

WINGING THE CHANGES

The *'Valley of the Crow'* has flown fast-forward into a new era. The old logo dating back to the 1970s, a simple angular picture of a static 'tired' old crow was replaced in 2004 with a more dynamic image. With its wings and tail spread wide, this 'young' crow is full of vitality and is swooping towards the town. Innovatively, it forms the 'C' of Cwmbrân. The new design is meant to symbolise the bird heralding a much-needed regeneration of the 'ageing' (?!) town. Some residents maintain it resembles ***'an evil vulture'***. Now that's an interesting comparison. With so much ongoing modernisation within the town centre it was only fitting that the logo should be given a fresh image. The new brand is certainly something to ***'crow about'***!

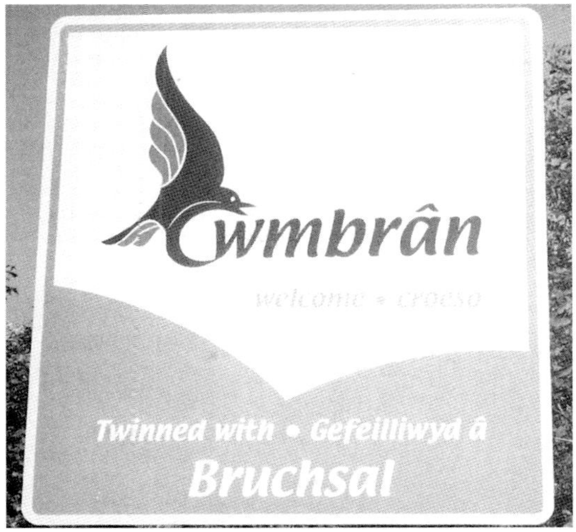

A new logo for a modern town.

AND TO THE FUTURE...

Recent years have seen major inward investment and redevelopment to transform certain areas of the town. The north-west quarter around General Rees Square has been completely rebuilt by owners Prudential to rejuvenate an ageing and run-down section of the centre to the tune of a whopping £21 million. Likewise, the south-west corner has also benefited from a major revamp and the impressive ***'vertical circulation tower'*** (who thinks up such a meaningless phrase?) fronting the section makes a fitting and contemporary new gateway to the Cwmbrân Shopping experience.

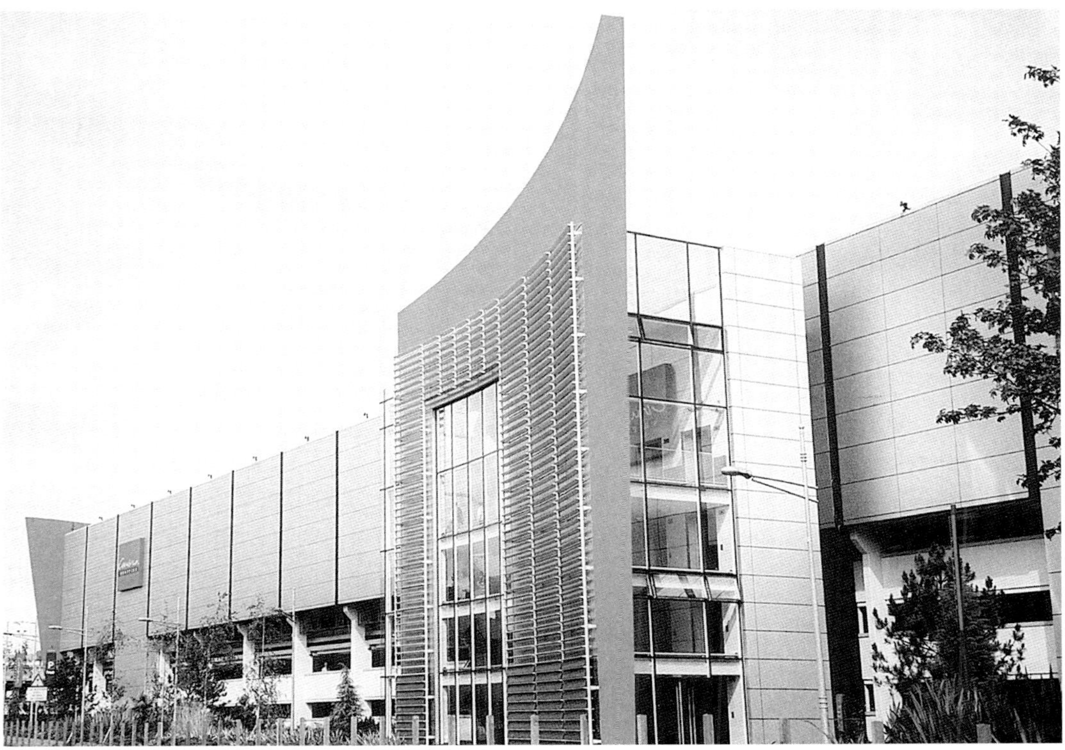

A rejuvenated town centre befitting the 21st century.

Despite the overwhelming success of the town centre during the day (which no-one can dispute), Cwmbrân lacks any real form of leisure facilities for families and night-life for youngsters who all too readily flock further down the valley to enjoy 'clubbing' in the nearby City of Newport. A shame that over very many years planners were unwilling to recognise the needs of those with ***'money to burn'***. After all, it's somewhat like going to a football stadium on a Tuesday night and wondering why it's empty. Food for thought. Yet highly relevant.

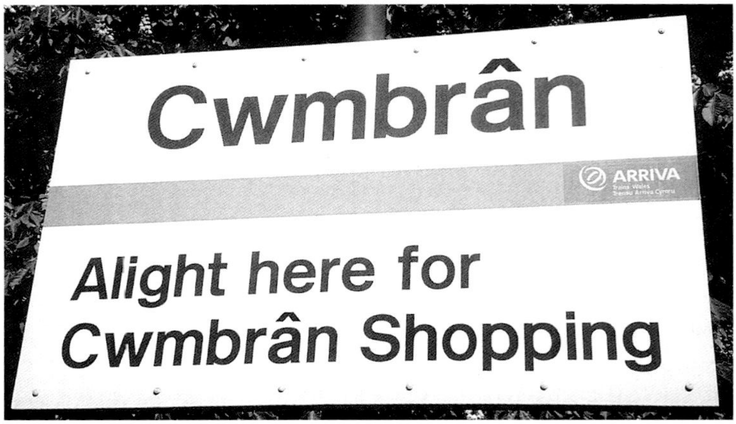

The sign says it all...

Somewhat belatedly, during 2005 plans were approved for a major new leisure complex on 'eyesore' derelict land adjacent to the town centre between St. David's Road and Glyndŵr Road to include a multi-screen cinema, a bowling alley, a nightclub, top-name restaurants including Portuguese restaurant chain Nando's and American eatery Frankie & Benny's, bars and - guess what? - even more office space. Work on the £15 million complex is finally well underway and promises to transform the heart of a bleak and lifeless night-time town. However, in 2006, the plan for a nightclub was rejected by a planning official claiming that this would have a ***'less potential impact on residential amenities'***.

Other proposals include the relocation of the railway station to a more central position, a much enlarged bus station at the south-east corner of the shopping centre, prestigious and luxurious new hotels to host visitors and business interests alike, to major canal-front developments including a marina and an additional expansion of shopping and commercial facilities. And to create a Parisian 'alfresco' café culture replete with wide open spaces offering relaxation and a sense of well-being on a summer's balmy evening. Well, anything is possible. A sense of vision holds the key to future aspirations.

The centre is further destined for massive inward investment and regeneration to the tune in excess of £100 million by 2016 - not all that far away in reality. The likes of Newport and Cardiff are presently rivals, but they should be wary - and envious. For neither can really compete with the infrastructure of virtually unlimited free parking and excellent public transport links by both road and rail. Yet Cwmbrân still deserves ***'a heart and a soul'***. This is long overdue. Merely a 'pipe-dream'? Who can say what the future holds? Cwmbrân is a modern progressive town with a well-integrated community possessing an identity of its own. For the people the New Town has heralded a new prosperity and introduced a better quality of life for its residents. Exciting times lie ahead. Watch this space! Iechyd Da! - Good Health!

ACKNOWLEDGEMENTS

We wish to thank the many individuals and organisations who have generously assisted in the preparation of this book. Their enthusiasm and support is surely fitting tribute to those who cherish the rich heritage of the area.

To Malcolm Thomas and Gwilym Davies of Old Bakehouse Publications for advice and their unstinting belief in the Authors' joint abilities to portray Cwmbrân's development from humble beginnings to the present-day success story that is indeed Cwmbrân New Town.

As ever, the late Mary Waithira John was undaunted by the complexities of proof-reading such a demanding work. For such dedication we extend to her memory our sincere appreciation. Likewise, to Stella Lawrence for her whole-hearted support and patience in also checking the manuscript.

To Robert Price, Chief Executive of Cwmbrân Library, for his patience and courtesy in finding often obscure documents/publications.

The photograph of Zoar Chapel, Henllys, was captured by a youthful Jonathan Samuel in 1986. To the late Brenda Samuel for so generously permitting extracts from her recollections ***'STORIES IN STONE'***.

The illustrations ***'School Pence'*** and ***'The Welsh Not'***, both by M. Mather, are taken from ***'CWMBRÂN - CHAPTERS IN ITS HISTORY'*** (1996) together with the photograph of ***'Tinplate Workers 1947'*** and appear courtesy of Cwmbrân Community Council.

To Jim Roberts whose pictures and memories are part of the legacy of Henllys. To Bryn Richards and his wife of Vale Farm for the photograph and information about ***'Mother Winsloe's Soothing Syrup'***; Mr. Evan Williams of Cock-y-North Farm for photographs of the Sheepdog Trials.

To the late Beverley Tomlin for the photograph of Porthmawr Colliery, Upper Cwmbrân, taken in 1997 and who died tragically young. To Eric Edwards for obtaining the moment of wedded bliss of Arthur Mann and his bride Peggy at Bethel Chapel in 1948.

To the poetess Audrey Donoghue for verses taken from ***'Growing Up In Pontnewydd'***; also, her recollections of village life as seen through the eyes of a greengrocer's daughter. To George Watkins for information and the 1954 programme of the former White Rose Cinema. To Roy Dixon, Secretary of Pontnewydd Male Voice Choir, for providing the excellent photograph of the group with full accompanying names.

The illustration of ***'Carved shields on the baptistery'*** at Llanfrechfa Church is taken from F[illegible]d J. Hando's ***'OUT AND ABOUT IN MONMOUTHSHIRE'*** (1958) R[illegible] Ltd.

To Margaret Pead for access to pictures and information on Llanfrechfa; Mr. & Mrs. Challenger for information and photographs of The Gate public house and Llanfrechfa School.

To David J. Orphan and Colyn Evans, respectively Clerks to Cwmbrân Community Council and Croesyceiliog & Llanyrafon Community Council, for uncovering hitherto virtually forgotten photographs of Garw Row and Jim Crow's Cottage; the former Grammar and Secondary Modern Schools; and the staged demonstration of the inadequacy of road transport at the railway bridge at Pontrhydyrun.

To Mrs. Edith Pontin for sharing her invaluable knowledge of both Jim Crow's Cottage and Llanfrechfa Grange.

To Gerry F. Keighley, Editor, ***South Wales Argus*** for permission to reproduce the following photographs: Graham Lawrence at the tombstone of Thomas and Elizabeth Morgan, Elim Independent Chapel, Cwmbrân Village; Madeleine Vowles at Llanyrafon Methodist Church.

To the poet Glynfab John for allowing ***'Worship'*** to be included within the pages on Llantarnam. To Mrs. Doris Tremlett for the photograph taken outside the Blacksmith's Shop at Llantarnam - the gentleman on horseback was her grandfather. To Mrs. Eileen Lawrence for photographs and details of ***'The Llantarnam Grand National'***.

To members of Cwmbrân Historical Society for freely sharing information on the area. Moreover, to the Gwent Record Office who remain helpful in subject matter relating to the development of Cwmbrân and surrounding area.

Photographs not acknowledged are derived from both Authors' vast collections of many years standing.

Finally, it is appropriate that we acknowledge those authors - far too numerous to mention - who down the centuries have been motivated to record the events that have shaped what today is regarded as Cwmbrân. Without them, we would remain 'in the dark' as to much of the Valley's Heritage. Hopefully, here's to a brave new world - in Cwmbrân, of course!

G.D.J.
G.L.
July 2007

